A Concise History
of the Crusades

Critical Issues in History

Series Editor: Donald T. Critchlow

The British Imperial Century, 1815–1914: A World History Perspective
by Timothy H. Parsons

The Great Encounter of China and the West, 1500–1800
by D.E. Mungello

Europe's Reformations, 1450–1650
by James D. Tracy

The Idea of Capitalism before the Industrial Revolution
by Richard Grassby

The Unfinished Struggle: Turning Points in U.S. Labor History, 1877 to Present
by Steven Babson

A Concise History of the Crusades
by Thomas F. Madden

A Concise History
of the Crusades

THOMAS F. MADDEN

ROWMAN & LITTLEFIELD PUBLISHERS, INC.
Lanham • Boulder • New York • Oxford

ROWMAN & LITTLEFIELD PUBLISHERS, INC.

Published in the United States of America
by Rowman & Littlefield Publishers, Inc.
A wholly owned subsidiary of The Rowman & Littlefield Publishing Group, Inc.
4501 Forbes Boulevard, Suite 200, Lanham, Maryland 20706
www.rowmanlittlefield.com

PO Box 317
Oxford
OX2 9RU, UK

British Library Cataloguing in Publication Information Available

Library of Congress Cataloging-in-Publication Data

Madden, Thomas F.
    A concise history of the crusades / Thomas F. Madden.
        p.   cm. — (Critical issues in history ; 105)
    Includes bibliographical references and index.
    ISBN 0-8476-9429-1
    1. Crusades.   I. Title.   II. Series.
    D157.M33   1999   99-27012
    909.07—dc21   CIP

Printed in the United States of America

♾ ™ The paper used in this publication meets the minimum requirements of American National Standard for Information Sciences—Permanence of Paper for Printed Library Materials, ANSI/NISO Z39.48—1992.

CONTENTS

MAPS

PREFACE

A ny historian who seeks to explain the crusades must first make peace with the length, breadth, and complexity of the subject. What were the crusades? When did they begin, and when did they end? What were the important milestones of the movement? Who was a crusader, and who was not?

Traditionally, authors have defined the scope of the crusades in terms of the expeditions to the Holy Land. In this, they are following the structure of sources like the *Gesta Dei per Francos*. The crusades, therefore, begin with Pope Urban II's call to arms at the Council of Clermont in 1095. The twin focuses of such studies are the major expeditions to the East (i.e., the "numbered" crusades) and the history of the crusader states in Syria and Palestine. The narrative thread then weaves itself between conditions in the Levant and conditions in Europe, bringing the two together in the events of the greater crusades. From this perspective, the crusades come to a close with the extinction of the mainland crusader states in 1291. The crusades, therefore, are nicely packaged in an organized fashion and in the space of two centuries.

In recent decades, this construction of the crusades has received some criticism. Although traditional histories usually include events like the Albigensian Crusade or Baltic Crusades, neither of which was bound for the East, they do so only peripherally. Modern scholarship has rehabilitated this periphery. Most scholars now accept that crusading took on many different forms; the general passage to the Holy Land was but one of them. Crusades against pagans, heretics, and enemies of the church were just as common by the thirteenth century as wars against Islam. Much of Europe's crusading energy was also devoted to removing Muslims from Spain.

Beyond broadening the definition of the crusade, scholars have also begun to reassess the neat organization of the major expeditions. The simplicity of the numbered crusades gives the impression that Europe periodically exploded with crusading zeal, sending large armies east to fight the Muslims of Palestine. As Jonathan Riley-Smith has argued, however, the crusades were not discrete campaigns but continuous streams of armies on the march. In between the major crusades were countless smaller expeditions to the Levant.

If one accepts that the crusading movement transcends the conquest of the Holy Land, then there is no reason its history should abruptly end in 1291. During the past century, much research has been done on these "later crusades." There is no doubt that crusading remained an important part of European thought well into the Renaissance and even beyond, into the Protestant Reformation and Catholic Counter-Reformation. At some point, though, the historian must accept that the trail has grown cold, and that crusade rhetoric has become merely that. If one insisted that the history of the crusades continued until the last crusader institution crumbled, then it would have to continue until the present so as to include the modern history of the Knights of Malta and the Teutonic Knights. Without a clear stopping point, it is up to the student to judge when the crusades ceased to be religious wars and transformed themselves into secular wars with religious trappings.

Despite the explosion in crusade studies over the past fifty years, the traditional construction of the crusades as a set of expeditions launched between 1095 and 1291 remains popular. There are good reasons for this. The traditional view introduces the student to the crusades in a way that is easier to grasp but does not distort the fundamental character of the movement. When one has a firm understanding of the crusades' peaks, one can then better descend into the foggy crevices of their valleys. For the interested student, that will require reading many more books than just one general survey.

For this concise history of the crusades, I follow in many respects the construction, if not the scope, of the traditional histories. My overriding objective is to relate the history of the crusades in a way that focuses on the events most important to Europeans at the time. Although political crusades and crusades against heretics were held to be valid, they were generally seen as derivative variations on the theme of the eastern crusades. The crusade, first and foremost, was a war against Muslims for the defense of the Christian faith; therefore, although I devote a chapter to crusading at home, the overall focus of this book is decidedly on the foreign expeditions. I do not deny the validity of the arguments that would bring other crusades to share the center stage, but I think that this can be done only when one has a solid grasp of the original intent of the holy wars.

The Spanish *reconquista* was a war against Muslims and was clearly seen by popes, clergy, and laity as equal in sanctity to the eastern expeditions. Nevertheless, I do not deal with these wars as broadly as they deserve. Unfortunately, the *reconquista* and its relationship to the crusading movement remains understudied. Only recently have scholars begun to investigate the archives of Spain to uncover the rich history of this centuries-long phenomenon. Until more of the fruits of that research are published, the *reconquista* remains on the periphery of crusade studies. It may or may not belong there.

In other respects, I part company with the traditional construction of the crusades. Because my concern is the crusades as an element in medieval European history, I describe the history of the crusader states only insofar as they make the crusades themselves more intelligible. The history of the Latin East is fascinating, but long and complex, and not all of it is relevant to the major expeditions. I also extend my treatment of the crusades well beyond the fall of Acre in 1291. Although the Holy Land was lost, it was not forgotten in Europe. After 1291, many crusades were planned, and some launched, to go to the aid of Palestine. Although by the fourteenth century turning back the Ottoman threat replaced the capture of Jerusalem as the primary motive of crusades, crusading remained a ubiquitous part of European thought and culture. I therefore follow the later history of the crusades until the point that (it seems to me) the Europeans themselves lost interest in them.

In summary, I have attempted to craft a history of the crusades that charts a middle course between the traditional and revisionist constructions. There is, after all, no contradiction between the two approaches: Both are merely different ways of understanding a complex set of events spanning centuries of Mediterranean history. In any general history, much of the story must be left out. It is my hope that readers will be sufficiently intrigued by the crusades to discover the rest for themselves.

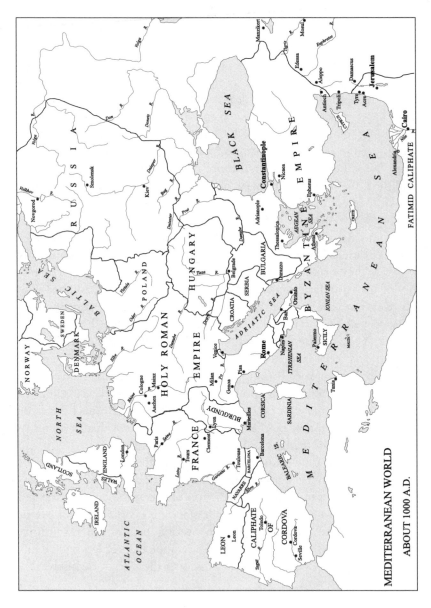

Map 1.   The Mediterranean world about A.D. 1000

1

THE CALL

"Crusade" is a modern, not a medieval, word. It derives from *cruce-signati* ("those signed by the cross"), a descriptive used occasionally after the twelfth century to refer to crusaders. Today, the term is commonly used to denote a grand enterprise, often with a moral dimension, as in General Eisenhower's "Crusade in Europe" or a "Crusade for Adult Literacy." When the crusades of the Middle Ages are remembered at all, it is usually with disdain and derision. In a post-Enlightenment world, the concept of religious warfare is odious, largely because most people no longer believe that one's religious beliefs are relevant to one's view of the world or place in it. Instead, modern wars are fought for political and ideological causes, like democracy or nationalism—ideas that would not seem worth the shedding of one drop of blood to most medieval men and women. War has not changed much in nine hundred years, only its weapons and tactics. Rather than fighting for a patriotic vision of a nation-state, thousands of medieval Europeans marched off to fight for Christ. In both cases, the soldiers felt similarly about their causes. They were willing to sacrifice their lives to defend what they held most sacred.

HOLY WAR

Unlike Islam, Christianity had no well-defined concept of holy war before the Middle Ages. Christ had no armies at his disposal, nor did his early followers. Only in A.D. 312, after the conversion to Christianity of the Roman Emperor Constantine I (306–337), did the religion come into direct contact with statecraft and warfare. Within a century, Christianity and the Roman Empire were fused tightly together. Christians in

1

government found themselves faced with questions of life and death, war and peace, questions that their religion had not wrestled with before. In the fifth century, St. Augustine outlined the necessary conditions for a Christian leader to wage a just war, but he was quick to insist that the faithful not engage in wars of religious conversion or for the purpose of destroying heresies or pagans. Warfare was a necessary evil sometimes forced upon a good leader—it was not to be a tool of the church.

The collapse of Roman power in the western Mediterranean did not spell a similar loss of power for Christianity because the Germanic barbarians who carved up the western empire were themselves Christians. The Christian faith, therefore, remained the faith of the large majority of people throughout Europe, the Near East, and North Africa.

Christianity's first serious competitor did not arise until the seventh century, when the prosperous Arab merchant Mohammed founded a new religion. Islam, or "submission to will of God," was and is a scrupulously monotheistic faith. Muslims believe that the God of the Jews and Christians made his word known to Mohammed, who then "recited" what he had been told. All these prophecies were carefully preserved and later written down in the Koran. Mohammed noted that God had frequently spoken to his people through the prophets of the Old Testament, but time and again the Jews had ignored these holy men. Mohammed accepted Jesus as a blessed prophet who was fundamentally misunderstood by both Jews and Christians: the former ignored him, and the latter proclaimed him God. Mohammed and his followers believed that God now bestowed his infallible word on a new people. Those who embraced the humble life of submission, good works, and prayer that the Koran enjoined would enjoy the riches of heaven for eternity after death.

Mohammed began his prophecies and preaching in Mecca, a trading city in Arabia. When he was expelled in 622, he fled to nearby Medina and became that city's ruler. There, Mohammed inspired more than just a religion. Because the Prophet was both a political and religious leader, Islam was at once a faith and a means of government. Commerce, justice, diplomacy, and war were built into the bedrock of the religion. Unlike Christian leaders, who tried to reconcile their prestige, power, and wealth with Christ's life of poverty, Muslims had in their founder a model of a worldly and spiritual leader. Mohammed waged war, first against Mecca and then against other Arab towns. He called each of these wars a *jihad,* or holy war. Soldiers who died in a *jihad* were thought to be martyrs of the faith. At the moment of their deaths, Muslims believed, the fallen in a *jihad* rose instantly from the sands of battle to their reward in a lush and sensual paradise. Yet not every war was a *jihad*. It could be waged only against unbelievers, those who refused to accept the one God. Jews and Christians, from the Muslim point of view, worshiped the true God, failing only to accept the prophecy of Mohammed. For that reason, they were misguided, but they were not pagans. They were the "People of the Book," who should remain free to retain their religious practices in the lands conquered by Islam. If they actively persecuted or hindered Islam, however, they too were legitimate targets of *jihad*.

After the conquest of Arabia, Mohammed envisioned the continued expansion of Islam, but in 632 he died. He was succeeded by a series of caliphs ("successors") who were to lead the Islamic state just as the Prophet had done. Islam grew with startling speed. Within a century, Arab Muslims had conquered Persia, Egypt, and Syria. Such rapid expansion led to rifts within the faith itself. The most important and long-lasting of these, the division between Sunni and Shia, occurred in the late seventh century. The original split was the result of a succession dispute, but the two groups soon began to drift apart theologically as well. The minority Shi'ites looked to their *imams,* who led them and attained for them the esoteric truths of the Koran. The majority Sunnites were much more conservative, shunning mysticism and other arcane practices and insisting on the political and religious unity of the Islamic state.

It would be too strong to say that it was the idea of *jihad* that later led to Christianity's own concept of holy war. The Christians of the eastern Roman Empire, known to historians as the Byzantine Empire, were willing enough to flirt with the idea of holy war during Emperor Heraclius's (610–641) campaigns against the Persians. When the forces of Islam exploded onto Byzantine lands shortly thereafter, however, the idea did not resurface. Christians were too fragmented into opposing sects to organize around such a fundamentally central doctrine. For minority Christian sects in Syria and Egypt, the arrival of Muslims was, in fact, good news. The new Arab leaders allowed them a freedom of worship that the emperor in Constantinople did not. Despite their close proximity to Islamic kingdoms, Byzantine Christians, it appears, never developed a religious rationale for waging or condoning holy war.

It was in western Europe that the concept of Christian holy war took root and grew. Muslim conquerors who swept through all of Christian North Africa also crossed the straits of Gibraltar and established their rule over Spain. By the eighth century, Muslim expeditionary forces were crossing the Pyrenees and marching into the heart of Catholic Europe. In 732, at the famous Battle of Tours, Frankish leader Charles Martel defeated the Muslims, driving them back into Spain. Spain was still Christendom, however, and Europeans believed strongly that Muslims should not be there. From their perspective, these lands were consecrated to Christ. It was not right that infidels should dwell there, let alone rule. Was it not self-evident that a Christian who fought to reclaim lands conquered by unbelievers was himself fighting for Christ? Thus, it was in dealing with the Muslim presence in Spain that Western soldiers and theologians first cut their teeth on the idea of holy war. The *reconquista,* or reconquest, was the training ground for the theological and moral justification of the crusading movement. Like the later crusades, the *reconquista* joined military campaigns with holy pilgrimage.

In the ninth century, in a thin strip of Christian-held territory in northern Spain, the bones of St. James the Greater were discovered at Santiago de Compostello. The cult of St. James flourished in Europe, and the shrine became a rallying point for warriors who were spurred to liberate the lands they believed that the apostle had claimed for Christ. During the first centuries of the *reconquista,* the church promoted the war as a just and appropriate reaction to Muslim aggression but did not articulate the kind of spiritual benefits that would signify a holy war.

TURKISH CONQUESTS

Like the *reconquista,* the crusades began as a result of a Muslim conquest, although not of the Holy Land. The Byzantine Empire had lost much in the storm of Muslim expansion but emerged with its most important regions intact, namely Greece and Asia Minor. The latter was essential for the recruitment of soldiers and the production of food to feed the great capital city of Constantinople. In the eleventh century, a new group, the Seljuk Turks, threatened Byzantium. The Seljuks were Muslims but not Arabs. They had swept into the region early in the century, conquering Armenia, Syria, and Palestine. Because they were themselves split into antagonistic factions, they disrupted the peace of the Near East that had been established by the Arabs. After their conquest of Jerusalem, many of the

Turks were amazed to find Christian churches and monasteries flourishing in Muslim lands. They destroyed some churches, murdered clergy, and seized pilgrims. It was not long, though, before the new conquerors learned what the Arabs had long known: Jerusalem was profitable only by virtue of its pilgrims. Great sums of money poured into the city from the pockets of Christian penitents eager to pray at the holy shrines. Soon the Turkish conquerors halted direct persecutions; nevertheless, the multiplicity of petty rulers and the relative instability of the region made pilgrimage to the Holy Land a difficult and often deadly task.

In 1071, Emperor Romanus IV (1068–1071) arrayed his forces against the Turkish assault on Asia Minor at the Battle of Manzikert. The Turks destroyed the Byzantine armies and captured the emperor. Beyond the body-strewn battlefield, the rich plains of Anatolia lay almost defenseless, and it took the Turks only a short time to capture them. Within a few years, the citizens of Constantinople could look across the Bosporus and see the land of the Turks. And they were not the only enemies. From the north, the Pechenegs were pressing south, and in the west, the Normans had ousted Byzantine troops from their last foothold in Italy. Many feared that the long-lived Roman Empire had finally come to its end. But, as so often occurred in Byzantine history, just as events seemed hopeless, a powerful emperor came to the throne to turn the situation around. Alexius I Comnenus (1081–1118) rallied Byzantine spirits and raised a large mercenary army to defend against the external threats. He also turned to the West for help. This was an action not lightly chosen. Byzantines viewed all of western Europe as Roman territory temporarily occupied by barbarians. Although Westerners were Christian, from the Byzantine perspective, they were misguided by various liturgical errors and heretical beliefs, chief of which was their insistence on the central authority of the pope over all Christians. Yet Alexius needed troops, and there were a good number of them in Europe. He therefore sent an emissary to the pope to request assistance.

POPE GREGORY VII

Byzantium's plight was well known in the West long before Alexius's envoy arrived. Pope Gregory VII (1073–1085) had made serious plans to raise an army against the Turks as early as 1074. For the pope, there was much to commend such a venture. In the aftermath of the Viking, Hungarian, and Islamic invasions of the ninth and tenth centuries, western Europe had become in many respects an armed camp. Fortified castles dotted the landscape. Armed knights and trained infantry were everywhere. Kings had almost no control over most of their vassals and therefore could claim sovereignty over only a small portion of their kingdoms. With no central authority and a proliferation of warriors, it is not surprising that the level of violence rose dramatically. Pitched battles and castle sieges were bad enough, but combatants were not above destroying villages and killing women and children. The church had attempted to reduce the violence with various initiatives, but none met with much success. The Peace of God movement threatened divine sanctions against those who attacked noncombatants, and the Truce of God attempted to put a stop to warfare on Sundays and holy days. The church, however, like the kings of Europe, had little control over petty knights and landed barons. If the martial energy of Europe's soldiers could not be siphoned off somehow, all of western Christendom would be harmed.

Gregory VII saw the Byzantine appeal for aid as the perfect opportunity to employ warriors in the service of God. When he envisioned the mighty army that he hoped would march to the East, he saw himself at its head. This fit well with the church's evolving view of its role in secular life during the eleventh-century reform movement. Reformers like Humbert of Silva Candide and Gregory himself had long argued that for the church to rid itself of sinful clerical abuses, it must first be free from the stain of lay control. Kings and emperors were ordained by God to look after the material needs of their people, but it was the pope and the church that had the greater responsibility for the care of the souls of Christendom. In the final analysis, these reformers maintained, it was the pope who wielded supreme power, even above that of an emperor. At least that was the theory, not at all subscribed to by Europe's ruling elite. A large army raised by the church and led by the pope against the enemies of Christ would be dramatic evidence of the reformers' contention.

Gregory also was concerned about the state of relations between the Christians of the East and West. Relations had been seriously strained by the reformers' renewed insistence on the primacy of the See of St. Peter. As the papacy sought to restore its ancient rights over the clergy in the West, it was natural that the universal character of Roman primacy as the reformers envisioned it would spill over into the Byzantine sphere. Matters had come to an unfortunate head when, in 1054, Humbert traveled to Constantinople and delivered a papal bull of excommunication to the patriarch in the great church of Hagia Sophia. Since then, both sides had tried to smooth over the situation, but few gestures would be as effective in restoring Christian unity as the destruction of Christ's foes by the combined forces of pope and emperor. Gregory may even have hoped that such a victory would once and for all settle the matter of papal authority.

Gregory did not characterize this planned expedition as a holy war. Instead, he saw it as an errand of mercy and an act of charity. The Christians of the East had suffered mightily at the hands of the Turks. It was only right then that their fellow Christians in the West should sally forth to help reclaim their lands and property. Although the pope seems to have envisioned a visit to the Holy Land after the defeat of the Turks, it was not the central focus of the expedition. While Gregory led the knights of Christendom east, he suggested leaving Germany's King Henry IV (1056–1106) to protect and guide the church in his absence. Henry was only too glad to oblige, but the period of friendship between pope and king was too brief. Soon, Gregory issued his decree against lay investiture of clergy. Henry replied with his letter condemning the pope as a power-hungry usurper of the throne of St. Peter. Thus began the great struggle between empire and papacy known as the Investiture Controversy (1075–1112). Matters in the East were, for the moment, forgotten.

THE COUNCIL OF CLERMONT

By the end of the eleventh century, the papacy was gaining the upper hand in its struggle with the Holy Roman Empire. Other European powers began to fall in line with papal directives lest they suffer the same destructive divisions that wracked the Germans. Pope Urban II (1088–1099) spent much of his life promoting the reform agenda in the church, above all working to remove lay control. By 1095, when Alexius I Comnenus sent an envoy to request aid against the Turks, the papacy had the moral and political authority to make Gregory VII's dream a reality. On November 27 of that year, at the Council of Clermont, Pope Urban II preached the First Crusade.

The precise wording of Urban's call, which he repeated at numerous other synods, meetings, and councils, is not preserved. It is clear, however, that he began where Gregory had left off. He called the knights of Christ to take up a war of liberation. The Christians of the East must be free from the brutal and humiliating conditions of Muslim rule. With the help of the West, Constantinople, the greatest Christian city in the world, could be liberated from the danger that beset it daily. As compelling as this message was, Urban knew that it was insufficient to stir men's hearts to bold action, so what was a mere possibility for Gregory VII became a focal point for Urban II: the Holy Land. The "soldiers of St. Peter," as he referred to them, would not only sweep away the festering presence of the Seljuk Turks in Asia Minor but also continue on to liberate the very lands of Christ. The goal was now Jerusalem. Byzantium was simply on the way.

Jerusalem and the Holy Land had a primacy of importance in medieval minds that is scarcely conceivable to moderns. Christianity had long placed a heavy emphasis on the inherent holiness of relics, the objects and bodies left behind by the saints. Pilgrimage to holy sites provided Christians with a means of penance, and the relics themselves were vital avenues of divine grace. The holiest sites were, of course, those in which Jesus himself had lived. Jerusalem, the holy city revered in the Scriptures, where Christ walked, preached, died, and was resurrected, was the greatest destination of any pilgrimage. For medieval people, Jerusalem lay at the very center of the universe. That it had been taken by Arab Muslims in the seventh century was scandal enough. At least they had allowed Christian pilgrims to visit the holy shrines unmolested, albeit for a price. Now the Turks occupied the region, and, as Urban recounted in graphic detail, they committed every kind of sacrilege and crime against Christ and his followers. In a summary of Urban's speech, Robert the Monk has the pope proclaim:

> They [the Turks] have completely destroyed some of God's churches and they have converted others to the uses of their own cult. They ruin the altars with filth and defilement. They circumcise Christians and smear the blood from the circumcision over the altars or throw it into the baptismal fonts. They are pleased to kill others by cutting open their bellies, extracting the end of their intestines, and tying it to a stake. Then, with flogging, they drive their victims around the stake until, when their viscera have spilled out, they fall dead on the ground. They tie others, again, to stakes and shoot arrows at them; they seize others, stretch out their necks, and try to see whether they

can cut off their heads with a single blow of a naked sword. And what shall I say about the shocking rape of women?[1]

For knights steeped in a culture of militant Christianity, these were stories to make the blood boil. The shouts of Europe's fighting men, filled with righteous anger, rang out across the land: "God wills it! God wills it!"

Urban could not preach to all of Europe himself, nor could his words alone have been responsible for the tremendous wave of enthusiasm that ensued. Bishops and preachers were sent out to spread the word. To their listeners, they quoted the words of Christ. "If any man will come after me, let him deny himself, and take up his cross, and follow me" (Matt. 16:24). "And everyone that hath forsaken houses, or brethren, or sisters, or father, or mother, or wife, or children, or lands, for my name's sake, shall receive a hundredfold, and shall inherit everlasting life" (Matt. 19:29). It was Christ himself, the preachers proclaimed, who called his warriors to the aid of Jerusalem. Preachers often employed feudal ideas familiar to their audience. Was it not the duty of every vassal to come to the aid of his lord if that lord's lands were unjustly taken from him? How much more, then, did the vassals of Christendom owe to their Lord and Savior Jesus Christ? Images of Christ carried by crusade preachers and manufactured in the workshops of Europe portrayed the Savior during the Passion and Crucifixion as a pitiful object of scorn and derision. Later, turban-headed Muslims in these depictions sometimes replaced the Roman torturers. The message was clear: Christ was crucified again in the persecution of his faithful and the defilement of his sanctuaries. The knights of Christ were called to be the avengers of an injured God.

CRUSADE AND PILGRIMAGE

Despite the emotional rhetoric, the crusade was not a holy war in the strictest sense of the word. Urban II did not overturn the teachings of Augustine but rather blended the Just War theory with other well-established principles such as Christian charity and pilgrimage. At Clermont, the pope issued the call that Gregory VII had crafted but not delivered. Urban's innovation was to emphasize the liberation of Palestine over the reconquest of Asia Minor and to tie it to the idea of pilgrimage. Each crusader joined the enterprise by taking a pilgrim's vow.

During that "taking of the cross," or "crossing," a crusader swore to make a pilgrimage to the Holy Sepulcher, the tomb in which Christ was laid and from which he rose. Because of the great expense and difficulties of such a journey, a crusader received a remission from sins, just as would a pilgrim who traveled to a holy shrine. As a pilgrim, a crusader's lands and properties were placed under the protection of the church until his return. The crusader's vow was frequently accompanied by other vows of fasting or abstention from sex or by special devotions to be performed during the course of the pilgrimage. Finally, a simple cross was sewn onto the shoulder of the crusader's garment to signify his status as a pilgrim. The distinction between holy war and pilgrimage was real. Crusaders usually referred to themselves as "pilgrims" or "cross bearers."

A pilgrimage the crusade might be, but it was a strange pilgrimage nonetheless. The many thousands who took the cross bore swords, armor, and other implements of war with them on their pilgrimage. Armed pilgrimages were nothing new. Given the unstable situation in the Near East, pilgrims to Jerusalem had often found it necessary to arm themselves for protection against pirates, highwaymen, unscrupulous officials, and every other sort of riffraff who preyed on foreigners with money in their purses. In this case, though, the pilgrims' party consisted of thousands of soldiers, trained in war and prepared not just for defense but for conquest.

From a distance, the crusades do look like great armies organized and directed by the church against the enemies of Christ, but from within the ranks it was a very different picture. Each crusader took a pilgrim's vow to reach the Holy Sepulcher. He was a pilgrim, first and foremost. The oath he swore was to God, not to the pope or to any other man. The only cohesion within a crusading army was that enforced by feudal obligations, family ties, friendship, or fear. A great lord who had taken the cross could command his own vassals but could not reasonably expect to command anyone else, least of all the other powerful lords who accompanied him on the crusade. Although it was customary to select a "commander in chief," the title was honorary. Even crusading kings found it difficult to maintain control over a crusade. Popes in faraway Rome never could. A crusade army was, in effect, a loosely organized mob of soldiers, clergy, servants, and followers heading in roughly the same direction for roughly the same purposes. Once launched, it could be controlled no more than the wind or the sea.

Because the crusade was preached as a pilgrimage, a holy act of charity, and a means of grace and penance, able-bodied men were not the only ones to heed the call. Women and elderly men had just as great an appetite for salvation as did their husbands and sons, and they too clamored to be crossed. Urban II ordered his bishops and preachers not to receive vows from those who could not participate in the army, and he dissolved those vows already taken. It was difficult, however, to make the case that some should be denied the right to make a pilgrimage simply because they could not fight. A great many of the poor, sick, and otherwise unfit donned the crusader's cross despite the papal pronouncements. Urban forbade monks to leave their monasteries or clergy to leave their parishes without proper permission. Those who could not wage the battle with swords should do so with prayers and devotions at home. Monks especially were enjoined to fulfill their role as "those who pray" rather than adding a burden to the tasks of "those who fight." The pope further directed that no Spaniards should take the cross. Their struggle against Islam was at home, not abroad. None of these prohibitions meshed well with the popular view of the crusade as pilgrimage, and so they were often ignored.

CRUSADER MOTIVATIONS

It was long believed by modern historians that the crusades were manned by Europe's castoffs: aristocratic second or third sons with no claim to their father's lands or title, robber barons, highwaymen, ne'er-do-wells, and greedy monks. In part, this interpretation was an assessment of demographic evidence. Europe's population soared during the tenth century, which suggested a need for more land. Thus, the crusades were often described as Europe's first colonial wars, a kind of proto-imperialism visited on the Muslim people. Men with little to lose and everything to gain, it was argued, took the cross merely as a pious pretext to enrich themselves with stolen booty and carve out a new home in a distant land. Historians who lived through Europe's scramble for empire or the subsequent dissolution of imperialism naturally saw the crusades in that familiar light. In addition, the post-Enlightenment and positivist view of religiosity too often presumed that medieval men and women could not possibly take seriously the pious words they uttered and wrote. For scholars of those schools, religion was not an impetus but a diversion, a ruse for those who spoke of the next world while profiting in this one. Unfortunately, this mistaken view is still dominant in popular works and even in many otherwise fine textbooks.

New developments in computer technology have allowed scholars like Jonathan Riley-Smith to analyze quantitatively large numbers of documents relating to the men and women who participated in the crusades. Rather than general impressions, we now have solid evidence concerning those who took up the church's call and the factors that motivated them. Approximately 150,000 people across Europe responded to Urban II's summons by donning the cross of the pilgrim. The vast majority of these were poor, and many were women or elderly (or both). During the course of the First Crusade, approximately 40,000 men marched to the East. Some left early, others late. Many did not make the entire journey. Only a small minority of that total were knights; nevertheless, it was the knights and barons who brought with them the armies, so their acceptance of the crusading vow was crucial to the success of the crusade. What is clearest in the documentary record is that the vast majority of these knightly crusaders were not spare sons but instead the lords of their estates. It was not those with the least to lose who took up the cross, but rather those with the most. Such men knew well the dangers of the proposed journey of some two thousand miles. A few of them were even familiar with the Turks, having served as mercenaries to the Byzantine Empire.

The cost of crusading was truly enormous. A knight who planned to bring a few family members (as many did) and an army appropriate to his position and authority would need to assemble funds equal to five or six times his annual income. Few had that sort of money lying around. They were forced to sell freeholds or settle property disputes to their disadvantage to raise the funds. In many cases, they also turned to their relatives, who liquidated their own assets to support the crusade. All of this represented a significant, in many cases dangerous, drain on the resources of a crusading knight and his family. And for what? All knew that a pilgrimage to Palestine was a treacherous undertaking even in the best of times. The tears that flowed when a crusader left his wife were not the result solely of an expected long absence but also of the strong likelihood that the soldier would never return. Although some hoped for the opportunity for plunder, the pope had decreed that all lands captured were to belong to the "prince" in command at the time. The expectation was that this "prince" would be the Byzantine emperor. In the event, very few crusaders remained in the Holy Land after their vows were fulfilled. The vast majority returned to Europe with neither riches nor land.

To impoverish one's family for the remote possibility of garnering wealth in Palestine would have been foolish in the extreme. The price was too great and the chances of return too slim. To understand why thousands of knights and their families made such profound sacrifices, one must remember that they were medieval, not modern, people. The culture of nobility in the eleventh century was one of public displays of piety. Lords were known as much for their love of God as for their skill on the battlefield. Indeed, the two were seen as different sides of the same coin, neither possible without the other. With open hands, these families had showered lands and wealth upon Europe's churches and monasteries for centuries. It was the duty of the nobility, who were blessed by God, to return the fruits of that blessing to God's people and his church. The crusade was simply another means of doing that. Knights were willing to make profound sacrifices for the crusade because it was in the nature of their class to do so. By expending great wealth, they were storing up treasure where rust and moth could not corrupt. By defending the church, they defended all that was good and true in their world. In short, most noblemen who joined the crusade did so from a simple and sincere love of God. As is still true, people gladly march off to horrible wars if they believe that the cause for which they fight is noble, true, and greater than themselves.

This is not to say that crusading armies were made up of saints, nor that these warriors were particularly saintly on the march. They were men of the sword: pious and idealistic, but also crude, arrogant, and, at times, savage. The crusade provided a means for such men to turn their talent for warfare and bloodshed into a means of their own salvation. One can presume that most of the lesser men, who made up the bulk of a crusade army, were motivated by many of the same pious principles that led their betters to take the cross, but undoubtedly those who had little must surely have hoped to gain something in the enterprise. Most, however, were beholden to the greater men who supported them, and most could not have made the journey without their largesse. A crusade army was a curious mix of rich and poor, saints and sinners, motivated by every kind of pious and selfish desire, yet it could not have come into being without the pious idealism that led men to risk all to liberate the lands of Christ.

NOTE

1. From the account of Robert the Monk, *Historia Hierosolimitana,* in James A. Brundage, *The Crusades: A Documentary Survey* (Milwaukee: Marquette University Press, 1962), 18.

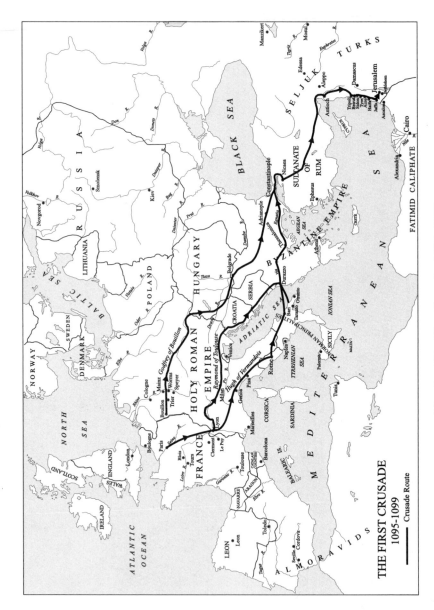

Map 2. The First Crusade, 1095–1099

2

THE FIRST CRUSADE

Pope Urban II set August 15, 1096, as the departure date for the armies of the crusade. Hurried and costly preparations were under way, not only on the estates of western knights but also in the cities of the Byzantine Empire, where citizens needed to gather provisions for the thousands of soldiers who would march across their lands. The First Crusade was shaping up to be the largest and most ambitious military operation launched from western Europe since the days of the Roman Empire. The costs in resources and manpower were enormous.

THE PEOPLE'S CRUSADE

Many in Europe wondered at the careful preparations for the holy enterprise. In the medieval worldview, it was right that made might. Just as David felled Goliath with only a sling and his faith, so God continued to bless his faithful with victory when they fought for just causes. This widespread belief would receive a vigorous shaking during the course of the crusading movement, but those days were still in the future. In 1095, optimism ruled. As thousands rushed to follow Christ to the place of his Resurrection, there was little thought of the possibility of defeat, particularly among those who understood warfare but a little. To many, the extensive preparations of the church and nobility for the crusade seemed not only superfluous but almost faithless. If Christ's soldiers marched to the Holy Land, would he not scatter the infidel Turks as he had the Philistines long ago?

This view was shared by one of the most popular crusade preachers, Peter the Hermit. Riding from town to town on his donkey, this ragged holy man mesmerized audiences with fiery and emotional sermons. Miracles followed Peter wherever he went. Demons were exorcised, sicknesses healed, and confirmed sinners turned to God. It was widely believed that Peter carried with him a letter sent down from heaven in which God exhorted all Christians to move quickly against the Turks so that he could take vengeance upon them. Peter's preaching drew thousands into the crusade. Many powerful lords took the cross after hearing Peter, or even simply hearing of him. The preacher's message, like his letter, was for all people, rich and poor, old and young, male and female. His sermons were not just an exhortation to go to the lands of Christ but an invitation to follow Peter himself. As a result, this charismatic man bore in his train a throng of people, predominantly French but of every social status. In April 1096, he left France for Cologne, where he preached to the Germans, also with great success.

Peter the Hermit's crusade preaching had become a crusade itself. Although there were knights and lords who followed the preacher on his march, the army (if it can be called that) consisted mainly of those who required little preparation to depart for an indefinite period of time to parts unknown. In other words, the large majority of his followers were relatively poor, and a great many were armed with only the crudest implements. Many were women and children. The crusade marched across Europe, a storm of religious enthusiasm impelled by simple faith and Peter's own spellbinding personality. It could not be slowed, let alone stopped. Long before the official departure date of August 15, Peter and his masses left western Europe on their long trek to meet the enemies of Christ.

Peter the Hermit's ragtag army was not the only group that left early. The French lord Walter Sansavoir (not Walter the Penniless, as he is often misnamed) led another large and ill-disciplined army of minor knights and enthusiastic peasants ahead of Peter the Hermit. Walter agreed to wait for Peter at Constantinople, where their combined forces would enter Turkish Anatolia. The march of these two armies across Hungary, Bulgaria, and Greece was not without violence. Emperor Alexius I had not expected crusaders so soon, and his government had not yet prepared the markets necessary to feed so large an army. As it happened, few of the crusaders in this "first wave" of the crusade, as Riley-Smith has called it, could afford to purchase food anyway. Foraging, theft, riots, and violence were the result. Matters could have been much worse had the emperor not moved quickly to make provisions available and had Peter and Walter not done their best to keep their rowdy followers in check.

Walter Sansavoir arrived in Constantinople in mid-July 1096. Peter the Hermit came a few weeks later, on August 1. Alexius was eager to meet them, particularly Peter the Hermit, about whom he had heard much. The emperor was clearly impressed with Peter's sanctity, but he expressed amazement that the preacher had come to Byzantium so quickly. Would it not be wiser, he asked, to wait until the main body of crusaders arrived before crossing into Asia Minor? Alexius succeeded where Urban did not, convincing Peter and Walter that it would indeed be better for them to tarry at Constantinople. Their followers were not so easily swayed. They had made a long journey through many trials and were now within sight of Turkish lands. Why should they wait until the stragglers caught up with them? Was God not calling to them even now to crush his foes? Would he not punish delay and cowardice? As subsequent events make clear, this was a crowd eager for glory, and they saw no reason to share it with those who mocked them when they left Europe with nothing but a prayer and a song. There was also the practical consideration of provisions. The crusade was camped in Constantinople's suburbs, where food was readily available in the markets, but the poor could not purchase it, and the rest did not think it right that they should have to impoverish themselves while waiting month after month for no good reason. Walter and Peter's pleas for patience fell on deaf ears. When they judged food prices to be too high, the mob began pillaging the suburbs for what they wanted. At last, Alexius allowed Peter to take his crusade to the Turks. It had done enough damage to the Christians.

On August 6, the "People's Crusade" was transported across the Bosporus. At last, the throng was on the Turkish frontier. No one seems to have come up with a plan for marching through Anatolia, a deficiency that was now all too apparent. Disputes about the proper course of action broke out, some of them violently. Regional sympathies began to tear the mob into two competing crusades, one of Germans and some Italians and the other of Frenchmen. Rather than advance, they took to raiding. When the French crusaders led a surprise attack on the suburbs of Nicaea and returned with plenty of loot, the Germans were beside themselves with envy. They quickly launched their own raid but were met by the Turks, who were now alive to the danger. They routed the Germans, capturing the entire army. Those who renounced Christ and converted to Islam were sent to the East; the rest were slaughtered. The Turks then sent a forged message to the French, purportedly from the

Germans, telling them of the riches of their captured citadel. With alacrity, the French headed off, despite the warnings of those better informed. Deep in Turkish territory, they learned too late the truth. In their rush, the French had blindly walked into an ambush. The entire army was wiped out.

Peter the Hermit avoided the massacre. Earlier, he had returned to Constantinople to discuss tactics with the emperor. There he received the news of the elimination of his crusade. Of all the thousands who had followed Peter from France to Asia Minor, he was virtually the only survivor. There was nothing for him to do but enjoy the emperor's hospitality while awaiting the arrival of the main body of the crusade.

The "People's Crusade" was not the only misfire of the movement. When Peter the Hermit made his way across Germany, in his wake sprouted a number of smaller crusade armies determined to catch up to the famous holy man. Some made it, but most did not. Instead, the lure of Jewish riches distracted some from their original purposes. Protected by the German crown and local lords, Jews were abundant in the thriving cities along the Rhine. They became a rich target for avaricious crusaders. The most infamous of the anti-Jewish crusade leaders was Count Emicho of Leiningen. On a rather pronounced detour, he and his followers marched down the Rhine plundering and massacring Jews in the cities of Speyer, Worms, Mainz, Trier, and Cologne. Some local bishops did their best to protect the Jews, but many were killed all the same. In Mainz, Emicho's men stormed the palace of the bishop, where the Jews had taken refuge. Albert of Aix described the terror:

> They killed the women, also, and with their swords pierced tender children of whatever age and sex. The Jews, seeing that their Christian enemies were attacking them and their children, and that they were sparing no age, likewise fell upon one another, brother, children, wives, and sisters, and thus they perished at each other's hands. Horrible to say, mothers cut the throats of nursing children with knives and stabbed others, preferring them to perish thus by their own hands rather than to be killed by the weapons of the uncircumcised.[1]

The pope harshly condemned the killings, but there was little more he could do.

Much has been written concerning the motivation behind these massacres. One must accept from the outset that just as there were many participants, there were also many reasons formulated for the attacks. For some, it was a matter of penury. Like the followers of Peter the Hermit, they lacked the funds to make it to the East. Here were Jews, they reasoned, many of whom had grown wealthy through the sin of usury. Why not take their ill-gotten gains and use them for this holy cause? Others considered the conversion or destruction of the Jews to be a first order of business. Why should Christians march two thousand miles to expel the enemies of Christ when there were so many dwelling here in their very homes? Undoubtedly the image of the crucified Christ employed by crusade preachers led some to look not to the Muslims but to the Jews, who, the Bible records, were responsible for the Crucifixion. As one of the crusaders explained to a Jewish rabbi:

> You are the children of those who killed the object of our veneration, hanging him on a tree; and he himself had said: "There will yet come a day when my children will come and avenge my blood."[2]

As it happened, none of these anti-Jewish "crusades" made it to the East. Most simply evaporated when resistance in the cities became too severe. Count Emicho pressed on to Hungary, where he continued his belligerence. There, his army was crushed.

To Constantinople

The main body of the First Crusade began to depart in mid-August 1096, just as the pope had requested. The plan was for the various armies to make their way to Constantinople, where they would combine their forces with the Byzantines for the march east. Among the greater lords was Godfrey of Bouillon, a member of the family of the counts of Boulogne. Godfrey was a second son, yet one with substantial resources. Henry IV had made him Duke of Lower Lorraine in 1087, and he had worked hard to consolidate and expand his other holdings. Once he took the cross, however, his efforts were transformed from consolidation to liquidation. To raise the sums necessary to transport himself, his brother Baldwin of Boulogne, and a sizable retinue of knights to the East, Godfrey sold off a number of properties and settled many ongoing disputes to his disadvantage. Although he made considerable financial sacrifice,

Godfrey clearly planned to come home after the crusade. He did not relinquish his claim to Lower Lorraine, nor to a nucleus of other rights and properties with which he could rebuild power upon his return. He traveled to Constantinople via Hungary. King Colman had already had his fill of crusaders destructively crossing his lands, but Godfrey gave over his brother Baldwin as hostage for his army's good conduct. His troops made their way in an orderly manner to Constantinople, where they arrived on December 23, 1096.

Godfrey was not the first crusader to make it to the great city. Hugh of Vermandois, the brother of the king of France, left Europe at the same time but took a more direct route and a much smaller force. For Emperor Alexius, the crusade presented both a challenge and an opportunity. On the one hand, he was pleased that his request for aid had met with such success. Thousands of Christian soldiers were now mobilized to fight the enemies of Byzantium. On the other hand, these western barbarians were not altogether trustworthy. He was quite concerned that the empire not exchange a Muslim enemy for a Christian one. When Hugh arrived, his men camped in the suburbs, while he was invited to the marvelously rich imperial palace in the city. There, Alexius engaged in the time-honored Byzantine practice of overawing foreigners with the fabulous wealth of their ancient empire. Hugh was impressed but not distracted. Like other crusade leaders, he was curious about the role the emperor planned to play in the expedition. Alexius bestowed rich gifts on Hugh and professed his desire to add imperial forces to the crusade's numbers and to lead personally the armies against the infidel. Before he transported foreign armies across the Bosporus, though, Alexius felt only justified in asking them to show their good faith. He politely requested that Hugh swear an oath that any lands the crusade should capture that had previously belonged to the empire should immediately be returned to the emperor. He also asked for an oath of loyalty to himself while the crusade remained in his domains. Since the crusaders had never planned to go beyond the far-flung borders of the old Roman Empire, this oath would effectively give all conquests to Alexius. Hugh stalled, not certain what other magnates had planned and not wanting to go out on a limb himself. In the meantime, the emperor kept him in sumptuous luxury in the city but refused to allow him to return to his troops. Under great pressure, Hugh at last relented and took the emperor's oath.

Shortly after Godfrey arrived in Constantinople's suburbs, he re-

Figure 1: **Land Walls of Constantinople.** The area near the walls, now under cultivation, was a moat during the middle ages. Photo by the author.

ceived a similar invitation to the palace of the emperor. From Hugh, Godfrey knew the emperor's intentions, and he did not much care for the particulars of the oath. He declined the invitation, but the emperor was not so easily put off. Alexius sent word that he would not transport Godfrey's army across the Bosporus until Godfrey had sworn loyalty and given his word that reconquered territories would not be stolen from the Roman Empire. When Godfrey remained aloof, the emperor cut off provisions to his army. In retaliation, the crusaders pillaged the suburbs, forcing Alexius to reopen the markets. For three months, the army stubbornly waited, all the while demanding to be taken to Asia. Exasperated, Godfrey finally ordered his troops to attack Constantinople itself. In January 1097, the crusaders assaulted the mammoth Theodosian land walls near the imperial palace of Blachernae. Godfrey's troops, however, were far too meager to seriously threaten the largest and best defended city in the western world. In retaliation, the emperor ordered a sortie of imperial soldiers to attack the Latin troops. After his forces were roughly pushed back from the walls, Godfrey at last decided to come to terms. On January 20, he took an oath to Alexius, and he and his men were promptly transported across the Bosporus.

The forty-year-old Bohemond of Taranto got a later start than Godfrey. Bohemond was the son of the Norman leader Robert Guiscard. Before his death in 1085, Guiscard had left his lands east of the Adriatic to Bohemond, and those to the west in southern Italy to his younger son, Roger. In 1082, that seemed a fair division, given that Robert and Bohemond had captured Durazzo and were in the process of the conquest of Greece, but by 1085 an allied force of Byzantines and Venetians had erased most of the Norman gains just before Robert Guiscard himself died of plague. Bohemond was left with practically nothing. Since then, he had managed to cobble together a lordship for himself in southern Italy, but it was not impressive. More than any other crusading leader, Bohemond was ambitious for personal gain. He had once believed that he would rule in Thessalonica or perhaps even Constantinople. Although his hopes had been dashed, he still looked to the east as his opportunity for power and wealth.

For the Byzantines, Bohemond seemed to present the most acute threat. Because Bohemond was a crusader, Alexius was obliged to make smooth his trip from Durazzo to Constantinople, a journey that Bohemond had fought his way across a little more than a decade earlier. The Byzantine citizens along the *via Egnatia,* the old Roman road that led to the eastern capital, could not help but look on the hated Normans with suspicion and dread. Bohemond, however, had his eyes on greater things. He carefully monitored his men, making certain that they were on their best behavior. He wanted to make clear to the emperor that his crusading army was no threat at all to the Byzantine Empire.

Bohemond arrived at Constantinople in early April 1097, not long after Godfrey's forces had been ferried across the straits. The Norman leader gratefully accepted the emperor's invitation to meet with him in the palace and listened intently when Alexius asked him to swear the same oath that Hugh and Godfrey had already accepted. From the emperor's perspective, the timing of the crusading leaders' arrival at Constantinople could not have been better. One by one, he was able to negotiate with them in isolation. As each leader agreed to take the oath, it made it more difficult for the next leader to refuse. Bohemond was not opposed to taking the oath in any event. It seems likely that the Norman prince suggested that Alexius appoint him commander in chief of the imperial forces in Asia, something that would have given Bohemond effective control over the entire enterprise. But Alexius was not willing to go that far in this friendly reconciliation. Instead, he replied cordially and in a noncommittal fashion, and Bohemond took the oath. His troops were then taken across the Bosporus to join the other crusaders assembled in Asia Minor.

By far the most powerful magnate to take up the cross was Raymond, Count of Toulouse. This fifty-five-year-old warrior had spent most of his life extending his power over thirteen counties in southern France—almost the entire region. His wealth, lands, and armies were greater than those of most kings, including the king of France. Moved by the preaching of the crusade, Raymond decided to finish his life in the service of God. He divested himself of all of his properties, giving them to his son, and with his wife prepared for the departure east. Raymond was among the first nobles to take the cross; indeed, he was probably informed of the crusade by Urban II before the Council of Clermont. It was probably the pope's desire that Raymond serve as a commander in chief, or at least principal leader, on the holy enterprise. To signify this papal favor, Urban appointed Adhemar, bishop of Le Puy, as papal legate to the crusade and instructed him to accompany the army of Raymond. It was a great army, far larger than any other single lord could muster. Raymond left in October 1096, but he had a difficult journey through the Veneto and Dalmatia before coming to Durazzo. For the remainder of his journey, he was given a Byzantine escort, whose mission it was to protect the local population from his army. There was more than one skirmish between the escorts and crusaders, and some pillaging did occur. At last, he arrived at Constantinople on April 21, 1097.

By now, Raymond had heard of the progress of the other crusading lords and was aware of the oath that they had sworn to the emperor. He probably also heard of Bohemond's attempt to take control of the crusade. Raymond was not like the other leaders. More mature and powerful, the count of Toulouse would not so easily be manipulated by this cunning emperor. When asked to take the oath, Raymond responded that he had come to serve God; he would not take another as his lord. The other crusading magnates across the Bosporus urged Raymond to relent so that they could get under way. He refused. Raymond clearly saw himself as the leader of the Latin forces. He did not want to be forced to accept Bohemond as commander in chief if Alexius decided to appoint him as such. Instead, Raymond proposed that if the emperor himself would take the cross and command the crusade, then he would gladly take his oath. Alexius replied that nothing would make him happier, but that he could not leave Constantinople at present. In the end, a compromise was reached. Raymond swore to respect the property and person of the emperor—a lukewarm oath not uncommon in southern France. With that, Raymond and his forces were transported across the Bosporus. The crusading army, what Riley-Smith calls the "second wave," was assembled.

From Constantinople to Antioch

The crusade's first objective was the city of Nicaea. The capital of the Turkish sultanate, Nicaea was an important strategic location for any further advances into Asia Minor. The heavily fortified city rested on the shores of a lake, making a complete investment of the city impossible until Byzantine vessels were sent overland to close off the city's ports. Having easily dispatched the crusade of Peter the Hermit, Sultan Kilij Arslan, who was not in the city, did not at first take this second army very seriously. He may even have heard that Peter was present and therefore assumed the caliber of forces to be poor. He learned differently, but too late. By the time he brought his army to relieve the city, the crusaders had established their siege. In a pitched battle on May 21, the crusaders decisively defeated the Turkish forces. In the mayhem, Kilij Arslan fled, leaving behind his wife, family, and treasury in the city.

With the defeat of the relieving forces, the Turkish garrison opened negotiations with Alexius for terms of surrender. The emperor guaranteed the life and property of all inhabitants and assured them that the Latin crusaders would not be allowed in the city. In the dead of night, the ports were opened to the Byzantine vessels. When the crusaders awoke, they found the imperial banners flying over the city walls. Alexius thanked the westerners for their assistance and bestowed rich gifts on their leaders. Many of the crusaders felt cheated. They had sworn to restore property like this to the emperor, and they were now robbed of the opportunity to break their oath. Surely a little plundering was justified, many grumbled, if only of the Muslim inhabitants.

On June 26, the crusading army departed Nicaea, bound for Antioch. Between the two cities lay the sun-baked expanse of Anatolia. Summers in Asia Minor are oppressively hot. What little food was in the fields had been destroyed by the retreating Turks. The crusaders decided to split their forces into two groups. The first was led by Bohemond and a few other lords. The second, which traveled a day behind, was commanded by Godfrey and Raymond. The wisdom of this deployment was demonstrated a few days later when Kilij Arslan attacked the first group, apparently believing that it was the entire force of the crusade. Bohemond lacked the manpower to defeat the sultan, but he could defend himself for a day while word was sent to Raymond and Godfrey. On June 30, the second group arrived, catching Kilij Arslan completely by surprise. He and his troops fled in panic, leaving behind their provisions and tents.

For the next four months, the crusaders made their way across Anatolia under horrible conditions. The heat was brutal, water scarce, and food scarcer. Repeatedly, the enterprise seemed doomed, yet in each case something allowed it to continue, if only just a little farther. For the crusaders, these were the miracles that God performed for those who marched to the land of his Son. Finally, on October 21, 1097, they caught sight of the great walls of Antioch. The crusaders were a large but pitiful force. A cleric, Fulcher of Chartres, recorded:

> Truly, either you would laugh or perhaps shed tears out of compassion, when many of our people lacking beasts of burden, because many had died, loaded wethers, she-goats, sows, or dogs with their possessions. . . . We saw the backs of these small beasts chafed by the heavy loads. Occasionally armed knights even used oxen as mounts.[3]

Meanwhile, Baldwin of Boulogne and Tancred, the cousin of Bohemond, had split off from the main body of the crusade to acquire assistance from Armenian Christian cities farther to the southwest in Cilicia. They were warmly welcomed, and both men soon found themselves caught up in local politics. Baldwin then headed east into greater Armenia, where he received a similar welcome. The capital of the region was the city of Edessa. It was ruled by Toros, who was officially a vassal of the Turks but in reality acted independently. He did not expect that situation to continue for very much longer without help, so he offered to adopt Baldwin as his successor. Baldwin accepted and entered Edessa among cheering throngs of citizens. Shortly thereafter, a coup toppled Toros, leaving Baldwin as the sole ruler of Edessa, where the Frankish knight settled permanently. The new County of Edessa was the first of the crusader states. It was to provide a valuable buffer against Turkish attacks on Antioch and other Christian lands. The means of Baldwin's acquisition nevertheless was a clear warning that relations between Byzantines and crusaders would not be smooth. Despite his oath, Baldwin made no attempt to restore Edessa to Alexius I in Constantinople.

One of the greatest cities of the ancient Roman Empire and one of the patriarchal sees of Christianity, Antioch was an imposing sight for the wearied crusaders. Its fortifications were massive, consisting of long walls studded with four hundred towers. The population was predominantly Greek and Armenian Christian, although it was garrisoned and ruled by Turks. The crusaders probably numbered around forty thousand souls, but they were incapable of completely investing the city for a siege. Raymond suggested an immediate attempt to take the city by storm, but Bohemond argued against it. The Norman leader clearly hoped to find a way to claim Antioch for himself, just as Baldwin had done at Edessa. If a direct assault were successful, the city would likely fall under the control of the most powerful lord. That would be Raymond. In any event, Bohemond did not think it possible to take the city so easily, and neither did a majority of the nobility. They decided to wait out a siege.

The winter of 1097–98 was a particularly cold and difficult one. Forty thousand people require a great deal of food, and there was little to be had. Foraging parties already had exhausted nearby lands, so they were sent ever farther in search of provisions. The leaders were often less concerned with the blockade of the city than the acquisition of supplies. Hunger, starvation, and disease descended on the soldiers. Many knights who had not lost their horses during the grueling journey were now forced to slaughter them for meat. This was a decision made only as a last resort, for the horse was not only the symbol of a knight's social station but also his principal means of combat. Fulcher of Chartres described the pitiful conditions:

> At that time, the famished ate the shoots of beanseeds growing in the fields and many kinds of herbs unseasoned with salt, also thistles,

which, being not well cooked because of the deficiency of firewood, pricked the tongues of those eating them; also horses, asses, and camels, and dogs and rats. The poorer ones ate even the skins of the beasts and seeds of grain found in manure.[4]

Some soldiers turned to cannibalism, making use of Turkish casualties. Many more simply died of starvation.

When it seemed that things could not get any worse, news from the East made it so. In 1098, the Fatimids of Egypt launched an attack against the Turks in Palestine, capturing Jerusalem and the surrounding region. Many of the Turks displaced from Palestine made their way to the greater Turkish lords in Damascus, Aleppo, and Mosul. The atabeg of Mosul, Kerbogha, combined these troops with others from Mesopotamia and began a march to relieve Antioch. When news reached the crusaders of the coming of Kerbogha, it created a panic. Decimated by hunger and disease, the crusade was in serious danger of being crushed between the Turkish forces and the walls of Antioch. Throughout the preceding winter months, many had been comforted by the visions of various holy men, who saw the saints and angels conspiring for the victory of the followers of Christ. Now that seemed foolish. So far from home, they were in desperate danger. Desertions reached an epidemic level. Even Peter the Hermit, the famed preacher who still bore his letter from heaven, slipped out of camp and ran for home; he was captured and returned. With profuse tears, he begged the crusaders to forgive him for his loss of faith, and they did.

Many others deserted more successfully. Professing to miss his wife, Stephen of Blois fled back across Anatolia. On the way, he met Alexius I and his troops, who were marching to Antioch to reinforce the crusaders. Stephen and his fellow deserters did not want to appear cowardly, so they professed to the emperor that the situation was so desperate that to go to Antioch would mean certain death. Would they have left their holy mission if there had been even the slightest hope? In rationalizing their decision to abandon their comrades, Stephen and his companions convinced the emperor that it was foolhardy and pointless to continue on to Antioch. The emperor returned to Constantinople. When the crusaders learned of Alexius's decision, they derided him as a coward, and many proclaimed their oaths to him void.

All was not as bleak as Stephen of Blois maintained. Bohemond had for some time been attempting to corrupt a captain of the guard in the city, and he had finally met with success. For a price, this captain was willing to allow Bohemond and his men to enter. The Norman leader called a meeting of the crusading lords. Without revealing his plans, he asked them to agree that if he and his men could take Antioch unassisted, then by rights the city should belong to him. All the barons were quite willing to agree to this—all, that is, except Raymond. The count of Toulouse reminded his fellow leaders that they had sworn oaths to restore this land to the emperor if it could be conquered; they had no right to promise it to a Norman adventurer. It is striking that although Raymond alone had refused to take the oath to the emperor, he alone insisted that it be honored. In part this was due to his own reluctance to let Bohemond acquire such a prize, but it was also motivated by what appears to have been a warm friendship that had materialized between Raymond and Alexius. At last, however, Raymond agreed that if Bohemond could take the city, he should have it until such time that the emperor could make his claim in person.

On the night of June 3, 1098, Bohemond and his men scrambled over the walls and opened the gates for their comrades. The crusaders spilled into the dozing city, capturing it in a matter of hours. Only the citadel held out. Antioch was in crusader hands.

Instead of heading straight for Antioch, Kerbogha first stopped off at Edessa in an unsuccessful attempt to wrest the city from Baldwin. He was delayed there for three weeks, a crucial delay that allowed the crusaders time to hole up in Antioch. Had the sultan not stopped, he would have caught the Christians outside the walls, just as they feared. When he finally arrived, Kerbogha completely invested Antioch. Now the former besiegers were the besieged. There was little food in the city, so starvation remained a severe problem. The forces of Kerbogha were awesome. Each day, the Turks took delight in describing the deaths they had in store for the Christians when the city inevitably fell. Fear, hunger, and despair wracked the city. Again desertions soared. Some deserters escaped; others were captured by the Turks and cruelly tortured and mutilated in view of their comrades on the walls.

It is not surprising that in such desperate straits, the visions that were always a part of the crusade increased in frequency. One visionary, Peter Bartholomew, proclaimed that St. Andrew told him the whereabouts of the Holy Lance, the implement used to pierce the side of Christ. Raymond was convinced by the story, but the papal legate, Adhemar of Le Puy, was openly skeptical. How could the Holy Lance be in Antioch, he asked, when he and others had seen it in Constantinople? News of the vision spread quickly and sparked other visions corroborating the first. On the night of June 14, a meteor streaked across the sky and landed in the camp of the Turks. The signs of heaven seemed clear. The next morning, Peter Bartholomew solemnly led Raymond and a procession of clergy into the Cathedral of St. Peter, where the visionary pointed to the spot where workmen should dig. Dig they did. Hour after hour passed with no sign of the relic. Raymond had lent his prestige to this search, and he was clearly irritated that it was revealing nothing. Finally, when the diggers were ready to quit, Peter Bartholomew himself jumped into the pit and began scrounging with his bare hands. After a few minutes, he cried in triumph and was pulled out of the hole holding a worn lance head. Raymond rejoiced at the find, which he quickly attached to a spear pole and carried around the city. Adhemar and others suspected that Peter Bartholomew had planted the spearhead, but nothing could stem the excitement that swept the crusade. Morale rose throughout the ranks. In the Holy Lance, they believed that Christ himself had given a sign of their impending victory.

Kerbogha's troops were numerous and his position strong, but within the Turkish forces there were internal divisions between jealous emirs, divisions that became more acute as the siege dragged on. In time, these factors might lead to the breakup of the besieging army, but the crusaders lacked the supplies to wait. Their only hope was to sally forth from the walls of the city and defeat the Turkish forces in a pitched battle. Because Raymond was bedridden with illness, it fell to Bohemond to lead the Christian forces against Kerbogha. On June 28, the assault began. Kerbogha watched as the crusading forces marched out of the city gates, banners flying, drawing up their ranks. Some of the emirs urged him to attack the Christians immediately, while they were still exiting the city, but the Turkish commander wanted to wipe out his enemy with a single blow. He may have believed that desertions and starvation had more seriously harmed the crusaders than was the case. Perhaps he also considered the reports of a very large army coming all the way from western Europe to be exaggerated. Whatever the reason for his decision, Kerbogha was plainly astonished when he saw the size of the forces assembling before him. Quickly, he sent an emissary to discuss truce, but the crusaders would hear none of it. They advanced in good order amid a torrent of arrows. When it became clear that a bloody and difficult battle was ahead, many of the Turkish emirs, who resented Kerbogha in any event, withdrew from the field. Their departure sparked a crescendo of panic in the Turkish forces, scattering them into the countryside. Miraculously, the fearful threat had disintegrated. With Kerbogha and his forces neutralized, the city's citadel surrendered to Bohemond. Antioch and its region were now safely in Christian hands. Against all odds, the crusaders had won a smashing victory, but not alone. Many of the combatants and those watching from the walls attested to the presence of armies of angels and saints, as well as the spirits of their fallen comrades, fighting alongside Bohemond's troops against the forces of the Turks.

The victory at Antioch placed the crusaders materially in their best position since leaving Constantinople. They now controlled a large port city and a strategic region stretching from Antioch to Edessa. The rich gains, however, were also the cause of internal strife. Raymond had opposed Bohemond's efforts to acquire Antioch from the beginning, but it was becoming increasingly difficult to do so now. The Norman leader had single-handedly captured the city and led the sortie that liberated it. From the point of view of most crusaders, Alexius and the Byzantines had forfeited their rights to Antioch when they turned their back on it. Since then, Alexius had declined an offer to garrison Antioch and lead the crusaders to Jerusalem. Surely, then, Bohemond deserved to have the city. Raymond disagreed. Even putting aside the oath the leaders had sworn to the emperor, Raymond stressed that they had also taken an oath to God to travel to Jerusalem and deliver the land of his Son. No crusader should be allowed to renounce that sacred vow for temporal gain. Raymond, therefore, insisted that Bohemond and his troops remain with the crusade as it headed south. Bohemond clearly did not want to do that, so the crusade stalled.

It was not an inopportune moment for it to stall. Summer had begun, and none of the soldiers were eager to march south into Syria's scorching desert heat. It was decided, therefore, to remain at Antioch until November 1. During the summer, a plague descended on the city, taking the life of the papal legate, Adhemar of Le Puy. This was a significant blow. Adhemar had been the voice of reason and common sense in the councils of the lords. When rivalries threatened to explode, it was always the papal legate who cooled heads. Along with Raymond, Adhemar opposed giving the city to Bohemond or to any crusader. Now the count of Toulouse stood virtually alone in that view. Nevertheless, Raymond was as determined as ever that the crusade would not leave without Bohemond, and that Antioch should not be given to the Norman leader. In council, the lords decided to send a letter to Urban II informing him of the death of his legate and asking him to come to Antioch to take the city himself and lead the army to Jerusalem. No one seriously believed that the pope would agree, but it did help to put the question off a bit longer.

November 1 came and went, and the crusade was no closer to leaving Antioch. The rank-and-file crusaders, exasperated with their leaders, demanded that they put aside their squabbles and prepare to march south. On November 5, the leaders met together in the Cathedral of St. Peter. After fruitless arguments, spokesmen for the army strode into the church and informed the lords that if they did not come to an agreement, the men would tear down the fortifications of Antioch. At last, Raymond agreed to a compromise of sorts. Bohemond could have Antioch provided he agreed to depart with the host and serve the crusade until the conquest of Jerusalem. Bohemond willingly agreed. The news was reported to the rank and file, who rejoiced.

All was not in readiness for departure. Over the course of November and December, preparations were made and a few nearby locations conquered. The soldiers were continually assured that their departure was forthcoming, but it became clear that Bohemond and Raymond were again attempting to outmaneuver each other. The Norman leader plainly had no intention of leaving Antioch, regardless of what he had agreed to previously. At last, the army offered to Raymond the title of commander in chief of the crusade if he would lead them to the Holy Land. He consented. The title, though impressive, was ornamental: Godfrey of Bouillon and Robert of Flanders had no intention of taking orders from the count of Toulouse. Raymond did acquire command over other nobles, but only because he paid money for it, not because of his designation as supreme commander.

From Antioch to Jerusalem

On January 13, 1099, Raymond, barefoot and in the attire of a pilgrim, led the army south into Syria. What the army found there were a number of petty emirs willing to pay if their towns were left unmolested. The course of the crusade's progress through the late winter and early spring was profitable and comparatively easy. The powerful Turkish emirs in Damascus and elsewhere had no interest in defending these rebellious small fry. Besides, Palestine was now in Shi'ite Fatimid hands. Why should the Sunni Turks lift a finger to protect them? On the contrary, many of the Turks watched with glee as the "Franks" (as they called them) bore down upon the Egyptians who had so recently taken Jerusalem from them. For his part, the sultan of Egypt had been sending envoys to the crusaders since their march across Asia. He applauded their martial prowess and offered to join with them in their war against the Turks, but his overtures were wasted on the westerners, who made few distinctions among Muslims. Now, as the crusade approached the newly won Fatimid territories in Palestine, the sultan again offered an alliance if the crusaders would remain outside his domains. Clearly, the Egyptians understood neither the purpose nor the motivation of the crusade.

On May 19, the crusade entered Fatimid territory just north of Beirut. Beirut and its coastal neighbors to the south—Sidon, Tyre, Acre, and Haifa—were willing to provide the crusaders with supplies on the condition that they leave the cities and their suburbs unmolested. Because the crusaders were interested only in reaching Jerusalem, they were glad to oblige. Just north of Jaffa, the army reached the inland road to the Holy City. It was June 3. Word had reached the leaders that the Egyptian army was mobilizing. Some argued that to head to Jerusalem now was foolhardy. The city's fortifications were immense, and a siege during the brutal summer would take a horrible toll on the army. When the Egyptian army arrived, the crusaders would be crushed beneath the walls of Jerusalem. If the Holy Land were ever to be secure, they must first destroy the Muslim power base in Egypt. Only then would Jerusalem fall into their hands. Strategically, this was a sound policy, and one that would inspire more than one future crusade, but it did not square with the crusaders' role as pilgrims. Their task was to make their way to the Holy Sepulcher, not the Pyramids. Had God not preserved them thus far? Would he not continue to do so if they remained brave and did not lose faith? The decision was made to march directly to Jerusalem.

Bethlehem, the birthplace of Christ, a city entirely Christian, hailed the crusaders as liberators on June 6. That night, the army was amazed to see a lunar eclipse—a clear sign from God, they felt, that the Muslim crescent was waning. The following day, the crusaders climbed the hill they later named Montjoie (Mount of Joy) and gazed at last on the imposing spectacle of the holy city of Jerusalem. Behind its monumental walls and spiring heights they could see the many domes of the city's rich mosques and churches. At last, they had come to their destination.

Even for a well-supplied army in the best of times, Jerusalem was a difficult nut to crack. These were not the best of times. The size of the city made a full-scale siege impossible, which was just as well since the news of the forming Egyptian army meant that the crusaders had no time to wait out the city's defenders. The Fatimid governor of the city had seen to the necessary preparations for the crusaders' arrival. He expelled all Christians, lest Jerusalem fall by the same treachery that sealed Antioch's fate. He was also careful to poison most of the wells around the city, thus forcing the crusaders to devote manpower to bringing in water from the Jordan River. If Jerusalem were to be taken, it would have to be soon.

It was decided to launch an all-out attempt to capture the city by storm on June 13. Despite the crusaders' brave effort, the city's defenders repulsed the attack with little trouble. The crusaders lacked sufficient scaling ladders and siege machinery to threaten seriously Jerusalem's towering walls. Without such equipment, the city could not be taken. Just then, almost miraculously, six Genoese and English vessels carrying building materials sailed into Jaffa. Praising God, the crusaders quickly set to work building catapults, ladders, and wooden castles on wheels that could be rolled up to the walls of Jerusalem. It was long, slow, and horribly hot work. Water was a constant problem. Tempers flared. Early in July, the crusaders received the news that the Egyptian army was on the march. It would arrive at Jerusalem within the month. Once again, their situation was desperate.

As had happened at Antioch, it was a vision that restored the spirits of the host and turned events around. On July 6, Peter Desiderius, a priest of Raymond's retinue, announced that he had seen the spirit of Adhemar, the late papal legate. Adhemar rebuked the crusading leaders for their quarreling and ordered them to turn their attention to the holy city that they had sworn to liberate. He further assured them that all was not lost. If the army would fast, do penance, and lead a procession around the city, Jerusalem would then fall nine days later. Immediately, a fast was proclaimed throughout the host. On July 8, the Muslim defenders on the walls of Jerusalem watched with astonishment as the army of the Franks became a barefoot, unarmed pilgrimage. Singing prayers and bearing relics, most prominently the Holy Lance, the army of the First Crusade walked around the walls of Jerusalem, coming at last to the Mount of Olives. There, Peter the Hermit delivered a sermon, inspiring the assembled thousands just as he had done on the plains of France so long ago.

With the siege machinery in readiness, the assault on Jerusalem began on the night of July 13–14. The hope of the crusaders lay in their great wheeled castles. All of July 14 was spent trying to bring them against the city's walls. By evening, Raymond's tower had reached Jerusalem's fortifications, but fierce resistance kept his men from gaining a foothold on the wall itself. Early in the morning of July 15, Godfrey also succeeded in bringing his tower against the wall, successfully defeating the defenders in that region. His men of Lorraine fought their way to the Gate of the Column, opened it, and allowed the main army to enter. In a flood, the crusaders rushed into the city. The governor was able to purchase his own freedom and that of his court, but many were not so lucky. Because the Christians had already been expelled, the crusaders saw no reason to temper their punishment of the inhabitants of the city. Men, women, and children were put to the sword until the streets were littered with corpses. Even Jewish inhabitants were killed. Raymond of Toulouse condemned the massacre, but there was nothing he could do to stop it. Turks and Arabs were shocked when they learned of the brutality of the crusaders at Jerusalem. It was not a wound that healed quickly.

The dream of Urban II had come true. Against all odds, this struggling, fractious, and naïve enterprise had made its way from western Europe to the Middle East and conquered two of the best-defended cities in the western world. From a modern perspective, one can only marvel at the improbable course of events that led to these victories. Medieval men and women did not marvel; they merely thanked God. For them, the agent of the crusade's victory was God himself, who had worked miracle after miracle for his faithful knights, delivering unto them the land of Christ.

NOTES

1. August C. Krey, *The First Crusade: The Accounts of Eye-Witnesses and Participants* (Princeton: Princeton University Press, 1921), 55.

2. Solomon Bar Simpson, "Chronicle," in Shlomo Eidelberg, *The Jews and the Crusaders: The Hebrew Chronicles of the First and Second Crusades* (Madison: University of Wisconsin Press, 1977), 25.

3. Martha E. McGinty, trans., repr. in Edward Peters, ed., *The First Crusade: The Chronicle of Fulcher of Chartres and Other Source Materials* (Philadelphia: University of Pennsylvania Press, 1971), 48–49.

4. Ibid., 55.

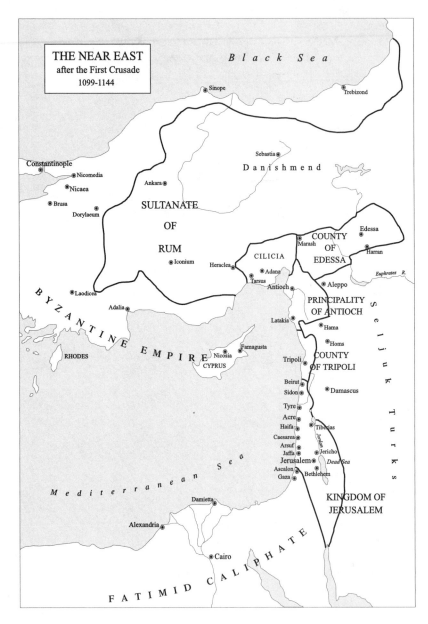

THE NEAR EAST
after the First Crusade
1099-1144

Black Sea

Sinope ⊚　　　　　⊚ Trebizond

Sebastia ⊚

D a n i s h m e n d

Constantinople
⊚
　⊚ Nicomedia　　　Ankara ⊚
　⊚ Nicaea

⊚ Brusa
　　Dorylaeum　　SULTANATE

⊚ OF

RUM　　　　　　　　COUNTY　　Edessa
　　　　　　　　　　　⊚ Marash　　OF　　⊚
　⊚ Iconium　　　CILICIA　　EDESSA　　Harran
　　　　Heraclea ⊚　⊚ Adana　　　　　　*Euphrates R.*
　　　　　　Tarsus ⊚　⊚ Aleppo
⊚ Laodicea　　　　　Antioch ⊚

B Y Z A N T I N E　Adalia ⊚　　　PRINCIPALITY
　　　　　　　　　Latakia ⊚　OF ANTIOCH

E M P I R E　　　　　　⊚ Hama

RHODES　　Nicosia ⊚ Famagusta　⊚ Homs

CYPRUS　　Tripoli ⊚ COUNTY
　　　　　　　　　OF TRIPOLI

Beirut ⊚　　　　⊚ Damascus
Sidon ⊚

Tyre ⊚
Acre ⊚
Haifa ⊚　⊚ Tiberias
Caesarea ⊚
Arsuf ⊚　　Jordan
Jaffa ⊚　⊚ Jericho
Jerusalem ⊚　*Dead Sea*
Ascalon ⊚
Gaza ⊚　Bethlehem

Damietta ⊚

KINGDOM OF
JERUSALEM

Alexandria ⊚

M e d i t e r r a n e a n S e a

⊚ Cairo

S e l j u k　T u r k s

F A T I M I D C A L I P H A T E

Map 3.　The Near East after the First Crusade, 1099–1144

3

THE RISE OF THE LATIN
KINGDOM OF JERUSALEM AND
THE SECOND CRUSADE

After more than four centuries of Muslim rule, Jerusalem was once
again in Christian hands. But for how long? The victories of the
First Crusade were impressive, yet they remained isolated conquests far
from home and deep in Muslim territory. Pious idealism had brought
these courageous knights to the Holy Land and convinced them of the
inevitability of their success, but it would take more than that to sustain
and extend a new kingdom planted on foreign soil. What was needed
was a strong ruler, ready troops, and abundant supplies. The crusaders
lacked all three.

BIRTH OF THE LATIN KINGDOM OF JERUSALEM

Pope Urban II never directly addressed the problem of the government
of Jerusalem. Back in 1096, when the crusaders were first leaving Europe, the pope expected that any conquered lands would be restored to
the Byzantine Empire. Since then, most of the crusade leaders had re-
pudiated their oaths to Emperor Alexius I. They would not hand over
their hard-won conquests to the man who left them to die at Antioch.
Who, then, should rule? Many assumed that the patriarch of Jerusalem
or perhaps a papal legate would govern the city, just as the pope governed Rome and the Patrimony of St. Peter. Should not the church rule
in Christ's Holy City? The crusade, however, had had no papal legate
since the death of Adhemar, and the Greek Orthodox patriarch of Jerusalem had died in exile a few days before the conquest. Although the crusading clergy insisted that a new patriarch be chosen before the election

of a secular ruler, the barons could not come to any agreement, so the matter was postponed.

The crusaders did not have the luxury of arguing for months over control of Jerusalem as they had done at Antioch. With a powerful Egyptian army on the march, they needed a ruler to organize the defense of the city and its lands. In council, the leaders decided to offer the crown to Raymond of Toulouse, still the wealthiest and most powerful of the crusade leaders. As commander in chief, Raymond had distinguished himself as a pious and effective leader. In addition, his troops were already in control of Jerusalem's citadel, the Tower of David, and it would be difficult to dislodge them. Raymond responded coyly to the offer, saying that he would not be king where Christ alone reigned. Given his material and strategic position, Raymond indulged in cleverness, piously refusing a crown that he knew would be pressed on him again. He was too clever. After his refusal, the council offered the crown to Godfrey of Bouillon. Godfrey was well liked by the rank and file, who knew him as a gallant and courageous warrior and the commander who had first led his troops into Jerusalem. Godfrey also refused the crown, but he took the city, saying that he would act as defender against the infidels. Later, he accepted the title *Advocatus Sancti Sepulchri,* Protector of the Holy Sepulcher.

When Raymond heard the news, he was incensed. He refused to recognize Godfrey as ruler or to remove his troops from the Tower of David. The latter was of serious consequence since Godfrey could never truly control the city without its military stronghold. Other leaders begged Raymond not to provoke a war among Christians when the Muslims were amassing against them. At last, the count of Toulouse agreed to put the citadel under the control of the bishop of Albara until a church council could decide the matter. The instant Raymond left the city, however, the bishop betrayed him, handing over the Tower of David to Godfrey. Disgusted, Raymond abandoned Jerusalem, taking with him all of his troops. He made a pilgrimage to the Jordan River, leaving Godfrey to fend for himself. When later he heard reports that a large Egyptian army was encamped near Ascalon, Raymond relented, bringing his forces back to join the other crusade leaders.

The Fatimid commanders expected the crusaders to hole up in Jerusalem, so they were caught completely by surprise when the Christian forces swept down on their camp at Ascalon on the evening of August

11. The sultan's soldiers were still asleep when the blare of the knights' horns and the rumble of hoofbeats woke them to their impending disaster. The entire Egyptian force was destroyed. For the moment, the conquest of the Holy Land was secure.

After the battle at Ascalon, most of the soldiers of the First Crusade boarded vessels for home. Each received a hero's welcome. The stories of these brave men marching two thousand miles across hostile terrain to redeem the land of the Savior stirred the imaginations of generations of Europeans. The exploits of the leaders, particularly Godfrey of Bouillon, were immortalized (and exaggerated) in epics and songs. Godfrey became the symbol of perfect Christian chivalry for centuries. Yet all of that was of little use to him in 1099. With the departure of most of the crusaders, Godfrey had the difficult task of extending control over a Muslim countryside with a mere three hundred knights and about two thousand foot soldiers. Of the original crusade leaders, only Tancred, the cousin of Bohemond of Taranto, remained in Jerusalem. By force of arms, Tancred carved out lands for himself in nearby Tiberias, which he held as a fief from Jerusalem.

Godfrey's reign was significantly complicated by the arrival of Daimbert, archbishop of Pisa and papal legate, who soon also became patriarch of Jerusalem. Daimbert firmly believed that Jerusalem and the Holy Land should be ruled by the church, something that Godfrey was naturally less willing to accept but hard pressed to resist. At stake was the nature of the forming crusader state. Godfrey was to play no further role in that drama. On July 18, 1100, the Protector of the Holy Sepulcher died.

Godfrey's death was welcome news for Daimbert, for he believed he could now take full control of Jerusalem. The patriarch was not in the city when Godfrey died, however, and Godfrey's friends and comrades were not willing to hand over Jerusalem so easily. They summoned Godfrey's brother, Baldwin of Edessa, to take the throne for himself. Baldwin gave the County of Edessa to his cousin Baldwin of Bourcq and prepared to travel to Jerusalem. Before leaving, he heard news that Bohemond of Antioch had recently led an expedition to secure his northern frontier and was captured by the Danishmends. Antioch was without a ruler and therefore vulnerable. Immediately, Baldwin marched to the city and secured it, before going on to Jerusalem. On Christmas Day of 1100, in the Church of the Nativity in Bethlehem, a reluctant patriarch crowned Baldwin I (1100–18) the first king of Jerusalem. Shortly thereafter, Daimbert was removed from office. His plan to place Palestine under ecclesiastical rule fizzled. Henceforth, the patriarch of Jerusalem was an important bishop in an important city, but no ruler.

THE CRUSADES OF 1100–1101

The departure of crusaders after the conquest of Jerusalem was partially offset by a steady stream of new crusaders arriving from the West. Most of these new arrivals were those who had earlier taken the cross but, for one reason or another, were delayed in their departure. Some constituted sizable forces. The only two European states to join the crusade officially, sending expeditions at government expense, were the republics of Pisa and Venice. For these maritime powers, preparation for the crusade was not simply a matter of assembling soldiers, supplies, and money: it required the construction of fleets. The northern Italian sailors were not unfamiliar with the ports of the Near East, and they knew well that the Franks could not hope to conquer and hold them without a powerful navy. Ships take time to build, so neither state was ready to depart in 1096. Pisa launched a very large war fleet of 120 vessels in 1098. Venice was further delayed by a ducal election, but, in July 1099, Doge Vitale I Michiel (1096–1101) led a massive crusader fleet of more than two hundred ships from the Venetian lagoon. The arrival of the Venetians increased Christian manpower in Palestine tenfold, giving Godfrey an effective army to extend his conquests. Michiel and Godfrey decided to attack the rich port city of Acre, but Godfrey's death complicated the situation. Instead, the Venetians captured Haifa for the Franks and then returned home.

News of the sweeping successes of the First Crusade stirred many thousands of previously hesitant knights and soldiers to take the cross, and thereby to share in the glory of the holy enterprise. Others had embarked on the original expedition but returned home before its completion. Stephen of Blois, the most famous deserter, was bitterly rebuked by his wife, family, and vassals when he showed up in France. He and other deserters were ordered by the pope to fulfill their pilgrim's vow to travel to the Holy Sepulcher. The sheer numbers of people who departed on crusade after the conquest of Jerusalem has led Riley-Smith to refer to the movement as the "third wave" of the First Crusade. It is more traditionally known as the Crusade of 1101. These new crusaders departed with a sure knowledge that God would work miracles for them just as He had done for the valiant soldiers who restored Antioch and Jerusalem to Christendom. They were to be disappointed. The First Crusade benefited from the fact that the Muslims did not understand the nature or scope of the enterprise, as well as the Muslims' inexperience with Frankish heavy cavalry. This new wave of crusaders could not rely on those advantages.

One of the largest groups of new crusaders came from Lombardy in northern Italy and was led by the archbishop of Milan. It left in the fall of 1100, passing through the Byzantine Empire and crossing into Asia at Constantinople. At Nicomedia, the Burgundian army of Stephen of Blois, as well as Raymond of Toulouse, met the Lombard crusaders. The new crusaders had heard of the recent capture of Bohemond and were eager to lead a mission to rescue this hero of the First Crusade. Speaking from experience, Raymond and Stephen strongly argued against a march into northern Anatolia, but the Lombards were determined. In mid-July 1101, they met a combined army of Turks on the field of battle. The Christians were destroyed; only a handful survived, including Raymond, Stephen, and the archbishop of Milan. None of the other new armies of crusaders met with any more success; all of them were crushed in Asia Minor before they could reach Antioch. In the failure of these expeditions, the largest that Europe had yet launched, the astounding success of the First Crusade seemed even more miraculous.

The failure of the follow-up crusades was a bitter disappointment to the barons and knights of the East. Without additional conquests, the newborn kingdom of Jerusalem could not survive. Overall, their strategy was to consolidate Christian conquests while further expanding to the south and east. If Ascalon could be taken, the Sinai desert would lie between the crusaders and the armies of Egypt. If Aleppo and Damascus were conquered, the Turks would lose their base of operations for an attack on Jerusalem or Antioch. The rich ports along the Mediterranean coast would also have to be captured if they were to cut off Turkish access to the sea. It was a tall order, and one that would have to be filled with a bare minimum of men.

Consolidation in the North

From Bohemond of Antioch's point of view, Aleppo was the greatest danger to the Christians. Shortly after he was released from captivity in 1103, he allied with Baldwin of Bourcq, the ruler of Edessa, and Joscelin of Courtenay, Baldwin's most powerful vassal, to wage war on their nearby enemy. The campaign was a disaster for the crusaders. Almost the entire army was killed, and Joscelin and Baldwin were captured. Bohemond managed to escape back to Antioch, but the northern states were in a dangerously weakened state. Quickly, King Baldwin dispatched Tancred to act as regent in Edessa and defend it against attack. The real threat came from a different quarter.

Despite his oaths, Bohemond had not moved to restore Antioch to the emperor in Constantinople. Tired of waiting, Alexius sent armies to take it by force. They captured Cilicia, but nothing else. Nevertheless, war between the Byzantines and Normans had once again been joined. Leaving Tancred as regent of Antioch, Bohemond swiftly sailed to Italy, where he prepared to invade the Byzantine Empire at Durazzo. In 1107, Bohemond led his Norman troops across the Adriatic, just as he had done with his father in 1082, but much had changed since then. Through careful administration, Alexius had restored the Byzantine army and navy to a respectable level. With Venetian assistance, the Byzantines easily repulsed Bohemond. In defeat, he was forced to accept the Treaty of Devol, stipulating that the Norman leader was to retain Antioch but only as a vassal of the Byzantine emperor. He was also to restore the Greek patriarch of Antioch, who had been ousted in favor of a Latin prelate. Humiliated by his defeat, Bohemond never returned to the East. In 1111, he died in Apulia, in southern Italy.

After returning to Palestine from Constantinople, Raymond of Toulouse made preparations to conquer some land for himself. He chose the strategic port of Tripoli. On a hill outside the city, which he renamed Mount Pilgrim, Raymond built a large castle to undertake the siege and protect the city after its conquest. Tripoli was a true prize. Not only was it a vital port, but its location also made it the natural membrane between the French in the south and Normans in the north. The siege was a long one, and Raymond, who was already an old man, did not have time to wait. He died on February 28, 1105, already styling himself count of Tripoli. Immediately after his death, a dispute broke out over the inheritance of the still unconquered county. There were two contenders: Raymond's cousin William, who had accompanied him on the crusade, and his son Bertrand, who had recently arrived from Toulouse. All the major princes, including King Baldwin and Tancred, as well as Baldwin of Bourcq and Joscelin, both of whom had recently been released from captivity, traveled to Tripoli to decide the issue in council. They followed the judgment of Solomon, splitting the inheritance between William, who would be a vassal of Antioch, and Bertrand, who would owe his allegiance to Jerusalem. With that decided, the Christian princes joined forces to attack Tripoli, which surrendered on July 12, 1109. The last crusader state was formed. As it happened, however, the struggle over Raymond's inheritance was moot. Shortly after the city's conquest, William died of an arrow wound. The entire County of Tripoli went to Bertrand, who held it as a fief from King Baldwin.

The capture of Tripoli was a great success for Baldwin I, not merely because of the addition of Tripoli to his feudal holdings but also because it was a clear demonstration of his royal power to settle disputes and lead Christian forces to important victories. Already he had won respect and approval by his conquests of the coastal cities of Arsuf and Caesarea in 1101. With the assistance of a Genoese fleet, he captured Acre in May 1104. After the fall of Tripoli, he continued his drive to capture the coast by marching north to Sidon and Beirut. There, with the help of a fleet of Norwegians led by King Sigurd, he captured both cities in 1110. In less than ten years, Baldwin conquered the entire Palestinian coast, with the exception of Tyre and Ascalon.

Over the next decade, the Christians of the Latin East lost many of the original crusade leaders. In December 1112, Tancred died, only one year after Bohemond. Because Bohemond's son was still a minor, the regency government of Antioch went to Roger of the Principate. Bertrand of Tripoli had died a few months earlier and was succeeded by his son, Pons. After extending his power farther to the south, King Baldwin I of Jerusalem led a small force into Egypt. He ventured as far as the Nile Delta before turning back because of illness. He died on the return journey, on April 2, 1118. The true founder of the kingdom of Jerusalem, Baldwin had transformed a tenuous arrangement into a solid feudal state. With brilliance and diligence, he established a strong monarchy, conquered the Palestinian coast, reconciled the crusader barons, and built strong frontiers against the kingdom's Muslim neighbors. The kingdom of Jerusalem clearly was not going away soon.

No precedent had yet been established for selecting a new king. Was succession to be hereditary or by election by the barons and clergy? Baldwin, who was childless, named his brother, Eustace of Boulogne, as his successor, but Eustace was in Europe and not overly enthusiastic about the inheritance in any event. Instead, the barons elected Baldwin of Bourcq, the ruler of Edessa. Baldwin II (1118–31) was an extremely pious man with a keen intelligence. He immediately handed over the County of Edessa to his former vassal Joscelin of Courtenay. In so doing, he hoped that the situation in the North would stabilize, but it did not. The following year, Roger of Antioch led his forces against Aleppo. On June 27, 1119, on the battlefield henceforth called the "Field of Blood," the Turks crushed the Christian armies. The enormous loss of life was a severe blow to the crusaders, whose numbers were small in the best of times. Antioch and Edessa were again in danger. Baldwin issued an urgent plea to the pope requesting aid.

In the aftermath of the disaster, Baldwin II was named regent of Antioch, which greatly enhanced his power and prestige but did not endear him to his local vassals. Much of the king's energy was now expended on the volatile situation in the North. In 1122, Balak of Aleppo launched a powerful attack against Edessa. Again the Turks defeated the Franks, although they did not take the city itself. In the melee, Balak captured Joscelin. Immediately, Baldwin marched against Balak in an attempt to free his comrade. He too met defeat. In April 1123, the ruler of Aleppo added the king of Jerusalem to his collection of crusade leaders in captivity.

THE VENETIAN CRUSADE OF 1122

Baldwin's request for help from Europe did not go unanswered. Pope Calixtus II (1119–24), preoccupied with the Investiture Controversy, passed the request on to the Republic of Venice. Again led by their doge, the people of Venice constructed a large fleet of 120 vessels and more than fifteen thousand men. Marked with the sign of the cross and carrying the papal banner, the armada left Venice on August 8, 1122. On the way, the Venetian crusaders decided to settle a score with the new Byzantine emperor, John II Comnenus (1118–43). The latter had refused to honor the trading privileges that Alexius granted to the Venetians after Byzantium's war with the Normans. During that war, the Venetians had conquered the island of Corfu for Byzantium, and they now meant to have it back. The fleet spent the winter of 1122/1123 unsuccessfully besieging the island's defenses. In early spring, word of Baldwin's capture reached the doge, so he ordered the fleet to sail immediately for the Levant. When the Venetians arrived in May, they learned that a large Egyptian fleet had abandoned a blockade of Jaffa and was returning to its base at Ascalon. Swiftly, the doge ordered his fleet to intercept the Muslim armada. The Venetian sailors brilliantly surrounded the enemy and destroyed them. Heralded by the devastation of the Fatimid navy, the men of the Republic of St. Mark arrived in Palestine for a second time. Next, the fleet sailed for Tyre, completely encircling it. With help from the Franks on land, the Venetians continued the siege for more than a year. Tyre at last surrendered on July 7, 1124.

The conquest of Tyre took place without Baldwin II. When Balak of Aleppo died later in the year, the king was released from captivity. The problem of his regency of Antioch resolved itself the following year when young Bohemond II arrived to claim his inheritance. The new heir had a rare moment of opportunity. The death of Balak had plunged Aleppo into a power struggle both internally and with Mosul in Mesopotamia, making it exceedingly vulnerable to attack. Thus, one of the major objectives of the rulers of Antioch was in easy reach. The inexperienced and headstrong Bohemond wasted the chance, preferring instead to wage war against his fellow Christian, Joscelin of Edessa. In the process, he weakened both states and gave the Muslims time to settle their disputes. By 1128, Imad ad-Din Zengi had succeeded in taking control of both Aleppo and Mosul, making him the most powerful Muslim the crusaders had yet faced. Zengi was a clever man, full of guile and ruthless ambition. He was determined to expand his territories into Syria and Palestine by whatever means necessary and against any foe, Christian or Muslim.

THE NEW CULTURE OF THE LATIN EAST

Bohemond II's poor leadership of Antioch ended in 1130, when he was killed fighting the Byzantines at Cilicia. He left a two-year-old daughter, Constance. Once again, the regency of the principate fell to King Baldwin II, who was very ill at the time. On August 21, 1131, the king died. A short time later, Joscelin also died, after bravely defending the increasingly defenseless Edessa. With the passing of these men went the last of the original crusaders. They were the warriors of Christ who had marched to the Holy Land and carved out a Christian state. They were the pilgrims who took the crusader's vow and restored Jerusalem to Christian rule. They were the heroes of a generation of knights, typifying the selfless virtues of a noble and chivalric Christian knight. The next generation of leaders in the crusader states were different. Many of them were born in Outremer; it was their native land.

A new culture was forming in the Latin East, one that combined elements of Christianity and Islam, Europe and Syria. Those who lived in the crusader states were no longer itinerant crusaders. To defend their homes, they were willing to negotiate with and even befriend their Islamic neighbors. And yet to sustain their state, they required assistance from Europe. As time passed, a gulf opened between the new crusaders, who arrived from the West to fight Muslims, and the local residents, who would have to live with the Muslims after the pilgrims returned home. In a sense, Europe was forming its first colonial expatriate population, a new people who stood between two cultures, never fully belonging to either. Fulcher of Chartres described it thus:

> I pray you, consider and reflect on how God has in our times changed West into East. For we, who were occidentals, have now become orientals. The man who was a Roman or a Frank has, in this land, been turned into a Galilean or a Palestinian. He who was once a citizen of Reims or of Chartres has now become a citizen of Tyre or Antioch. We have already forgotten the places where we were born; many of us either do not know them or have never even heard of them. One among us now has his own houses and retainers, just as if he possessed them through hereditary or family right. Another takes as his wife, not a woman of his own stock, but rather a Syrian or Armenian, or even, occasionally, a Saracen who has obtained the grace of baptism. . . . Men address one another in turn in the speech and idiom of various languages. The several languages of various nations are common here and one joins faith with men whose forefathers were strangers. For it is written: "The lion and ox shall eat straw side by side."[1]

Usama, an Arab writer and courtier, agreed that "there are some Franks who have settled in our land and taken to living like Muslims," but he was quick to point out where the two cultures parted company. One of these was in the divergent attitudes of Christians and Muslims toward women. Usama wrote:

The Franks are without any vestige of a sense of honor and jealousy. If one of them goes along the street with his wife and meets a friend, this man will take the woman's hand and lead her aside to talk, while the husband stands by waiting until she has finished her conversation. If she takes too long about it he leaves her with the other man and goes on his way.[2]

The Military Orders

It was during the reign of Baldwin II that the first military orders were formed. In them, monastic discipline and martial skill were combined for the first time in the Christian world. In a real sense, the military orders brought the idea of the crusader to its logical conclusion. Here were fighting men who went beyond the quasi-monastic nature of the crusader's vow by fully accepting a lifetime of service to Christ. Hugh of Payns, a knight of Champagne, founded the first of the orders. He and eight of his companions traveled to the Holy Land with the desire to devote their lives to Christ and turn their swords to acts of pious chivalry. The patriarch of Jerusalem, Gormund, administered to them the three monastic vows of poverty, chastity, and obedience, as well as a fourth vow to protect pilgrims on their way from the port of Jaffa to Jerusalem. Baldwin II gave the company rooms in the former mosque of al-Aqsa, which the crusaders called the Temple of Solomon. From their new headquarters they derived their name, the Knights Templar. Back in Europe, Bernard of Clairvaux, a famous churchman, lent his considerable rhetorical skills to the advancement of the new order. With his help, the Templars received a Rule and formal papal acceptance in 1128. Bernard brought waves of recruits to the order through his preaching and writing on the "New Chivalry," a knighthood dedicated to God. Soon, these armored men, donning white tunics emblazoned with a red cross, could be seen throughout the crusader states and across Europe. Their duties in the East rapidly expanded as subsequent kings assigned them strategic areas to safeguard. The castles they built were enormous fortresses, dwarfing anything that could be found in western Europe. On both sides of the Mediterranean, they built monastic houses and round churches modeled on the Church of the Holy Sepulcher. Those in Europe were meant to raise funds for ac-

Figure 2: **Templar Church of the True Cross in Spain.** Templar churches in Europe were often modeled on the Church of the Holy Sepulcher in Jerusalem. Photo by Alfred J. Andrea.

tivities in the East, but they also provided services for pilgrims. In time, these services included the ability to deposit money in a Templar convent in Europe and collect it in the Levant, minus a service charge. This convenience put the Templars in the unlikely business of banking, thus sowing the seeds of their ultimate demise. Yet those days were far distant. In the twelfth century, the Knights Templar were a truly international order of warriors, independent of episcopal control, who devoted themselves to monastic discipline and military service.

Another military order active in the crusader states was the Knights of the Hospital of St. John, or the Hospitallers. Unlike the Templars, the Hospitallers did not start out as a military organization—far from it. Shortly after the capture of Jerusalem, monks from the abbey of St. Mary of the Latins founded the Hospital of St. John, an institution dedicated to the care of sick pilgrims. Their special concern was for the "holy poor," whom they treated with every kindness and offered every luxury. With the surge in pilgrim traffic to Jerusalem in the first decade of the twelfth century, the need for the hospital grew. Soon it had more than two thousand beds and an army of men and women who selflessly cared for the sick and dying. Accommodations were extravagant. Few of the poor who flocked to the hospital had ever slept in a proper bed, let alone consumed the meats, vegetables, and wines that were the standard fare. In all this, the hospital staff remembered the words of Christ: "Whatsoever you do to the least of these, so you do unto me." In 1113, the Hospitallers became a religious order separate from the monastery of St. Mary of the Latins, but they did not become involved in military affairs until much later. In 1136, King Fulk gave control of a fortress near Ascalon to the Hospitallers, but they probably hired mercenaries to man it. Other responsibilities followed. During the course of the twelfth century, additional castles were turned over to them, forcing the Hospitallers to create a military arm of the order. By the beginning of the thirteenth century, military responsibilities overshadowed, yet never fully extinguished, the care of the poor and sick.

With the Templars and Hospitallers, the crusader states had a permanent, reliable presence of expert soldiers dedicated to the defense of the Christian East. In a place where large crusades came and went, the military orders provided stability otherwise impossible to maintain.

THE RISE OF ZENGI

Baldwin II had made careful preparations for the succession of the crown of Jerusalem. Although he had no son, he married his daughter Melisende to the powerful lord Fulk of Anjou. The kingdom was to go jointly to Fulk, Melisende, and their two-year-old son, Baldwin. Fulk took the royal title, but authority over the kingdom was shared between him and his wife. King Fulk (1131–43) also inherited the regency over Antioch. For too long, this important city had been ruled by regents and absentees. With the alarming growth of Zengi's power, it was necessary to give the region a solid ruler. At Fulk's command, Bohemond II's younger daughter, Constance, now nine years old, was married to the thirty-four-year-old Raymond of Poitiers, the son of Duke William IX of Aquitaine. Raymond arrived from Europe in 1136.

Ominous tidings continued to come from Zengi's growing state. Among his subjects, he preached a *jihad,* a holy war against the Christians. To the relief of Raymond of Antioch, Zengi remained preoccupied with Muslim Damascus. Repeated sieges failed, but they took a hard toll on the city. Zengi was momentarily distracted when the Byzantine emperor John II unsuccessfully attempted to capture Aleppo in 1138, but he remained undeterred. The following year, Zengi prepared again to attack Damascus. Weakened by previous assaults, the city seemed certain to fall. The people of Damascus were terrified of the fate that awaited them under so brutally cruel a man. Desperate, the emir of the city turned to the Christians. King Fulk also had no desire to see Zengi extend his power to the borders of the Latin kingdom, so an alliance between Jerusalem and Damascus was forged. Fulk mobilized his troops to assist in the defense of his Muslim neighbors. Foiled by the alliance, Zengi turned his attention to affairs in Mesopotamia. For the moment, the threat was averted.

Like his predecessors, Fulk knew that the security of the crusader states depended on strong borders. Capturing Damascus would provide a solid defense on Jerusalem's eastern flank, but a firm alliance with the city was the next best thing, at least from a strategic point of view. New crusader arrivals from Europe were routinely shocked that the king of Jerusalem made peace with Muslims of any stripe, particularly when they controlled a city made holy by the life of St. Paul. To the north, Aleppo and Mosul continued to pose a danger, but there was nothing to be done about it while Zengi held them in his grip. To the south, Ascalon remained a thorn in the side of the Christians. Egyptian troops could land there at will, raiding the countryside and causing enormous damage. Without a fleet at his disposal, Fulk had no hope of capturing Ascalon, so he made provisions to isolate it. A ring of castles was constructed around the city between 1136 and 1142. Some of these were given to Fulk's vassals or friends, others to the Hospitallers. These were not the only castles built or improved during Fulk's reign. Across the landscape arose powerful fortresses, strategically positioned to defend commerce and property. The most famous of them, Krak des Chevaliers, commanded the important roads running from Hama and Homs to the coast of the Mediterranean. In 1144, it was given to the Hospitallers, who spent the next century expanding and strengthening it. Even in the best of times, Latin Christians were a tiny minority in the East. Mammoth fortifications like these were essential if they were to defend their kingdom.

In November 1143, King Fulk, while hunting, was thrown from his horse and killed. Queen Melisende retained control of the kingdom. Her eldest son, Baldwin III (1143–63), was still only thirteen years old. Melisende was an able ruler, but the kingdom needed more. Already the crown's vassals were testing their independence; with a woman and a minor on the throne, that trend would only accelerate. More worrisome was the continued ill will between the prince of Antioch and the count of Edessa. The two were within a hair's breadth of open war. Jerusalem needed a strong king to end these quarrels and enforce discipline.

The death of Fulk did not go unnoticed by Zengi. With his operations in the East concluded, he was now in a position to lead his *jihad* once more against the crusaders. With a woman ruling in Jerusalem and Christian leaders fighting among themselves, the time was ripe for attack. His object was Edessa, which he besieged in late November 1144. The city was well fortified, but Joscelin was absent, keeping his best troops at nearby Turbessel. The count of Edessa begged Raymond for reinforcements to break the siege, but the prince of Antioch refused. Queen Melisende dispatched a relief force, but it was too little and too late. On Christmas Eve, Zengi's Turkish and Kurdish army breached the walls and captured the city. The first of the crusader states was the first to fall. The buffer state that had disrupted communications between Muslims and provided a strong flank for Antioch was now gone, putting the northern territories in grave danger.

News of the fall of Edessa had a profound effect on Christians and Muslims alike. It was the first loss of territory the Christians had suffered since their arrival more than four decades earlier. Their aura of invincibility was shattered. A new generation of Muslims who had thought of the crusader states as permanent entities now began to think again. Zengi, of course, was the biggest winner. His power was unmatched in the Muslim world. Behind his rhetoric of *jihad,* he planned to wipe the Franks off the map, sending them back to distant Europe. His official title, *atabeg* of Mosul, was now replaced with *king* and *conqueror.* The apex of his power, however, was also its end. On September 14, 1146, Zengi was murdered in his bed by a slave, who was angry for having been scolded for drinking wine. Zengi's kingdom immediately unraveled as petty Turkish leaders fought among themselves for the scraps.

THE SECOND CRUSADE

In Europe, the fall of Edessa and the rise of Zengi was stunning news. The barons of the crusader states did not exaggerate when they reported that all of the Latin East, including Jerusalem itself, was in mortal danger. They were desperate for help. No major crusading effort had been undertaken since just after the conquest of Jerusalem. With the Holy City in Christian hands and the crusader states in stable condition, there were few clear objectives around which a grand enterprise could crystallize. In the intervening four decades, an entire generation of Europeans had been born and raised on the epic stories of the First Crusade. It was now the stuff of legend. There was scarcely a Christian knight who did not know by heart the exploits of Godfrey of Bouillon and long for the opportunity to imitate them. Here was the spark that could reignite the fire of crusade.

On December 1, 1145, Pope Eugenius III (1145–53) issued the papal bull *Quantum praedecessores*. It was reissued in a modified form on March 1, 1146. As the title suggests, the bull looked back to the glorious victories of the First Crusade and called the knights of Christendom once more to take up the cross of Christ, following him to the land of his birth and Resurrection. After a narration and exhortation, *Quantum praedecessores* laid out the crusading privileges that henceforth became standard. These included protection of property as well as suspension of interest and debt collection. Eugenius was eager to see the new crusade preached in France and Italy, but he plainly did not want the Germans to take part. The pope needed German emperor Conrad III (1138–52) to support him in his quarrels with the Normans in southern Italy; he did not want his allies leaving him in the lurch to fight in distant Palestine. The devout and pious King Louis VII of France (1137–80) had for some time been considering the idea of leading an expedition to the East, although his barons and advisers continued to dissuade him. Even after the formal declaration of the crusade, the king's chief counselor, Abbot Suger of St. Denis, urged him to remain at home.

The Second Crusade was born by papal pronouncement, but it drew breath from the words of Bernard of Clairvaux. As described earlier, Bernard had already developed and embraced the idea of a "new chivalry" as a means of doing God's work while purifying Christian society. He now put his substantial prestige behind the new crusade. In a very real sense, it was his crusade. He and his Cistercian brothers fanned out across France preaching the cross. Because Jerusalem was the seat of a Christian kingdom and had been so for nearly half a century, the exhortations used by the preachers of the First Crusade were no longer appropriate. Soldiers could not be asked to forsake all to reclaim the lands of Christ when those lands were still in Christian hands. Instead, Bernard and his brothers portrayed the crusade as a means of redemption:

> Again I say, consider the Almighty's goodness and pay heed to his plans of mercy. He puts himself under obligation to you, or rather feigns to do so, that he can help you to satisfy your obligations toward himself. . . . I call blessed the generation that can seize an opportunity of such rich indulgence as this, blessed to be alive in this year of jubilee, this year of God's choice. The blessing is spread throughout the whole world, and all the world is flocking to receive this badge of immortality.[3]

In his mercy, Bernard proclaimed, Christ called those who lived their lives by the sword to use their martial skills to fight for him in the East. Of course, Christ could restore Edessa, indeed all the world, to his rule if he so chose, but instead he gave a rare gift to his children: the opportunity to show their faith by taking on the mantle of the cross. In return, he would shower victory, glory, and salvation on them forever. There was no question about the outcome of the crusade for Bernard. Just as God had performed miracles for the heroes of the First Crusade, so now he was eager to do the same for a new generation of pious Christians.

Louis VII received the crusader's cross from Bernard himself, as did his wife, Queen Eleanor, the heiress of the Duchy of Aquitaine and niece of Raymond of Antioch. The king and queen were an odd couple, Louis austere and pious, Eleanor cultured and extravagant. By all accounts, Louis loved Eleanor deeply, but the crusade was to be a strain that the marriage ultimately could not bear. At an assembly of Louis's nobles, Bernard administered the vow to so many that he ran out of cloth crosses and was forced to tear them out of his own habit. With the crossing of the king and his barons, the crusade quickly picked up steam across France. Bernard did his best to keep enthusiasm levels high, traveling across northern France preaching tirelessly.

In one sense, Bernard was repeating the role played by Peter the Hermit during the preaching of the First Crusade. He was keenly aware of this and eager that the similarity not extend to Jewish massacres or a premature and ill-equipped crusade. Repeatedly, Bernard stressed that the Jews were not to be persecuted:

> Ask anyone who knows the Sacred Scriptures what he finds foretold of the Jews in the Psalm. "Not for their destruction do I pray," it says. The Jews are for us the living words of Scripture, for they remind us always of what our Lord suffered. They are dispersed all over the world so that by expiating their crime they may be everywhere the living witnesses of our redemption. . . . Under Christian princes they endure a hard captivity, but "they only wait for the time of their deliverance."[4]

Like Peter, Bernard found that his best efforts were not enough. Radulf, a fellow Cistercian monk, had begun preaching in northern France against the Jews. By the time that the renegade reached the German Rhineland, his words were having an effect, sparking massacres of Jews in the same cities that had suffered similarly fifty years earlier. Bernard's repeated letters to the people of the Rhineland to desist in these persecutions fell on deaf ears. Finally, he went there himself. When he caught up to Radulf, Bernard bitterly rebuked him and sent him back to his convent. Although he was able to put a stop to the persecutions, Bernard could not quell the enthusiasm for the crusade that now spread into Germany.

Bernard knew well that Eugenius wanted Germany kept out of the crusade, but now that it was plainly involved, Bernard intended that it go all the way. Conrad III resisted Bernard's first attempts at enlistment, but he was weakening. At Christmas Mass, Bernard directed his sermon to the emperor, asking him to imagine the Last Judgment, when he would approach the throne of Christ. There, the Savior would recount the many gifts he had bestowed on Conrad during his life: kingship, wealth, wisdom, courage, and strength. Then, remembering that the emperor would not take up the crusader's cross, Christ would ask him, "Man, what should I have done for you that I did not do?" Conrad collapsed in tears. When he looked up again, he replied simply, "I am ready to serve Him." So, too, were hundreds of German nobles, who took the cross along with their king.

Bernard continued his preaching in Germany. On March 13, 1147, a large body of German (mostly Saxon) crusaders requested that they be allowed to fulfill their crusading vow by waging war on the pagan Wends living east of the Elbe River. This was a logical request, given that Bernard

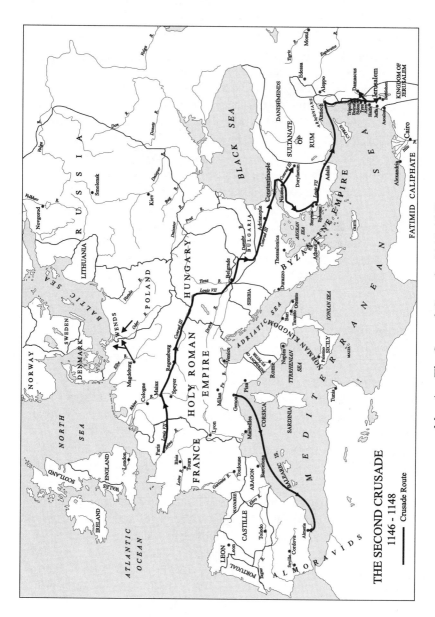

Map 4. The Second Crusade, 1146–1148

preached a war of redemption rather than armed pilgrimage. If God offered salvation to soldiers who fought for his causes, why should those causes be only in the Levant? That was how Bernard saw it, anyway. He immediately forwarded their request to the pope, whom he convinced to accept the plan. The Wendish Crusade, as it called, is really just another manifestation of the Second Crusade. Although its destination and objective were different from those of the crusade to the East, the motivation, as described by Bernard and the other Cistercian preachers, was identical. The Saxons who fought the Wends did so to win the same salvation as their colleagues who marched to Syria. There was, however, one important difference: The objective of the Wendish Crusade was not to displace infidels but to convert them by the sword. Bernard himself forbade the crusaders from accepting peace from the Wends unless they were baptized as Christians:

> We utterly forbid that for any reason whatsoever a truce should be made with these peoples, either for the sake of money or for the sake of tribute, until such a time as, by God's help, they shall be either converted or wiped out.[5]

In short, they were to be given a choice: Convert or die. Here was a true Christian holy war.

The Second Crusade went in three directions at once. Aside from the movements to the east and north, there was also a major offensive in the southwest. Eugenius issued a separate bull authorizing a crusade in Spain against the Muslims. Lords in northern Spain and southern France joined with the Genoese to continue the long struggle to remove Islam from the Iberian peninsula.

The pope's Norman enemy, Roger II of Sicily, saw opportunity in the forming crusade. As an ally of the king of France, Roger offered his fleet to transport the French forces to their destination in the East. Along the way they could further the cause of Christendom by conquering what was left of the Byzantine Empire. Just as the virtuous deeds of Godfrey of Bouillon had been exaggerated by poetic license in the West, so were the putative transgressions of the Byzantine emperors. Sly, cowardly, double-dealing: These were the adjectives that best described a Byzantine for most Europeans who had never met one. Roger was not as concerned with the Byzantine attitude toward the crusader states as he was about the chance to at last make good on the century-old Norman desire to capture Constantinople and her empire. There was a strong anti-Byzantine party in the French court that urged Louis to accept the Norman offer. In the end, though, the desire to take the overland road made famous by the pilgrimage of Godfrey was too great. Louis declined Roger's offer.

In Constantinople, Emperor Manuel I Comnenus (1143–80) was plainly irritated by the Second Crusade. He had painstakingly organized an anti-Norman alliance with the Germans, the papacy, and Venice. Now his plans lay in ruins. He was also not eager to disrupt his peaceful relationship with the Turkish sultan of Rum. Given the conduct of past crusades, it was clear to the emperor that the Westerners had no intention of returning captured territories to the empire. He therefore made a truce with the Turks to forestall any Muslim attacks on Byzantine territory. Strategically, this was sound policy, but for the crusaders it was additional evidence of the apostasy of the Greeks. Rather than fighting the enemies of Christ, the Byzantines made deals with them.

The first band of crusaders to depart was a diverse collection of northerners, including Flemish, Norman, and English soldiers. They left Dartmouth on May 19, 1147, and sailed south along the coast of France and the Iberian peninsula. While passing Portugal, they heard reports that King Alfonso I was conducting a siege of Muslim-held Lisbon and that he hoped the crusaders would assist him. Some opposed any delay in reaching the Holy Land, but the majority favored helping Alfonso when the king promised they could plunder the city after its capture. After a three-month siege, Lisbon surrendered to the crusaders on October 24, 1147. In the spring, the crusade fleet continued on its way, laden with riches.

Conrad and his German armies left Regensburg in May 1147. They arrived at Constantinople in September. Manuel was displeased by the Germans' unruly passage through his empire but eager to salvage his relationship with Conrad. The German emperor remained aloof, eager to cross over into Asia Minor. In the city's suburbs, the Germans troops and noncombatant followers repeatedly attacked Byzantine citizens, their businesses, and their homes. At last, Manuel sent the army across the Bosporus to meet the Turks.

Conrad should have waited for the French to join him, but he did not. After arriving at Nicaea, he decided to make his way to Antioch across central Anatolia along the same path that the First Crusade had traversed. Just as had occurred in the First Crusade, Conrad's troops met a Turkish army near Dorylaeum, but the result was not the same. Surrounded by Turkish light infantry, Conrad's forces were virtually defenseless. The carnage was horrible: Almost the entire German army was killed. Conrad and a few other survivors struggled back to Nicaea, where they decided to await the arrival of the French.

Louis VII and his crusading army left France on June 11, 1147. They arrived at Constantinople on October 4. Some members of the royal court continued to advise the king to join forces with Roger II of Sicily and attack the capital city in a land/sea operation, but Louis would not hear of turning his holy army against a Christian empire. Manuel invited the king and queen into Constantinople, where they were housed in a lavish palace and treated to every luxury and entertainment that the wealthy and cosmopolitan city could offer. Louis was pleased and Eleanor enchanted, but the party soon ended, and the French forces were ferried across the Bosporus to continue their pilgrimage.

Louis met Conrad at Nicaea, where the two kings discussed their situation. After his defeat at Dorylaeum, Conrad commanded only a tiny force. If the crusade were to succeed, it would rest with the French to make it happen. For obvious reasons, the rulers decided not to venture into central Anatolia again. Instead, they made preparations to march along the Aegean and Mediterranean coasts of Asia Minor, thus remaining in Byzantine territory as long as possible. Leaving Nicaea, the crusaders marched to Smyrna and then Ephesus, where Conrad fell gravely ill. At Manuel's invitation, the German emperor sailed to Constantinople, where he was nursed back to health by the emperor and empress themselves. Relations between the two men were thus repaired. When he was healthy enough, Conrad sailed directly to Palestine from Constantinople.

Although the French army remained in Byzantine territory, their progress was anything but easy. The Turks continually harassed them and raided the cities on which the crusaders depended for provisions. Disagreements between the Greeks and Latins broke out regularly, often ending in bloodshed. Manuel ordered his troops to protect Byzantine citizens, which meant that the French spent more time fighting Christians than Muslims. Rumors spread quickly that Manuel was purposefully attempting to weaken the crusade so that it could be crushed by his friends, the Turks. Letters that Louis sent home make clear that the king believed that the Byzantines were no small part of the problems that beset his forces. At last, the crusade made it to Adalia. Antioch remained distant, and the king learned of the dire risks involved in marching further along the coast into Turkish territory. He therefore contracted for a fleet of Byzantine vessels to transport his army safely to Antioch.

This was easier said than done. Although Byzantine and Italian ships were summoned throughout the region, there simply were not enough of them to carry so many people. Someone would have to stay. Louis put the clergy on the first boats. When the second group of vessels assembled and it was clear that no more were coming, he boarded along with his wife, court, closest friends, and assorted high nobles. The bulk of the army, including all the foot soldiers, remained in Adalia. The king provided them with money and what little provisions he could muster, and ordered them to march to Antioch. As his ship sailed out of the harbor, Louis looked on his great army for the last time. Early in 1148, while marching east, the French soldiers were massacred by the Turks at Laodicea. Only a handful of survivors made it to Antioch to meet their king.

The Christians in the East were heartened by the death of Zengi, but they remained in difficult straits. Joscelin II already had made one attempt to recapture Edessa and failed. Zengi's son, Nur ed-Din, now the ruler of Aleppo, subsequently ordered the massacre of all Christians in the city. Raymond of Antioch and Joscelin remained on bad terms. All parties waited expectantly for the enormous Christian army led by the kings of France and Germany. Instead, Louis and his court arrived at Antioch with but a remnant of the crusade armies that left Europe. The rest lay dead on the fields of Anatolia.

There was no longer any question of attempting the recapture of Edessa, the original goal of the Second Crusade. Nevertheless, the king had a good contingent of knights and money and could therefore still do much good for the Christian states. Raymond warmly welcomed the monarch and especially his own niece, Queen Eleanor. The prince explained to Louis the current state of affairs, pointing out that Nur ed-Din did not have the resources of Zengi, because Mosul was under the control of his brother. Now was the time to strike against him by leading an army against Aleppo.

Louis and Raymond were men cut from very different cloth. The austere and pious king neither liked nor trusted the handsome, swashbuckling, and sophisticated man of Aquitaine. He particularly resented the spell that the count seemed to cast over Eleanor, who naturally enough admired her cosmopolitan uncle. When Louis proved reluctant to assent to Raymond's plans, the prince made his case to the queen, who agreed with him completely. Rumors began to circulate that Raymond's relationship with Eleanor was something more than avuncular. The final straw came when Eleanor proclaimed that if Louis did not lead his men against Aleppo, as Raymond requested, she would seek an annulment of their marriage on the grounds of consanguinity, taking rich Aquitaine with her. Heartbroken and angry, Louis placed the queen under house arrest and immediately left Antioch bound for Palestine.

Conrad had already arrived in Jerusalem with an army of mercenaries. When Louis joined him, the French forces were increased by the late arrival of crusaders from Provence. On June 24, 1148, the two kings convened an assembly at Acre of all the barons and leading clergy of the kingdom of Jerusalem. It was the largest such group ever assembled. Together, they commanded a powerful force. The question was what to do with it. Many options were debated, although the original purpose of the crusade, the recapture of Edessa, was not among them. Aleppo was the obvious target, but it received minor consideration. Louis probably was not eager to see Raymond's plan endorsed by the assembly when he had already rebuked it at Antioch. At last, they settled on an attack on Damascus.

Jerusalem and Damascus were allies, of course, but that was easily dispensed with. It had not escaped the notice of King Baldwin III, who had just reached the age of majority, and the other Palestinian lords that Nur ed-Din had recently married the daughter of the *atabeg* of Damascus. Although the people of Damascus hated the son of Zengi as much as his father, many Christians felt that it was only a matter of time before Nur ed-Din captured the city, putting Jerusalem in danger. Still, it was a risk. In an attempt to shore up a firm defensive line against Nur ed-Din, the knights of Palestine would have to chance creating a new and nearby enemy. For the recently arrived crusaders, there were no such qualms. They did not understand how a treaty with infidels could have been made in the first place, and they saw no reason to honor it now.

On July 24, 1148, the siege of Damascus began. It lasted four days. In a supremely foolish move, the Christian army gave up a highly defensible position to attack a weaker portion of the city's defenses and thereby found themselves in an untenable location. They had no choice but to retreat, intensely humiliated. The greatest Christian army ever to assemble in Outremer bungled its way to Damascus and back again, gaining nothing except the enmity of an ally. For the Muslim world, this was the strongest evidence yet that the Franks could lose, and lose big.

Conrad left in disgust on September 8, sailing first to Thessalonica and then to Constantinople. There, he again became the houseguest of the emperor. Now fully reconciled, and indeed good friends, the two men made their plans to destroy the Norman kingdom of Roger II. King Louis remained in Palestine until Easter of 1149. Although Abbot Suger repeatedly wrote to him requesting his prompt return, the king remained, trying to find some good that he could do after doing so much harm. Still under armed guard, Eleanor was more determined than ever to end her marriage as soon as she reached Europe. That too kept Louis in Palestine, as he tried to convince her to change her mind. Throughout, he blamed Manuel and the Byzantines for his misfortunes, and he meant to make them pay.

The Second Crusade was over. By any measure, it was a disaster. Not only did it fail to recapture Edessa, but by its blundering attempt to take Damascus, it strengthened the Christians' greatest enemy, Nur ed-Din. It is no exaggeration to say that crusader states would have fared better had the crusade never been launched. When Louis returned to Europe, he proclaimed his firm intention to once again take up the cross and, with his Norman allies, crush the real enemy of Christ, the Byzantine Empire. The pope did not support the plan, so it came to nothing, but the perception that the Byzantines were part of the problem rather than the solution became widespread. Instead of promoting Christian unity, the crusades were driving East and West farther apart.

No one was more disappointed than St. Bernard. The crusade built on his prestige and reputation had been an unmitigated fiasco. The question all of Europe asked, Bernard continually asked himself: Why? Why would God call his knights to the East to be butchered by the infidels? Why would he bring dishonor and blame on Christian kings seeking to do his will? Why would he allow their pious efforts to harm that which they had come to save? For his answer, Bernard looked no further than the Old Testament. The armies of Christendom failed because of the sins of Europe. God withheld victory from his knights to chastise them and all Christians. The fault lay not with Bernard or the pope, but with every sinful man and woman who brought down the wrath of God. If crusades were ever to succeed, he argued, Europe must purify itself.

NOTES

1. Fulcher of Chartres, *Historia Iherosolymitana*, in Brundage, *The Crusades: A Documentary Survey*, 74–75.

2. Francesco Gabrieli, *Arab Historians of the Crusades*, trans. E. J. Costello (New York: Routledge, 1969), 77.

3. Bernard of Clairvaux, in Brundage, *The Crusades: A Documentary Survey*, 92.

4. Ibid., 93.

5. Ibid., 94–95.

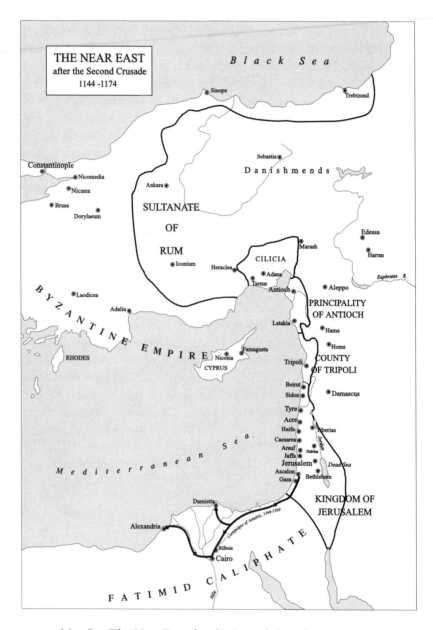

Map 5.   The Near East after the Second Crusade, 1144–1174

4

THE DECLINE OF THE LATIN KINGDOM OF JERUSALEM AND THE THIRD CRUSADE

NUR ED-DIN

While Europe mourned the defeat of the Second Crusade, the crusader states were left with its bitter legacy. The people of Damascus now deeply distrusted the Christians, although they hardly liked Nur ed-Din much better. More important, momentum had shifted from the crusaders to the Muslims. Unlike any enemy the crusaders had yet faced, Nur ed-Din energized Islamic religious zeal, using it for his own advancement and as a weapon against the Christians. Like Zengi, his father, Nur ed-Din preached the *jihad,* a holy war against the infidel invaders. Like St. Bernard, Nur ed-Din believed that victory on the battlefield required religious purification. He founded numerous schools, mosques, and Sufi convents, and he persecuted Shi'ite Muslims. Throughout it all, he continued to beat the drum of holy war, proclaiming that Muslim unity and piety would stir God to expel the Christians from his sanctified lands.

While Nur ed-Din unified, the crusader states crumbled apart. Baldwin III (1143–63), like any young man in his teens, was eager to go his own way without parental meddling. Unfortunately for him, his mother, Queen Melisende, was not merely a regent but a coruler. She could not simply be brushed aside. Relations between mother and son eroded rapidly. The nobility split into factions favoring one or the other. Tensions between the parties grew so severe that civil war seemed imminent, and in isolated areas it did break out. By 1152, however, the political struggle was over. Melisende was removed from power and given the town of Nablus, where she lived out the remainder of her days. For his part, Baldwin had grown into a vigorous man, fair haired with a thick beard. He was intelligent and well educated, with a winning personality and a diplomat's guile.

With his mother out of the way, Baldwin prepared for his first great initiative, the capture of Ascalon. This heavily fortified port city was the last remnant of Muslim power on the Palestinian coast. The Egyptians had long used it as a base for raiding. Although the raids had subsided with the construction of crusader fortresses around the city, it remained a strategic port where Fatimid rulers could station their fleets to disrupt Christian shipping. It would also make a useful beachhead for a Muslim invasion. In January 1153, Baldwin put all the resources of his kingdom into the siege. Month after month the city held out, but on August 19 it finally surrendered. The captured booty was enormous, the first such haul crusaders had seen in several generations. The Christian conquest of Palestine was complete.

The capture of Ascalon had a price: Nur ed-Din took advantage of the diverted attention of the crusaders by marching on Damascus. Baldwin had no resources to assist in its defense. Although the *atabeg* of Damascus had patched things up with the crusaders, the people of the city no longer trusted them after the Second Crusade. Nur ed-Din's religious rhetoric swayed others. A few months after the fall of Ascalon, the people of Damascus opened their gates to Nur ed-Din. He was now the unquestioned master of Muslim Syria.

Ascalon carried an additional price, although none could then see it. For the first time, Egypt was in reach of the crusaders. The temptation to expand into the rich lands of the Nile was enormous. Rather than preserving a balance of power at home, the Christians of the kingdom of Jerusalem would find themselves drawn powerfully into Egypt. The same lure would animate many of the later crusades from Europe, with disastrous results.

King Baldwin was eager to foster good relations with the Byzantine Empire. Byzantine armies were an effective tool in preserving a balance of power in Syria, and the Byzantine navy would be indispensable in an attack on Egypt. Relations between the two states were strained, however, over the matter of Antioch. Prince Raymond had been killed fighting Nur ed-Din in June 1149. His widow, Constance of Antioch, was determined to marry for love. She chose Reynald of Châtillon, a handsome, dashing, and reckless adventurer. It was a disastrous choice. According to his nature,

Reynald acted impulsively and without thought. He was grotesquely cruel, painfully bombastic, and politically tone deaf. In 1156, joining forces with Prince Thoros of Armenia, he led three weeks of plundering expeditions against Byzantine Cyprus. With joy, Reynald presided over and took part in brutal murder, rape, and destruction across the Christian island. Emperor Manuel was enraged, and so was King Baldwin. The two leaders formed an alliance in September 1158, while the emperor and his troops were already on the march. Baldwin agreed to do nothing while Manuel waged war on Antioch. In return, the emperor promised to assist the crusaders in their struggle with Nur ed-Din. To cement the agreement, Baldwin married Manuel's niece, Theodora.

Thoros fled, leaving Reynald to face the imperial army himself. Although adept at killing the defenseless, the prince of Antioch had no stomach for fighting men with swords. It was, in any case, a hopeless fight. Without help from Jerusalem, Antioch would fall. Reynald left the city, making his way to the emperor's camp. There he groveled at the emperor's feet, begging for mercy. He got it; in fact, more than he deserved. Manuel agreed to allow Reynald to hold Antioch as an imperial vassal, provided that the citadel was handed over to Byzantine troops. On April 12, 1159, Manuel I made a triumphal entry into the ancient city. After securing the citadel, he marched toward Nur ed-Din's stronghold at Aleppo.

Once again it seemed that Aleppo would fall, and once again it did not. Manuel was not as interested in capturing the city as he was in securing peace for the crusader states. In return for the emperor's retreat, Nur ed-Din agreed to a truce with the Christians, preserving the current borders. He also agreed to assist Manuel in an attack on the Seljuk Turks of Anatolia. Although some knights muttered bitterly about the emperor's withdrawal, the truce was honored almost everywhere. Predictably, Reynald did not honor it. In 1160, he was captured by Muslim forces and held for ransom. No one was willing to pay, so he remained in captivity for the next sixteen years.

King Baldwin III died in February 1163 after a short illness. He was greatly mourned by Christians and Muslims alike. Having no children, he had named his younger brother, Amalric, to be his successor. Twenty-seven years old, Amalric (1163–74) was much like his brother in many ways. The two looked quite alike, except that Amalric was much heavier. There was some opposition among the nobility to Amalric taking the crown. In 1157, he had married Agnes of Courtenay, the daughter of Joscelin II of Edessa.

The patriarch had condemned the marriage because they were too closely related. To obtain the throne, Amalric agreed to an annulment, provided that his two children, Baldwin and Sibylla, were declared legitimate. It was during his reign that Archbishop William of Tyre was commissioned to write a history of the crusader states and a history of Islam. The former remains an important and valuable source. The latter is lost.

THE LURE OF EGYPT

Before taking the throne, Amalric had been count of Jaffa and Ascalon. It is not surprising, then, that when he thought of the future of his kingdom, he looked to Egypt. The time seemed ripe for an invasion. The Fatimid caliphate had disintegrated into factional warfare between two viziers, each in search of allies to use against the other. Nur ed-Din had tried to end the struggle by sending his Kurdish general, Shirkuh, into Egypt to place the vizier, Shawar, in power, but once this was accomplished, Shirkuh and Shawar became bitter enemies, and war again seemed likely. Shawar appealed to Amalric for help. In 1164, the king led his troops into Egypt, besieging Shirkuh at Bilbeis. The situation was desperate for Shirkuh. In an attempt to break the siege, Nur ed-Din attacked the crusaders near Antioch, decisively defeating their army and capturing their leaders. To restore the truce, Amalric agreed to withdraw from Egypt provided that Shirkuh did the same. For the moment, the balance of power was maintained, but the continued instability of the Fatimid caliphate threatened all.

Three years later, with his position better consolidated in Syria, Nur ed-Din prepared to snatch the Egyptian prize before it could fall to the Christians. Once again, he sent Shirkuh into Egypt, and again Shawar turned to Amalric for assistance. The king sent Hugh of Caesarea to Cairo to negotiate a treaty in which the vizier agreed to pay 400,000 gold dinars in return for Christian aid. Boldly, Hugh insisted that the caliph himself ratify the agreement, even demanding that the sheltered potentate shake hands on the deal. With the treaty signed, the Christian forces marched into Egypt and besieged Alexandria, which Shirkuh had previously captured. After a brief siege, the city capitulated. It was a great moment for the crusaders as they strode victoriously into the city of St. Mark, the last of the ancient patriarchal sees not already in Christian hands. Alexandria was restored to the Fatimid caliphate, but the Franks were allowed to fly their standard over the famed Lighthouse. In addition, they stationed a garrison of soldiers in the capital city, Cairo, to defend against further attacks from Nur ed-Din. For this protection, they were to receive an annual payment of 100,000 gold dinars. For all practical purposes, Egypt had become a Christian protectorate.

With courage and skill, Amalric had reversed the kingdom of Jerusalem's downward slide, bringing it to a new apex of power and prestige, but he wanted more. Control over Egypt was one thing, but he, like Nur ed-Din and Shirkuh, dreamed of capturing it outright. To that end, Amalric sent William of Tyre to Constantinople to negotiate a joint attack on the Fatimids. Earlier, the king had married the great niece of the emperor, Maria Comnena. The Hospitallers strongly favored the conquest of Egypt, arguing that the terms of the Christian withdrawal were too lenient. Egypt was weak and ready for conquest, they argued. Shawar was unreliable, and his son, Kamil, was known to be negotiating with Nur ed-Din. Would the crusaders wait until Egypt could rebuild its strength, or would they capture it now for the good of all Christendom? The power of the crusaders, the Hospitallers argued, was more than sufficient to perform the task. There was no reason to wait for the emperor in Constantinople to arrive and claim the prize for himself. The Templars disagreed, opposing the expedition to Egypt altogether. They insisted that the crusaders not repeat the mistake of Damascus of attacking an ally and thus driving him into the bosom of their enemy. Amalric agreed with the Hospitallers. Without waiting for word from Constantinople, the king began the invasion of Egypt. The Templars refused to take part.

When Shawar learned that his allies were now his enemies, he turned immediately to his enemy, Nur ed-Din. With promises of rich rewards and a third of Egypt, the Muslim leader again sent Shirkuh to Egypt with a large war chest and the army of Damascus. In November 1168, the crusaders captured Bilbeis and began their trek to Cairo. They were delayed, however, getting their fleet down the Nile. In the interim, Shirkuh's forces arrived in the vicinity. He did not venture to attack the crusaders directly, because there was really no need. Both sides knew that the crusader assault had run out of steam. Amalric attempted to extract money from Shawar for his withdrawal, but the vizier put off the matter with negotiations, knowing that the Christian threat was largely neutralized. At last, Amalric ordered the retreat of his forces from Egypt. It was a bitter defeat.

THE RISE OF SALADIN

Shawar was saved from the Christians, but not from Shirkuh. Days later, the general murdered his old enemy and took the title of vizier for himself. He did not hold it long; two months later, he died too. His nephew, al-Malik al-Nasir Salah ed-Din Yusuf, known to the Christians as Saladin, succeeded him. Saladin had been at his uncle's side during most of the Egyptian campaigns. There was nothing about him or his early career to suggest to the crusaders that he was a particularly gifted or effective leader, but he was. As vizier, Saladin began the process of putting Egypt back together again. He reorganized the Egyptian army and began work on a citadel and other fortifications to defend Cairo against future attacks. He secured the lucrative Red Sea ports, including one controlled by the Franks. In September 1171, he boldly deposed the Fatimid caliph, removed all Shi'ites from power, and placed Egypt under the nominal rule of the Sunni Abbasids in Baghdad. Theoretically, Syria and Egypt were at last united into one Islamic empire, under the overlordship of Nur ed-Din. In reality, though, Saladin was master of Egypt. Tensions between the two men increased, particularly as Nur ed-Din extended his own power over Mosul and Mesopotamia.

King Amalric had by no means given up on Egypt. In 1169, he and Manuel Comnenus launched a joint land/sea attack on Damietta. The greatest obstacle to their victory was not the enemy but themselves. Amalric and the Hospitallers did not trust the emperor, fearing that he would capture the city and exclude them from the spoils. The utter lack of cooperation between the two forces doomed the enterprise from the start. When the rains came, Amalric ordered his army home. The Byzantine fleet also returned home, although many of their ships were lost in a sudden storm.

Recriminations for this latest defeat were heard all around Jerusalem and Constantinople. Among the crusader nobility, most blamed the Byzantines, although some criticized the delays and tactics of their king. For his part, Amalric still refused to abandon his dream of conquering Egypt. Despite the bad feelings generated at Damietta, he continued to seek good relations with Manuel in the hopes of another joint attack. He also opened negotiations with Byzantium's enemies, the Normans. Here he was more successful. In 1174, King William II of Sicily led a massive fleet against Alexandria. Amalric and his troops planned to join the Normans there to assist in the siege, but on July 11, before he could arrive, the king of Jerusalem died of dysentery. His troops returned home. Alone, the Normans prepared for an assault, but a surprise sortie from the city drove them back to their boats and to Sicily.

For Saladin, all the news was good. The death of Amalric left the kingdom of Jerusalem to the king's thirteen-year-old son, Baldwin IV (1174–85). Although the young man possessed a keen intelligence, he was very sickly. In fact, he had already contracted leprosy, a disease that was to cripple, disfigure, and ultimately kill him. On May 14, 1174, the great Nur ed-Din died, leaving behind a young son and a host of Zengid family members vying for control of his kingdom. Saladin took advantage of the strife by posing the argument that he was the rightful heir of Nur ed-Din. He occupied Damascus swiftly, thus gaining a military foothold in Syria. Two years later, he settled the power struggle by allowing two Zengids to take Aleppo and Mosul, while the Abbasid caliph named Saladin overlord of Syria and Egypt. To make the case further, he married Nur ed-Din's widow. The crusaders' greatest fear was thus realized—the Muslim kingdoms were united not only in theory but also in fact.

Saladin continued the propaganda of *jihad* and Muslim purification that Zengi and Nur ed-Din had begun. This is not to say that Saladin was insincere in his rhetoric. He truly believed that his state must abide by the laws of Islam if it were to prosper. At great detriment to himself and his administration, he abolished all unlawful taxes. Like his predecessors, Saladin gave generously to pious causes and spent freely on the building of new mosques, libraries, and convents. He was a deeply religious man who genuinely hoped to reunify Muslims into a powerful state holy before God. When he spoke of holy war, he did so with passion. His friend and biographer, Baha ad-Din, recorded:

> The Holy War and the suffering involved in it weighed heavily on his heart and his whole being in every limb; he spoke of nothing else, thought only about equipment for the fight, was interested only in those who had taken up arms, had little sympathy with anyone who spoke of anything else or encouraged any other activity.[1]

Jerusalem, the third holiest city in the Muslim faith, became the center-piece of his rhetoric. He looked forward to the day when the Christian conquerors would be driven from the city, back to the European lands whence they had come three-quarters of a century earlier. Indeed, he hoped for a great deal more:

> While I [Baha ad-Din] was standing thus Saladin turned to me and said: "I think that when God grants me victory over the rest of Pales-tine I shall divide my territories, make a will stating my wishes, then set sail on this sea for their far-off lands and pursue the Franks there, so as to free the earth of anyone who does not believe in God, or die in the attempt."[2]

The problem of the Byzantine Empire's protection of the crusader states resolved itself for Saladin in 1176 at the crucial battle of Myrio-cephalum. There, the Seljuk Turks of Anatolia crushed the imperial armies. The emperor's dream of recapturing Asia Minor disintegrated. More important for Saladin, the defeat put Byzantium on the defensive at home, removing it as a player in Palestine and Syria. Faraway Europe was also not a problem. Crusader requests for aid to the pope, France, England, and Germany had been met with sympathetic words but little else. Europe's leaders were too preoccupied with their own struggles to be concerned with the Levant. The pope and the Lombard League were at war with the German emperor in the north of Italy, and France and England were on very poor terms with each other. The crusader states would have to stand on their own.

Saladin could not lead a *jihad* against the Christians until he consoli-dated his power in Muslim lands. He must be the champion of Islam in word and deed. In 1180, he allied with Sultan Kilij Arslan II of the Seljuks. Three years later, he captured Aleppo, and in 1185 he made an alliance with Mosul. In the same year, he struck a four-year truce with the Franks, giving him time to improve his position in Syria. Simultaneously, he entered negotiations with Emperor Andronicus I Comnenus (1183–85) in Constantinople. The latter was in a difficult position, squeezed by the Turks from the east and the Normans from the west. An-dronicus and Saladin signed a treaty of friendship, leaving the crusaders farther out in the cold. Unlike John II and Manuel I, Andronicus had nei-ther the opportunity nor the will to assist Christian Palestine. Although he was himself once given a fief in the Latin Kingdom, the emperor had risen to power on a wave of vehement anti-Latinism in Constantinople. In 1182, he had encouraged the urban mobs to massacre thousands of western Europeans living in the capital, an event that embittered the crusaders against the Byzantines even further. No longer was the emperor seen as a friend of the crusader states; he was now their betrayer.

THE REIGN OF THE LEPER KING

Because of his leprosy, there was no question of Baldwin IV producing offspring, nor was there an expectation that he would live for very long. Because he was unable to rule directly, his reign was one of regents and factions vying for control of the kingdom and jockeying for position while the king approached death. The first regent was Count Raymond III of Tripoli, a sober and intelligent man. Raymond attempted to deal with the problem of a royal heir by marrying the king's sister, Sibylla, to William Longsword, the powerful and wealthy marquis of Montferrat in northern Italy. The two were married in October 1176. William died in June of the following year, but not before Sibylla conceived a son, whom she named Baldwin.

Dark intrigue walked the hallways of the royal palace in Jerusalem while the leper king reigned. On one side was the faction of Raymond of Tripoli, made up of members of the "old families" of the crusader states. They were the pragmatists, the diplomats, the conservatives. Because they owned much, they wanted to safeguard the status quo. Stability and security, they believed, was best achieved through diplomacy with the Muslims and close ties to Europe and Byzantium. Among the members of this faction was Archbishop William of Tyre, and it is from this perspective that he wrote his history of the Franks in the Levant. On the other side was a more diverse collection of adventurers, ne'er-do-wells, and royal family members whom historians have called the "court party." A good many of these lacked the pedigree of the old families, but they longed to win fortune or glory for themselves. Prominent among the members of this faction were Agnes of Courtenay, the mother of the king, who kept a close eye on her son, restricting access to him as best she could. Joining her were Reynald of Châtillon, the former prince of Antioch, who was released from captivity in 1176 and by another marriage became lord of Transjordan and Hebron, as well as Joscelin III of Courtenay, titular count of Edessa and uncle of the king. Because of their tight control on Baldwin, the court party quickly acquired power in Jerusalem after Raymond of Tripoli's regency expired in 1176.

A natural for inclusion in the court party was the recently arrived Guy of Lusignan. Guy and his brother Amalric had been expelled from their fief in Poitou for attacking the agents of their lord, Richard the Lionheart. Although disgraced and penniless, Guy had a daring and swashbuckling demeanor that endeared him to some, but by no means all, of the court party. Sibylla, the young and recently widowed sister of the king, was captivated by Guy and soon acquired permission to marry him. Guy thus became one of the most important men in the kingdom: brother-in-law to the king and guardian of the royal heir. It was not surprising, then, that when leprosy claimed the king's sight, Guy was named regent. He also acquired a fief, becoming lord of Jaffa and Ascalon.

Mere months went by before Guy of Lusignan ran afoul of the king. In September 1183, Saladin crossed the Jordan with a large force and plundered Baisan. Quickly, Guy summoned the armies of the crusaders to move into position to defend their kingdom. He commanded a sizable force of more than fifteen thousand soldiers. Although Saladin did his best to provoke a fight, Guy kept his distance, ensuring that the Muslim leader could do nothing more than petty mischief. The regent knew well that Saladin's militia troops could not remain in the field for extended periods, so he simply waited them out. After a few weeks, Saladin and his army withdrew. When Baldwin IV heard of the engagement, he flew into a rage, accusing Guy of treason and cowardice for not attacking Saladin when he had the chance. At once, he dismissed Guy as regent and took control of the kingdom himself. He even attempted to obtain a divorce for Guy and Sibylla—something neither of them wanted. In this, Baldwin was unsuccessful, but his attempts to harm Guy led the latter into open disobedience to the crown. The court party, many of whom had never liked Guy of Lusignan, began to break apart.

Despite Baldwin IV's determination to rule, it soon became clear even to him that he really did need a regent. Earlier, he had crowned his young nephew as coruler, so a regent was doubly necessary to manage affairs for the leper while he lived, and the child after that. With the court party in shambles, there was no realistic candidate but Raymond of

Tripoli. Raymond agreed to take up the reins of state again, but only on the condition that his regency would last a decade, thus extending into Baldwin V's majority. He also insisted that all swear that if Baldwin V should die before the age of majority, a committee of the pope, the German emperor, and the kings of England and France should decide which of Amalric's two daughters, Sibylla or Isabella, had claim to the throne. This was a real possibility, because the child was already in poor health. Raymond did not want suspicion cast on him if the youth were to die, so he refused to be his regent, preferring instead to confer that title on Joscelin III of Courtenay. The partnership of Raymond and Joscelin, prominent members of the two struggling factions, seemed to mark the end of the bitter political feud. Despondent over the arrival of Raymond, Agnes of Courtenay died.

In March 1185, the long-suffering Baldwin IV died. In August 1186, Baldwin V followed his uncle to the grave. According to the agreement, Raymond was to remain regent of the kingdom until the pope and kings of Europe could decide the question of the royal heir. Matters never got that far. On the suggestion of Joscelin, Raymond made a trip to Tiberias. No sooner had the regent left Jerusalem than Joscelin closed the capital and seized control of Acre and Beirut. Raymond was betrayed. Enraged, he summoned all the nobles of the kingdom to Nablus to make war on the traitors, but only the members of his party complied. The kingdom of Jerusalem was again torn by factionalism, only this time both sides were armed and ready for war. Saladin watched with glee as the Christians prepared to destroy themselves.

Now back in control, the court party in Jerusalem, led by Reynald of Châtillon and Patriarch Heraclius, moved quickly to crown Sibylla queen of Jerusalem. There was, however, a small problem: her husband. Many in the party had never liked Guy of Lusignan, and others shunned him as a coward after Baisan. They would not have him as king now. Sibylla's love for Guy was undiminished, so it was with grief that she learned that she could be queen only if she agreed to a divorce. After extracting promises for the continued legitimacy of their two daughters and a guaranteed livelihood for her former husband, Sibylla at last agreed to the divorce on the further condition that she could choose her next husband freely immediately after her coronation. So ardently had Sibylla bargained for Guy's upkeep that the nobles felt secure in granting her the matrimonial freedom she requested. But the negotiations were only a clever ruse. No sooner was the crown on her head than she announced that she would marry Guy of Lusignan. With her own hands, she crowned her beloved husband, having outmaneuvered his enemies. Given little choice, the court party accepted Guy (1186–90) as king. When Raymond received word of Guy's coronation and the subsequent support of the nobility, he withdrew his forces to Tiberias. There, he made a formal alliance with Saladin, who readily supplied him with troops to prosecute his war against Jerusalem.

THE HORNS OF HATTIN

It was not long before relations between the erratic Reynald of Châtillon and the new king broke down. In a rage, Reynald returned to the Transjordan and audaciously declared that his lands were independent of royal control. For income and enjoyment, Reynald and his men preyed on tradesmen and other travelers making their way from Syria to Egypt. For Saladin, this was more than an annoyance: Those trade routes were the principal means of communication between his two kingdoms. Because Saladin was already looking for an excuse to break his truce with the Christians, the raids of Reynald were a serious threat to the kingdom of Jerusalem as well. Despite warnings, Reynald attacked a large and wealthy caravan bound for Egypt in early 1187. To avoid war, Guy ordered Reynald to make restitution to Saladin, but Reynald ignored the order. The Transjordan, Reynald insisted, was independent and therefore not bound by Jerusalem's truces. His foolhardy recklessness had already visited violence and destruction on Cyprus and Antioch. Now Reynald's actions were to doom Jerusalem itself. With Islam united, Saladin declared war on the Christians.

The crusader states had prospered because of their relative unity in the face of Muslim chaos. Now the situation was reversed. Syria and Egypt were under one ruler, a man who filled the Muslims with the same kind of religious zeal that had animated crusader conquests for almost a century. Saladin's war was a countercrusade, aimed at removing the Christians from Jerusalem and all the Holy Lands. For their part, the Christians were broken into warring factions. Seeing the grave danger, Raymond of Tripoli finally ended his alliance with Saladin and offered his services to the king of Jerusalem.

Both sides quickly brought their forces together. The crusaders' army was the largest they had ever assembled, totaling approximately twenty thousand men, including twelve hundred heavily armored knights. Saladin's forces were greater, numbering around thirty thousand men, almost half of whom were light cavalry. Near Nazareth, the two armies made camp. King Guy's strategy was simple and proven effective: He would deploy the army defensively, letting the clock tick away. He knew from experience that Saladin's militia could not remain in the field indefinitely. This was the strategy that had stopped Saladin at Baisan four years earlier, although Guy had suffered a political defeat for employing it.

Saladin could not let matters rest as they were. He needed to provoke the Christians into attacking before the season was over. In a desperate move, he marched against Raymond's city of Tiberias. The city fell, but the citadel, commanded by Raymond's wife, Eschiva, held out. Here was a powerful inducement to attack the infidels! Not only had they captured a Christian town, but they also were besieging a noble woman. But it was Raymond himself who insisted that the king must not allow his chivalric zeal to dictate military strategy. Between the crusader camp and Tiberias was a barren, waterless plain. In the summer sun, the army would need a great deal of water to make the crossing, and delay would be perilous. Let Saladin send his armies across the plain if he wished to fight, Raymond argued. The Christians should not make the trip. King Guy agreed with Raymond's wise but painful advice.

Later that same night, the king was visited by Gerald, the Master of the Temple. Gerald was a member of the court party, but he had other reasons for hating Raymond of Tripoli. During the latter's alliance with Saladin, a party of Templars had been massacred by Muslim raiders allowed into Christian lands by Raymond. From Gerald's point of view, Raymond was a traitor and an agent of Saladin: Of course Raymond urged the king to refrain from attacking the Muslim army, for he knew that the crusaders could destroy it. It is also likely that Gerald reminded Guy of the bitter scorn he had received after failing to attack Saladin at Baisan. Here was his chance to disprove those who called him a coward. Guy was convinced by Gerald's words. In the morning, he ordered the army to prepare for the march across the desert plain.

Saladin was surprised and delighted when he heard that the Christians were on the march. Quickly, he prepared to spring his trap. In the baking sun, the crusaders made slow progress along the desert just west of the Sea of Galilee. On the afternoon of July 3, 1187, at the waterless place near Hattin, the crusaders met the first parts of Saladin's army. King Guy gave his exhausted and thirsty troops the order to make camp. It was a hellish night. The soldiers were parched, yet there was no water. In the darkness, the Muslims surrounded the campsite, tormenting the Christians with taunts and threats. They also lit large brushfires, filling the crusader camp with horrible heat and choking smoke.

In the morning, the weakened army prepared for a hopeless battle. All around them on the scorched plain were fresh troops prepared for the slaughter. It was a heartbreaking and heroic battle. The crusaders rushed to an extinct volcano, known as the Horns of Hattin, where they fought off the onslaught as long as they could. In the end, though, the defeat was total. Only Raymond of Tripoli and a few friends were able to break through Saladin's forces and escape. The rest of the massive army was either captured or killed. King Guy was among those captured, as were the Master of the Temple and many other barons. They were all given a comfortable confinement—all, that is, except Reynald of Châtillon. Saladin had sworn to behead this criminal with his own hands, and he did so with satisfaction. He also ordered the mass execution of all captured Hospitallers and Templars, with the exception of the Master himself. Saladin's secretary, Imad ed-Din, described the scene:

> He [Saladin] ordered that they should be beheaded, choosing to have them dead rather than in prison. With him was a whole band of scholars and sufis and a certain number of devout men and ascetics; each begged to be allowed to kill one of them, and drew his sword and rolled back his sleeve. Saladin, his face joyful, was sitting on his dais; the unbelievers showed black despair.[3]

Thousands of common foot soldiers who could not purchase their freedom were sold on the slave markets. Saladin also won for himself a great symbolic prize. The True Cross, carried into battle by the king of Jerusalem, was paraded through the streets of Damascus upside down.

The Horns of Hattin marked the greatest defeat in crusading history. Almost all the fighting men in the kingdom were lost, leaving Christian lands defended only by small garrisons in towns and forts. In one disastrous battle, the kingdom of Jerusalem had lost not only its ability to wage war but also its power to defend itself. The storm of Saladin's

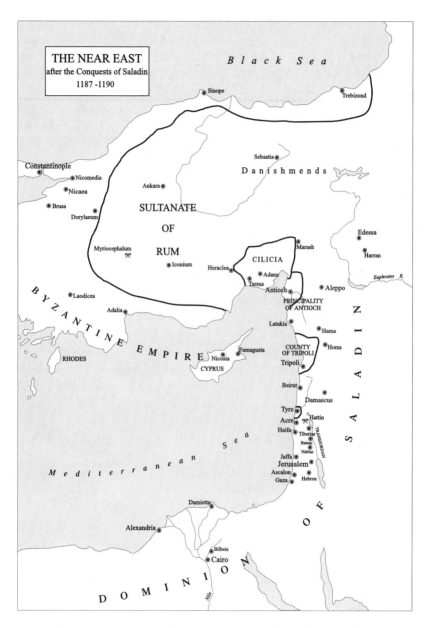

THE NEAR EAST
after the Conquests of Saladin
1187 -1190

Black Sea

Sinope

Trebizond

Sebastia

Constantinople

Nicomedia

D a n i s h m e n d s

Nicaea

Ankara

Brusa

Dorylaeum

SULTANATE

OF

Edessa

Myriocephalum

RUM

Marash

Harran

Iconium

Heraclea

CILICIA

Adana

Euphrates R.

Tarsus

Antioch

Aleppo

Laodicea

B Y Z A N T I N E   E M P I R E

Adalia

PRINCIPALITY
OF ANTIOCH

Latakia

Hama

Homs

RHODES

Famagusta

COUNTY
OF TRIPOLI

Nicosia

CYPRUS

Tripoli

Beirut

S A L A D I N

Damascus

Tyre

Hattin

Acre

Tiberias

Haifa

Baisan

TRANSJORDAN

Nablus

Jaffa

Jerusalem

Ascalon

Gaza

Hebron

O F

M e d i t e r r a n e a n   S e a

Damietta

Alexandria

Bilbeis

Cairo

D O M I N I O N

Nile

Map 6.   The Near East after the Conquests of Saladin, 1187–1190

armies was poised to wipe away the Christian presence in the Levant. This was not lost on the garrison commanders and citizens of the kingdom's cities. They knew well that Saladin was an honorable man who would keep a promise. They therefore sought immediately to make favorable terms on which they could surrender. Like a row of dominoes, the great cities capitulated one by one: Acre on July 10, Ascalon on September 4, and finally Jerusalem itself on October 2. Saladin had planned to avenge the First Crusade's massacre of Muslims in 1099 by killing the Christians of Jerusalem in 1187. He abandoned the idea, however, when the commander of the Jerusalem garrison, Balian of Ibelin, threatened to destroy the Holy City and kill its Muslim inhabitants before Saladin could capture it. Instead, the sultan agreed to leave all Christians of Jerusalem unmolested, giving them safe passage to the coast after they had purchased their freedom. Many could not afford the cost. Some of these Saladin granted release; others eventually were sold into slavery.

All that Saladin had foretold for a united Islam became so. With unbounded joy, he entered Jerusalem and restored the al-Aqsa mosque, which had been the home of the Templars, to a place of Muslim worship. Many of the churches were pillaged and all had their crosses removed. The Church of the Holy Sepulcher was left untouched, but its clergy was reduced to four Syrian priests. The great Hospital of St. John was rededicated as a Shafi'ite college. Streams of Christian refugees fled to Tyre while Saladin continued his campaigns across the crusader states. With ease, he captured almost everything in his wake. Two years later, all that remained to the Christians were the cities of Tripoli, Antioch, and Tyre.

Tyre came within a hair's breadth of falling. After a long siege, its citizens concluded negotiations with Saladin for their surrender. Indeed, Saladin had already sent his standard to be flown from the city walls. Just then arrived Conrad of Montferrat, the younger brother of William Longsword. Conrad was renowned across the Mediterranean for his skill and bravery. He had taken the crusader's cross several years earlier but was delayed when he stopped in Constantinople to marry the sister of Emperor Isaac II Angelus (1185–95). There, he defended the imperial city against an armed revolt, earning the gratitude of his brother-in-law. When he heard of the defeat at Hattin, he immediately set sail for the Levant to fulfill his vow. He took charge of the city's defense, repudiating the surrender and personally throwing Saladin's standard into the city ditch.

CALLING THE THIRD CRUSADE

The bravado of Conrad was inspiring, but his efforts were only a stop-gap. If the crusader states were to survive, they would need far more as-sistance from Europe. The Christians of the East had been requesting help for many years, but it had not been forthcoming. King Henry II of England (1154–89) was preoccupied with his rebellious sons and a war with King Philip II Augustus of France (1180–1223). The German em-peror, Frederick I Barbarossa (1152–90), himself a veteran of the Sec-ond Crusade, promised much but never delivered anything substantive. All of that was about to change. The crushing defeat at Hattin, the loss of Christianity's most precious relic, and the Muslim capture of the Holy City of Jerusalem shocked and horrified western Europe. Pope Urban III (1185–87) died of grief when he heard the news on October 20, 1187. Nine days later, his successor, Gregory VIII (1187), issued *Audita tremendi*. A beautifully crafted document, it became the model for all sub-sequent crusading bulls. It imposed a seven-year truce throughout Eu-rope so that rulers could concentrate on the Levant. It accepted the for-mulation of St. Bernard, that the success of a crusade was linked to the spiritual well-being of Christendom. All Europeans, whether they could fight or not, should contribute to the crusade through purification, fast-ing, and prayer. Jerusalem fell because of the sins of Christ's followers, the pope maintained. Only through their penance could it be redeemed.

The Third Crusade marks the height of the crusading movement. With the crusading idea now mature, the Third Crusade harnessed west-ern Europe's religious faith and chivalric virtue into the largest military enterprise of the Middle Ages. From the beginning, it was a high-profile crusade, led by kings and the highest elites. King William II of Sicily was the first to heed the call, sending an imposing fleet of Norman crusaders to Tripoli. It arrived just in time to save the city from capture. Shortly thereafter, William died, so the Normans played no other role in the Third Crusade.

Vital to the success of any crusade were the warriors of France, but until a truce could be imposed on the Angevin/Capetian struggles there, few knights were free to take up the cross. After papal legates brokered intense negotiations, Henry II and Philip II finally signed a truce on January 21, 1188. Both kings then took the cross. They agreed to leave on Easter of 1189. In the meantime, a general tax was imposed across the land. This "Saladin Tithe" was extremely successful. So too were the batteries of crusading preachers that quickly fanned out across Europe gaining enthusiastic recruits for the holy struggle.

The Germans of the Third Crusade

In April 1189, Frederick Barbarossa also took the cross. Although nearly seventy years old, Frederick remained vigorous and eager to use, in the service of Christ, the considerable power he had built up in Germany. As a crusading veteran, he knew that one of the greatest challenges was moving a large force across southeastern Europe and Asia Minor with as little damage as possible. He sent out his envoys, who made treaties for safe passage with all the potentates on the long journey, including even the Turks of Anatolia.

In Constantinople, Emperor Isaac II had nothing but suspicion for Frederick, who had recently made an alliance with Byzantium's enemy, the Normans. With so large an army, Frederick could cause untold damage in Greece or Thrace, and perhaps even threaten Constantinople itself. It was also troubling to Isaac that Frederick insisted on being called "Roman emperor," a title that the rulers of Constantinople naturally reserved for themselves. Isaac did not want to see rebellions crystallize around this German ruler that might threaten his own position in the imperial city. He turned, therefore, to Frederick's new enemy, Saladin. In a secret treaty, Isaac II agreed to do all that he could to hamper or harm Frederick's crusading host on its way to the East. When news of this treaty later leaked out, it only added to the deep sense of betrayal Latin Christians felt toward their brethren in the East.

Frederick Barbarossa left Regensburg on May 11, 1189. He was accompanied by his son, Duke Frederick of Swabia, most of the upper German nobility, and a massive crusading army—the largest yet to leave Europe. It was a glorious moment, the culmination of a long and successful reign. Surely, they reasoned, this powerful army, led by so bril-

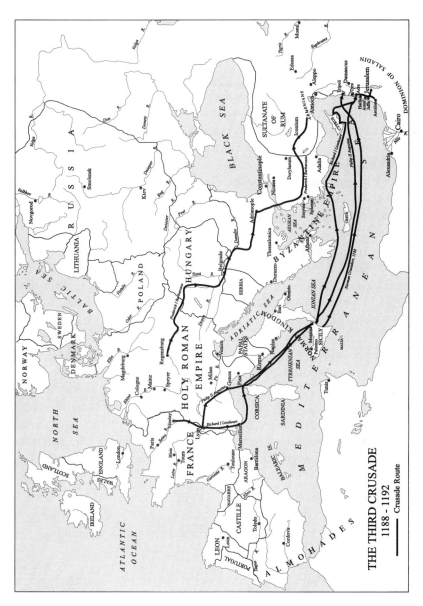

Map 7.   The Third Crusade, 1188–1192

liant a leader, would avenge the humiliations of Christ! Troubles began for Frederick, however, as soon as he entered the Byzantine Empire. As Isaac had promised Saladin, the emperor did all that he could to hinder the German army. Provision markets failed to appear, and imperial forces openly harassed the crusaders. Frederick wrote an angry letter to Isaac warning him to cease these impediments or risk an attack on Byzantine territories. Isaac responded with a call to negotiations, which were quickly bogged down in the question of Frederick's imperial title. The German emperor would discuss nothing unless Isaac recognized him as a brother emperor of Rome. Isaac refused, and his diplomats stalled. Exasperated, the German crusaders captured Adrianople, the capital of Thrace. Finally, in February 1190, Isaac agreed to provide provisions and transport across the Hellespont for Frederick's forces in return for the surrender of the captured city.

On April 25, 1190, the Germans entered Turkish lands. Frederick's treaty of safe passage from Kilij Arslan II proved worthless. The Turks met the Germans in battle on May 18, ending in a resounding victory for the Christians. The Turks scattered, the Germans captured Iconium, and Kilij Arslan once again promised safe passage. A few weeks later, the crusaders entered Christian Armenia. There, on June 10, Frederick Barbarossa drowned in the River Saleph while crossing on horseback. It is not clear precisely what happened: He may have been affected by the heat, his horse may have lost footing, or the old emperor may have suffered a heart attack. Whatever the case, the life of the celebrated emperor had come to a most anticlimactic end. Without the powerful figure of Frederick Barbarossa to lead it, the German crusading army evaporated. Most sailed home. Only a few continued their march to the Levant under the command of Duke Frederick.

Division between Guy of Lusignan and Conrad of Montferrat

News of the death of Frederick Barbarossa came as a bitter disappointment to the embattled defenders of the last Christian strongholds in the East. Still, they looked with hope to the arrival of other crusaders, particularly the promised armies of Henry II and Philip Augustus. King Guy and most of the other crusading barons were released from captivity in June 1188, after swearing never to take up arms against Saladin. Once freed, they quickly gained absolution from that vow. Guy and his small force marched to Tyre, a royal fief and the last Christian city in Palestine. He did not find the homecoming he was expecting. Conrad of Montferrat had no intention of handing over the city that he had saved. He refused to recognize Guy as king of Jerusalem, forcing him to camp outside the walls for month after humiliating month.

As a stream of crusaders began to arrive from Europe, they were surprised to see the king of Jerusalem at odds with the self-proclaimed lord of Tyre. Invariably, they sided with the king. Guy was more concerned with the attitude of the kings of England and France when they arrived, so he made every attempt to demonstrate that he was the true defender of the Holy Places. In August 1189, a Pisan crusader fleet arrived, placing itself at Guy's disposal. He seized the moment. With his meager land forces, he marched to Acre, making camp at a fortified base on a hill of Toron. The Pisan fleet blockaded the port, and the king prepared for an assault on the city. From a military point of view, the move to Acre was pointless and futile. Saladin had greatly strengthened the city's fortifications and its garrison. Indeed, the garrison of Acre alone outnumbered Guy's besieging army. Saladin had brought additional troops to break the siege, although the Christians' fortified encampment made that impossible.

Militarily futile it might be, but Guy's move to Acre was politically brilliant. It graphically cast him as the crusader king, fighting the hated Saladin in an attempt to reconquer a Christian city. Holed up in Tyre, Conrad of Montferrat no longer looked chivalric and daring, but cowardly and craven. New arrivals from the west, eager to prove their mettle against Saladin, went immediately to assist in the siege of Acre. The prestige of Guy grew along with the size of his army. Finally, Conrad himself was forced to join the siege in September 1189. By spring 1190, Conrad had formally accepted Guy as the rightful king of Jerusalem. What had been a small expeditionary force became a large and powerful threat to Acre. Various attacks on the city were repulsed, but the Pisan fleet kept the pressure on by starving out the city's defenders. On October 7, Duke Frederick of Swabia arrived with the pitiful remnants of the German crusade.

Everything unraveled that fall, when Queen Sibylla and her two daughters died. Although the siege of Acre made Guy look like a king, the fact remained that his sole claim to the throne was through his marriage to Sibylla. The only surviving member of the royal family was now Isabella, the daughter of Amalric. Isabella was already married to Humphrey of Toron, who had long ago forsworn the throne. Humphrey was a man of kindness, chivalry, and honor, and Isabella loved him greatly. Conrad quickly realized that Isabella was the key to his own aspirations. Against her will, Conrad had Isabella's marriage to Humphrey annulled. On November 24, 1190, he married Isabella himself—despite the fact that the bride was unwilling, the two were within prohibited degrees of blood relationship, and Conrad was himself married to a Byzantine princess. As husband to Isabella, Conrad claimed the throne of Jerusalem and withdrew from the siege of Acre to await the arrival of the kings of England and France.

It was during this siege that another of the major military orders was born. A group of German merchants from Bremen and Lübeck bound themselves into a pious fraternity dedicated to caring for the sick outside Acre. Later, they took possession of a hospital in Acre, which they called the Hospital of St. Mary of the German House in Jerusalem, and continued their mission. Like the Hospitallers before them, the fraternity soon grew into its own religious order. With the approval of Pope Clement III (1187–91), they adopted a rule very similar to the original rule of the Hospitallers. Following further in the footsteps of the Knights of St. John, the new order was militarized in 1198, adding to its charge the defense of the Holy Land. The Teutonic Knights, as they were subsequently called, received substantial lands in the Levant and Germany over the years, becoming an important element in the history of the crusades in the East and Europe.

THE KINGS OF ENGLAND AND FRANCE

Easter of 1189 came and went with Henry II and Philip Augustus no closer to leaving their kingdoms for the Holy Land. The painstakingly negotiated truce between England and France collapsed when Henry's son, Richard the Lionheart, perceived that his father was favoring his brother, John, to be heir to the throne. Legally speaking, Richard was the vassal of Philip (as was Henry II) for his lands in the kingdom of France. Fearful of losing his claim to the English throne, Richard allied himself with Philip and made war on his father. The matter settled itself in July, when Henry II died and Richard was anointed king of England.

Richard I (1189–99) was the epitome of French chivalric culture. Well educated, well spoken, and even an accomplished poet, the Lionheart was also a man of bold action. A young man of 32 when he took the throne, Richard was an imposing figure—tall, blond, and physically strong. Like the knights of the *chansons de geste,* he was a daring figure, placing himself in personal danger without a thought, always eager to take part in any clash of arms. He was also a brilliant general, perhaps the best military mind of the Middle Ages. Although careless of his own safety, he was obsessed with the safety of his troops. This quality endeared him to his men and fostered intense loyalty. As a man of chivalry, Richard was enthusiastic about the opportunity to crusade against the infidel Saladin. Indeed, against his father's wishes, he had taken the cross shortly after hearing of the defeat of Hattin. As king, Richard was well positioned to make good on his vow. The Saladin Tithe had reaped rich returns in England. To that sum, Richard added his own funds; he sold off many of his rights and properties to increase his war chest. Richard did not hesitate to spend generously from this impressive pot of money.

Philip II Augustus was nothing like Richard. A younger man of 25, Philip was small, sickly, and nervous. He had a sardonic wit and cynical style that was all the more unattractive when compared with Richard's hearty and flamboyant personality. Although Philip was Richard's lord for his French holdings (a fact that Philip reminded Richard of frequently), even a casual observer saw that Richard's charisma and presence far outshined that of Philip. The king of France had no war chest to compare with Richard's, nor did he have the control over his French vassals that Richard enjoyed with his men. As a result, Philip was to remain in Richard's shadow throughout the Third Crusade.

On July 4, 1190, both kings left Vézelay. Before departing, they agreed that all conquests of the crusade would be split evenly between them. They had also decided to abandon the traditional land route through Byzantium and travel to the Holy Land by sea. Philip led his troops to Genoa, where he contracted for vessels and provisions. Richard marched south to Marseilles, where he awaited the arrival of his own fleet. It was late, having stopped off in Portugal to fight Muslims. Tired of waiting, he at last hired some vessels and sailed to Messina in Sicily, where the army was to spend the winter. There, Richard rendezvoused with his tardy fleet.

Matters had recently changed in the Norman kingdom of Sicily. After the death of William II, the throne was seized by Tancred of Lecce. The German king, Henry VI (1169–97), who was married to Constance of Sicily, claimed Sicily for himself and was preparing to launch a campaign to make good on that claim. Richard was not overly concerned about the power struggle. What he wanted from Tancred was money. William II had been married to Richard's sister, Joan. Richard wanted her dowry back. Tancred stalled while attempting to bring Philip into the quarrel. As weeks passed, riots erupted in Messina against Richard and his men. With his patience exhausted, Richard attacked the city, capturing it on October 4. Philip refused to take part in the attack, but he demanded his half of the city all the same. Tancred moved quickly to defuse the situation, agreeing to repay Joan's dowry for the return of Messina. Outrageously, Philip now demanded that Richard hand over half of the dowry money, classifying it as war booty. Clearly, Philip had no right to the money, but Richard gave him one-third anyway in the interest of peace.

The rest of the winter did not go much better. Philip continued to squabble with Richard over any perceived slight, prerogative, or privilege. He became particularly angry when he learned that Richard's mother, Queen Eleanor of Aquitaine (herself a participant in the Second Crusade), was shopping around for a wife for her son. She found an excellent match in Berengaria, the daughter of King Sancho VI of Navarre. Because she was nearby, Eleanor picked up the bride-to-be and prepared to transport her to Messina to join Richard on the crusade. What bothered Philip was the fact that Richard was long ago engaged to marry Philip's sister, Alice. Philip demanded that Richard make financial restitution for breaking the engagement. Richard agreed. On March 30, 1191, Philip and his fleet left Sicily, bound for Acre. Richard waited for the arrival of Berengaria, then set sail himself on April 10.

King Philip found a difficult situation at Acre when he arrived on April 20. Already he had been apprised of the dispute over the crown of Jerusalem between Conrad of Montferrat and Guy of Lusignan. Philip backed Conrad. Although Guy had a title, Conrad had the support of the native barons and, since his marriage to Isabella, the majority of the crusading lords. Conrad was also a proven general, whereas Guy had been the commander at Hattin. With Philip's support, Conrad rejoined the siege of Acre. It had grown into a very large affair, with the city completely invested and Saladin and his troops hovering outside. Still, Philip brought them no closer to taking the city.

Richard had a more exciting journey to Acre. A powerful storm disrupted his tightly ordered fleet, causing a few of the ships to become separated from the main body. Some of these vessels, including one of the treasure ships, wrecked on the coast of Cyprus. Many survived, but many were drowned, including the warden of the Great Seal of England. Since 1184, the island of Cyprus had been ruled by Isaac Comnenus, a Byzantine rebel who styled himself the true emperor of Constantinople. When he discovered the misfortune of the crusader vessels, Isaac quickly looted the treasure and imprisoned the survivors. Among the vessels that were not wrecked was the royal ship transporting Joan and Berengaria. It cast anchor off the coast, helpless to assist those captured by the Cypriotes. Isaac used sweet words to entice the ladies ashore, but they wisely refused. When Richard arrived with the main fleet, he was outraged. He demanded that Isaac hand over all that he had taken and return the crusader captives. Isaac refused, instead marshalling his troops to defend against an attack. He did not have to wait long. A number of the king's vessels were brought to shore for an amphibious assault. When the Greek troops saw the strength and ferocity of the western knights, they scattered. With little resistance, Richard and his men quickly captured the entire island. In May 1191, Isaac Comnenus surrendered on the condition that he not be put into irons. Richard complied, ordering him to be placed in shackles of silver.

The capture of the island of Cyprus was an important milestone in the history of the crusades. The island would remain under Latin rule for the next four centuries. Richard found it immediately useful as a rich source of provisions very close to the coast of Palestine. It would remain his chief source of supplies throughout the Third Crusade. Indeed, it is hard to imagine how the crusaders could have continued their war against Saladin without their base in Cyprus.

While at Cyprus, Richard received a visit from King Guy. The latter was understandably upset by the turn of events at Acre, which now favored Conrad as king of Jerusalem. It would be interesting to know how these two men greeted each other at this first meeting. Richard, after all, had expelled Guy from Poitou for attacking his agents. Now the disloyal vassal begged his former lord for support. Richard listened to Guy's relation of events at Acre with interest. It was disconcerting to him that Philip Augustus had already announced his support of Conrad of Montferrat. Leopold V of Austria, the leader of the Germans, had done the same. It would have been easy for Richard to send Guy packing, but he did not. Instead he assured him of his support. Why? Perhaps he naturally opposed the candidate of Philip. Perhaps he simply warmed to Guy, who was, in culture and temperament, not unlike Richard himself.

Philip's command of the Christian forces at Acre produced nothing of value. It irritated him to hear among the soldiers the great anticipation they had for the arrival of the Lionheart. True to form, Richard arrived with a flourish. On June 7, his fleet discovered a large Muslim vessel transporting nearly a thousand reinforcements to the Acre garrison. The English galleys quickly moved into position and rammed the vessel, sending it to the bottom of the sea. The loss of the reinforcements was a serious blow to the already desperate defenders of the city.

Both kings fell ill shortly after Richard's arrival. By the end of June, Philip was sufficiently recuperated to demand that Richard hand over half of Cyprus. The request was ignored. Once Richard was well enough to consider an attack on the city, things began to pick up at Acre. Saladin was helpless to supply the city or break the siege. On July 12, the day after a fierce but unsuccessful attack by the English and Pisans, the city's garrison asked for terms of surrender. It was agreed that in return for the lives of the Muslim garrison, Saladin would return the True Cross, render 200,000 dinars, and release all of his Christian hostages—still more than a thousand men. The gates were opened, and the crusaders took back the city. When Saladin later did not make his first installment payment on schedule, Richard flew into a rage. He ordered twenty-seven hundred members of the Muslim garrison marched outside the city and executed in view of Saladin and his army. Clearly, the deal was off. Saladin responded by massacring most of his Christian hostages.

Shortly after the capture of Acre, Philip Augustus announced that he would be returning to France. Despite fervent entreaties by his countrymen, the crusader barons, and Richard, Philip would not hear of remaining. The Levant did not agree with the king of France. He had been sick almost since his arrival, and he was tired of playing second fiddle in what had become Richard's crusade. He probably also planned to move against Richard's domains in France while the latter remained engaged in the Holy Land. He swore that he would do no such thing, but subsequent events proved otherwise.

Before his departure, Philip was eager to clear up the problem of the crown of Jerusalem. Richard and Philip sat in judgment of both men's claims. After hearing the arguments, they at last settled on a compromise: Guy would remain king as long as he lived. After his death, the crown would pass to Conrad of Montferrat or his heir. With that settled, Philip bade a hasty farewell to the crusaders and headed back to France. He left the French forces in command of Hugh of Burgundy, who was even poorer than Philip. With large doses of charisma and money, Richard quickly took command of the entire crusade. Conrad of Montferrat, angry over the royal decision, returned to Tyre, refusing to assist the crusade in any way.

RICHARD THE LIONHEART

Saladin controlled the countryside, forcing Richard to rely on his fleet for supplies. Unfortunately for the crusaders, the object of the crusade, Jerusalem, was not on the coast. Any march inland would require a secure port and defended lines of supply. Richard therefore decided to march south to Jaffa, the port closest to the Holy City. Saladin and his armies trailed the crusaders, hoping to capitalize on any mistake. Richard allowed none. He ordered the crusading army to draw up its ranks in tightly controlled columns, with the most vulnerable portions marching along the shores. Farther inland were the infantry and cavalry, and on the outside of the column the archers, crossbowmen, and spearmen. Marching in the hot summer sun was exhausting, so Richard kept the day short to make certain that all soldiers were fit and healthy. Saladin harassed the crusaders with his light Turkish cavalry, who fired arrows at the mounted forces. Knights were often hotheaded and eager for glory, and Saladin hoped to lure at least a few of them into breaking ranks and charging into his trap. Saladin's biographer, Baha ad-Din, described the scene:

> I saw some of the Frankish infantry with between one and ten arrows sticking in them, and still advancing at their usual pace without leaving the ranks. . . . One cannot help admiring the wonderful patience displayed by these people, who bore the most wearing fatigue with-

out having any share in the management of affairs or deriving any personal advantage.[4]

It is a testament to Richard's command skills that none of the crusaders took the bait.

The sultan was running out of time and under increasing pressure from his emirs to launch an all-out attack on the Christian forces. He carefully chose a wooded area just north of Arsuf as the best place to meet Richard in battle. Richard expected the attack and prepared his armies for it. On September 7, Saladin's forces engaged the Christians in battle. Richard orchestrated the event brilliantly. The only discordant note came when the Hospitallers disobeyed Richard's orders to delay their counterattack. Their premature mounted charge could have been disastrous, but the king quickly ordered the general attack and salvaged the situation. The heavily armored knights crushed the Turkish light cavalry. At the end of the day, Saladin's losses were heavy and Richard's very light. The prestige that Saladin had acquired at Hattin was shattered. In the wake of their recent victories, Muslims had begun to count the Frankish charge of no consequence. They were reminded at Arsuf of its devastating potential under the control of an able commander. Saladin would never again risk battle with Richard the Lionheart.

There was now no doubt that the crusaders would recapture Jaffa. Saladin, therefore, destroyed the city's fortifications and withdrew his forces to Ascalon. When they arrived, Richard's men began rebuilding the walls. At Jaffa, Richard had three options, all of which Saladin also understood perfectly. He could lead an attack on Jerusalem. This was certainly the option favored by the French, but Richard knew that it would be an intensely difficult enterprise. Supply lines from Jaffa to Jerusalem would have to be defended by a string of fortifications. Furthermore, if Jerusalem were taken, the majority of the host would return to Europe, leaving the crusader barons with little means to defend the hard-won victory. A second option was to march south to Ascalon. With possession of this key port, the Christians could disrupt communications between Saladin's Syrian and Egyptian kingdoms, thus greatly harming his ability to bring reinforcements and supplies from the latter. Clearly, if the Third Crusade's conquests were to outlast the crusade itself, the crusader barons would need control of Ascalon. Nevertheless, few of the rank-and-file crusaders favored an attack on a coastal city when Jerusalem was within their grasp. Finally, Richard could pursue diplomacy, negotiating a settlement with Saladin. The latter had an army that was increasingly demoralized and a council of emirs that wanted peace with the Christians as soon as possible. Most of all, the Muslim lords wanted Richard I to go away.

Richard pursued all three options simultaneously. Because Saladin lacked sufficient forces to defend both Ascalon and Jerusalem, the sultan abandoned the former, destroying its fortifications. Although Richard favored garrisoning Ascalon and rebuilding its defenses, the crusading majority remained steadfast in their desire to march to Jerusalem. Bowing to their will, in October 1191, Richard prepared the army for the inland trek. At the same time, he sent envoys to Saladin with a plan for peace. In a bold move, Richard proposed that Saladin's brother, Saphadin, marry the king's sister, Joan. The couple would then jointly rule all the land west of the Jordan River. Saladin was intrigued by the idea, but negotiations faltered when Richard insisted that Saphadin also convert to Christianity. While talks continued, Saladin also contacted Conrad of Montferrat, offering to ally with him against Richard and his crusader army. The lord of Tyre was willing to plot against Richard but not to meet him on the field of battle.

The march to Jerusalem was excruciatingly slow. Before advancing, Richard insisted that fortifications and castles be repaired to defend the route to Jaffa. Only when all was secure would he continue the march. In January 1192, the army reached Beit Nuba, just twelve miles from Jerusalem. The weather was terrible. Hailstorms and torrential rains battered them, but the spirits of the soldiers remained high. Here at last was the object of their quest. With the conquest of the Holy City, they could return to their homes as glorious victors like the legendary heroes of the First Crusade.

Before advancing, Richard called a council of barons to decide on the best course of action. The Hospitallers and Templars argued strenuously against an attack on the city. Already the supply line to Jaffa was dangerously harassed by Muslim raiders. Even if they could defeat Saladin's garrison in Jerusalem, they argued, the native lords could never hold the inland city after the crusading host returned to Europe. Most of the crusade leaders agreed with this calculus. They recommended that the army retreat to Ascalon, where they could rebuild the fortifications of that strategic city. Richard accepted their counsel, but when the decision was announced to the rank and file, it evoked bitter recriminations against Richard and the other leaders. After months of hardship, they were deprived of their holy victory. Many, including some nobles like Hugh of Burgundy, refused to go to Ascalon, returning instead to Jaffa or Acre.

Richard arrived in Ascalon on January 20, accompanied by his nephew, Henry of Champagne. Immediately, his men began the difficult task of reconstructing the walls of the city. At Ascalon, Richard continued negotiations with Saladin as well as Conrad of Montferrat. Neither of the talks went anywhere. Saladin hoped to pit the two Christian factions against each other, and Conrad refused to assist an army associated with King Guy. Complicating matters were reports that Richard received in April of his brother John's attempts to ally with Philip Augustus in a bid to capture Richard's Angevin lands. The clock was ticking for the king of England. The longer he remained in the Levant, the more he would be harmed in France, yet he could not leave matters as they were. Conrad of Montferrat enjoyed so much support among the native barons that as soon as Richard departed, the Christians would be plunged into civil war. Saladin would be the ultimate victor in that war.

Richard convened a council of barons and prelates to reconsider the question of the kingdom of Jerusalem. They advised that the only means of healing the division among the Christians was to bestow on Conrad of Montferrat the crown of Jerusalem. Richard accepted the decision with grace. As a consolation prize, he gave the island of Cyprus to the deposed Guy of Lusignan. In Tyre, Conrad received the news of his elevation with great satisfaction. The victory was short-lived. On the evening of April 28, 1192, the king-elect was murdered in the street by two members of the Assassins cult. Some suspected Richard of hiring the assailants, but it was not so. The Assassins had their own reasons for wanting Conrad dead: He had recently seized a ship that belonged to them and refused to return it. Saladin had also offered the Assassin leader, known as the Old Man of the Mountain, a large sum of money for the murder of Conrad or Richard.

Henry of Champagne arrived in Tyre shortly after Conrad's death and was immediately offered the throne by the crusader barons. He was a natural choice. Henry was able, respected, and the most powerful lord in France, after Richard himself. He was also unmarried, which led the barons to offer to him the hand of Isabella, the last surviving heir of Jerusalem. Isabel was more than pleased with the match to this dashing young man. Henry took up the reins of state, but it appears that he never officially took the title of king of Jerusalem. It is not clear why.

With the accession of Henry, the factional division between the Christians disappeared. The count of Champagne put all the armies that had stood aloof with Conrad at the disposal of King Richard. In a general council, the barons urged Richard to seize the moment and lead an attack on Jerusalem. This put Richard in a difficult bind. He continued to receive reports of his brother's treachery in France. If he remained in the East much longer, Philip Augustus would have his hands on most or all of Richard's Angevin lands. After some consultation, he agreed to remain in the Holy Land until Easter of 1193 and to lead an attack on Jerusalem if it seemed feasible.

On June 7, the crusading army marched from Ascalon toward Jerusalem. They encountered no resistance, arriving at Beit Nuba in just four days. The garrison in the Holy City was considerable, and Saladin had poisoned all the wells in the surrounding countryside. Richard was thus faced with the same problem and at the same place he had stood five months earlier. If the crusaders attacked Jerusalem and it did not fall immediately, Saladin could attack the host in a waterless expanse, trapped against the walls of the city. If Jerusalem did fall, Saladin could cut off the city from the coast and recapture it easily. Because neither of these was an attractive scenario, Richard offered a third. Since Jerusalem could never be secure until Saladin's power was broken, he let the crusaders turn their swords against Egypt. Once that rich country was theirs, Jerusalem would fall to them like a ripe apple. A council of barons and prelates considered the proposals and found the Egyptian plan preferable.

Hugh of Burgundy and the French crusaders were disgusted by the decision. Once again, Richard had led them to Christ's holy city, and once again he had turned his back on it. They swore that they would never take part in an attack on Egypt. Richard understood and shared their disappointment. He proclaimed that if the crusaders were determined to attack Jerusalem, he would join but not lead them. As a soldier and pilgrim, he was willing to lay down his own life, but he would not be responsible for the deaths of so many good men in a plan that was sure to fail and would weaken the crusader kingdom in the bargain.

Grieved and embittered, the crusaders again turned their eyes from Jerusalem and trudged back to the coast.

In the face of fierce opposition among the crusaders, the Egyptian campaign never advanced beyond the planning stage. The idea, however, would survive long after the dissolution of the Third Crusade. In the following months, Richard resumed his stalled negotiations with Saladin. He had come to the bitter conclusion that while Saladin remained sultan of Egypt, the Christians could never take and hold Jerusalem. He therefore attempted to broker a truce that would allow the Christians to at least retain the reconquered coast of Palestine. Saladin, whose armies were exhausted and eager for peace, was agreeable in principle. The sticking point was Ascalon. The sultan could not afford to have the crusaders in possession of the linchpin of his empire. He insisted that the city be returned to him. Richard refused.

In August 1192, Richard became very ill. While bedridden, he received additional reports from home—all bad. Philip was now actively engaged in carving up Richard's domains. It seemed that there was no longer any reason for Richard to remain in the Levant. He had done all that he could; he must return now to save his own kingdom. On September 2, he concluded a formal three-year truce between the Christians and Muslims. Saladin agreed to respect Christian territories along the coast from Tyre to Jaffa. Christian pilgrims could henceforth travel freely throughout Palestine to all holy sites, including Jerusalem. The lords of Tripoli and Antioch were also to be included in the truce, if they so wished. For his part, Richard agreed to hand over Ascalon after his men destroyed the rebuilt fortifications. Many of the crusaders took advantage of the truce, journeying to the Holy Sepulcher before returning home to Europe. Richard was not among them. He had sworn to restore Jerusalem to the hands of Christ. He would not enter the city until that came to pass.

On October 9, 1192, Richard I boarded his vessel and headed home. The Third Crusade was at an end, but Richard fully expected to return.

> [The king's] legates informed Saladin in the hearing of many of his satraps, that Richard had in fact sought this truce for a three year period so that he could go back to visit his country and so that, when he had augmented his money and his men, he could return and wrest the whole territory of Jerusalem from Saladin's grasp if, indeed, Saladin were even to consider putting up resistance. To this Saladin replied

through the appointed messengers that, with his holy law and God almighty, as his witnesses, he thought King Richard so pleasant, upright, magnanimous, and excellent that, if the land were to be lost in his time, he would rather have it taken into Richard's mighty power than to have it go into the hands of any other prince whom he had ever seen.[5]

Despite its failures, the Third Crusade was by almost any measure a highly successful expedition. Most of Saladin's victories in the wake of Hattin were wiped away. The crusader kingdom was healed of its divisions, restored to its coastal cities, and secured in a peace with its greatest enemy. Although he had failed to reclaim Jerusalem, Richard had put the Christians of the Levant back on their feet again.

It is tempting to imagine what might have happened if Richard had remained in Palestine until Easter of 1193, as he had promised. Three weeks before that date, on March 4, 1193, Saladin died. Muslim unity died with him.

NOTES

1. Gabrieli, *Arab Historians of the Crusades,* 100.
2. Ibid., 101.
3. Ibid., 138.
4. Quoted in John Gillingham, *Richard the Lionheart* (New York: Times, 1978), 187.
5. *Itinerarium Peregrinorum et Gesta Regis Ricardi,* in Brundage, *The Crusades: A Documentary Survey,* 186.

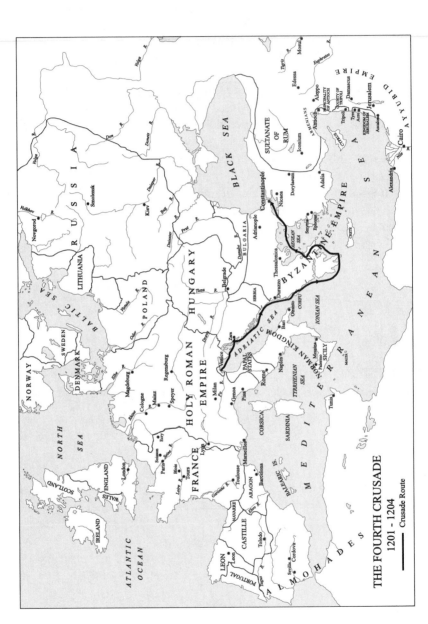

Map 8.   The Fourth Crusade, 1201–1204

5

THE FOURTH CRUSADE

The successes of Richard the Lionheart were impressive, but they did not include the redemption of Jerusalem. From the medieval perspective, the purpose of the crusader states was the protection of the holy sites; they were not an end in themselves. Although Jerusalem was once again open to Christian pilgrims, it remained in Muslim hands.

INNOCENT III

Shortly after his election in 1198, Pope Innocent III (1198–1216) proclaimed a new crusade. Innocent was a very young pope, only in his thirties at his accession. He was keenly intelligent and politically astute. During his pontificate, he expanded papal power and influence throughout western Christendom. Above all, Innocent was determined to restore Christian control over the Holy Land. No goal was nearer to his heart than the reconquest of Jerusalem. He was convinced that all Christendom would need to be mobilized for the effort. Those who could not fight should fast and pray. He ordered collections to be taken up in every church, and even the clergy and monasteries were instructed to render a portion of their income for the sake of the crusade. Innocent meant for his new crusade to overshadow all others.

Innocent faced the same kinds of problems that plagued Gregory VIII when he called the Third Crusade. Once again, the kings of England and France were at war. Richard I was busy reclaiming the lands that Philip II took from him while the former was on crusade. Although eager to return to the Levant, Richard would not leave France until he had restored his domains and had his revenge on Philip. Germany was in even worse condition, torn between two rival claimants to the imperial throne: Philip of Swabia and Otto of Brunswick. These power struggles and others occupied many of the fighting men in Europe.

No crusade could begin until some measure of peace was restored in the West. Innocent sent out papal legates to negotiate the necessary truces. In France, Richard received Cardinal-legate Peter Capuano, who urged him to make peace with Philip so that he or his vassals could travel to the land of Christ. The king angrily pointed out that were it not for the treachery of Philip, he could have remained in the Holy Land and would by now have restored Jerusalem. What had the church done to safeguard his lands while he was away? Now the pope wanted him to strike a truce while Philip still held some of those stolen territories? So great was Richard's storm of fury that Peter fled lest the king carry out his threat to castrate him.

Despite a rocky start, the truce negotiations did bear fruit. Richard and Philip agreed in principle to a five-year truce, although the exact parameters were still problematic.

But, in March 1199, the odds finally caught up with Richard. While surveying a castle siege without donning his armor, he was hit by a crossbow bolt. The surgeon's knife did the rest. In April, he died of gangrene. With the death of the crusader-king, many despaired that Innocent's new crusade would ever materialize.

THE TREATY OF VENICE

The Fourth Crusade was saved by the actions of two men. The first was a spellbinding crusade preacher, Fulk of Neuilly, who filled the French countryside with the pious zeal to risk all for the good of Christ. Thousands took the cross after hearing him speak, although most were poor and therefore of no military use. Nevertheless, the enthusiasm sparked by Fulk also recommended the languishing crusade to the chivalric minds of the nobility. One of those was Count Thibaut of Champagne. Thibaut was the brother of Henry of Champagne, who ruled the kingdom of Jerusalem from the death of Conrad of Montferrat in 1192 to his own death in 1197. Like his brother, Thibaut was a good warrior, intelligent, and attractive. On November 28, 1199, Thibaut hosted a knightly tournament at his castle at Ecry-sur-Aisne. It was a gay event, although overshadowed by the recent death of the most chivalric of kings (and Thibaut's uncle), Richard I.

During the revelry of the tournament, Thibaut announced that he would no longer use his weapons in sport, but instead would place them in the service of the Lord. Immediately, he was joined by his cousin, Count Louis of Blois. Many more of the participants followed suit, each taking the vow of the cross. The crossing of Thibaut and Louis gave the foundering crusade a foundation on which to build. Enthusiasm among the nobility swelled. In February 1200, the illustrious Count Baldwin of Flanders also took the cross and was joined by his wife, Marie, the sister of Thibaut. Many other Flemish nobles joined him. Although they were not kings, Thibaut, Louis, and Baldwin were among the three most powerful lords in France. All three were young men in their twenties, eager to finish the work of Richard I in the East. At last, the Fourth Crusade was coming to life.

A council of the leading crusading barons met at Soissons in early 1200. There they discussed the timetable and goals of the new crusade. At once, they agreed that they would not venture down the land route across the Byzantine Empire but would instead follow King Richard's example and travel by sea. Unlike the king of England, none of these feudal lords possessed a sizable fleet. They decided, therefore, to contract vessels from a maritime port. Thibaut, Louis, and Baldwin each appointed two of their men to a six-man committee with full powers to make contracts in their names. These six were to travel to whatever port seemed best and make whatever arrangements they thought wise and prudent. One of these men was Geoffrey of Villehardouin, the marshal of Champagne. His memoirs are one of the most valuable sources for the Fourth Crusade.

The envoys chose the Republic of Venice because they knew that it had an established crusading tradition and sufficient resources to provide a large fleet for the forming crusade. During the winter of 1200–1201, the envoys crossed the Alps and made their way to the lagoon city. The doge of Venice, Enrico Dandolo (1192–1205), was extremely old (probably in his nineties) and blind; nevertheless, he remained intellectually vigorous, shrewd, and perceptive. He received the French envoys with joy and listened intently to their request. It was a weighty one. The men told the doge of the great crusade that was forming across Europe and their need for vessels and provisions. They begged him to take pity on the land of Christ and assist them in their holy task. It was probably at this point that the envoys revealed to Dandolo that the barons planned to take up the strategy of Richard I by attacking Egypt before moving on to capture Jerusalem. The crusade's destination, however, was to remain secret, because the barons feared the rank and file would oppose it. Dandolo agreed with the envoys and promised to do all that he could to gain the assent of the people of Venice to their proposals.

After some negotiation, the Republic of Venice agreed to supply the crusaders with one year's provisions and sufficient vessels to transport forty-five hundred knights and their horses, nine thousand squires, and twenty thousand foot soldiers to Egypt in return for eighty-five thousand marks of Cologne. In addition, the Venetians agreed to supply fifty manned war galleys at no cost, provided they received an equal share of war booty. The fleet would be ready to sail on June 29, 1202. The envoys enthusiastically signed the treaty, and the pope subsequently ratified it.

Meanwhile, Thibaut of Champagne had fallen ill. Although bedridden when the envoys told him of the treaty with Venice, the news of the great fleet so lifted his spirits that the young count leapt to his feet and rode his finest horse. His illness remained serious, however, and he finally died on May 24, 1201. He was laid in a tomb with the inscription:

> Intent upon redeeming the Cross and the land of the Crucified
> He paved a way with expenses, an army, a fleet.
> Seeking the terrestrial city, he finds the heavenly one;
> While pursuing his goal far away, he finds it at home.[1]

The loss of Thibaut was a serious blow to the forming crusade. The barons decided to offer the titular command of the enterprise to another great lord. As with any crusade, the title of commander in chief was only honorary, but it could be used to entice another baron to take the cross, one who would bring with him additional troops.

After some discussion, it was decided to offer the command to Marquis Boniface of Montferrat. Unlike the barons of France, Boniface was a mature man in his fifties with a lifetime of practical experience. His family was no stranger to the crusader states. Boniface's brother was Conrad of Montferrat, the savior of Tyre, who received the crown of Jerusalem only to be murdered by the Assassins. Another of his brothers was William Longsword, the husband of Sibylla and father of King Baldwin V of Jerusalem. Boniface readily accepted the barons' offer.

Venice put all of her energies into preparing for the new crusade.

The fleet that the crusaders had contracted was truly enormous, exceeding five hundred major vessels. The republic suspended all merchant activity, pressing all of her trading vessels into service for the crusade. In addition, many new ships were built and enormous stores of provision purchased. With unshakable determination, the Venetians completed their task. The largest fleet assembled in Europe since antiquity stood ready to transport the Fourth Crusade across the Mediterranean to Egypt.

The crusaders were not quite so conscientious in keeping their part of the bargain. According to the treaty, they were to have paid the Venetians for the fleet in four installments by April 1202; yet, when the first crusaders arrived in Venice in June, they had made only a small down payment. Furthermore, although the fleet was to depart on June 29, only a fraction of the crusaders arrived in Venice by that date. Even the papal legate did not show up until July 22. By that time, it was clear that the crusade was in trouble. Without a king like Richard I to lead them to a single port, many crusaders felt justified in making whatever arrangements seemed best for their own transportation. As long as they joined the host in the Levant, they reasoned, what difference did it make where they embarked on their journey?

To the leaders of the Fourth Crusade, it made all the difference in the world. The envoys had contracted for a fleet and provisions for 33,500 men. The cost of the fleet was to be collected from the individual crusaders. As it happened, only about 11,000 arrived at Venice. With only one-third of the projected number, when transportation costs were collected, it amounted to only one-third of the promised payment. In short, the crusaders could not pay their bill. For his part, Doge Dandolo could not renounce payment for the fleet. To do so would represent an enormous, possibly ruinous financial injury to Venetians across the lagoon. Venice was a republic, and Dandolo did not have the power to place the crusaders' debts on the backs of his own countrymen.

In his memoirs, Villehardouin blames the crusaders who sailed from other ports for all the crusade's subsequent troubles. In fact, even had every crusader who avoided Venice arrived there, the host would still have failed to reach its projected size. The real blame lay with Villehardouin himself and his fellow envoys, who drastically overestimated the number of crusaders who would be ready to depart in the summer of 1202. In the medieval West, an army of 11,000 was enormous, an army of 33,500 almost unprecedented. The envoys probably were guided by the widespread enthusiasm for the crusade that swept France in 1201 and the reports of Fulk of Neuilly crossing more than 200,000 people. Perhaps they even considered 33,500 to be a conservative figure. The facts, however, were different. Although the Fourth Crusade was large, it was only one-third the size needed to pay for the fleet it had leased.

It was a difficult summer for the crusaders. They camped on the Lido, a sun-baked and barren island at the edge of the lagoon. There they waited week after week, staring at the magnificent fleet and going nowhere. They naturally became restless and rowdy, and they began to blame the Venetians for the delay. The Venetians, for their part, were exasperated with the northerners for their failure to keep their bargain. Matters could not stay as they were. A disgruntled army in the lagoon could cause enormous damage to the maritime republic. The crusaders needed to depart.

In August, Dandolo met with the crusade leaders. He pointed out that the Venetians had met their obligations to the letter and reminded them of their great patience thus far. Payment was already four months late, and they could wait no longer. He demanded that the crusaders pay what they owed. The leaders agreed with the doge, so the word was sent to the host that all should pay not only their passage but all that they could afford to complete their covenant with Venice. Many of the poorer crusaders had nothing more, and others indignantly refused to pay anything beyond their individual passage. The barons set the example by handing over large sums of money and gold plate. The crusading bequest of Thibaut of Champagne was also rendered. Still, in all, it was only half of what they owed.

DIVERSION TO ZARA

Dandolo met with his ducal council to discuss the dire situation. The crusaders had paid all they had; there was simply no way for them to meet their obligations. A solution was needed—and right away. Soon it would be October, when voyages on the Mediterranean stopped altogether. The council suggested a compromise. There was a city on the Dalmatian coast, Zara, that had rebelled against Venetian rule. Venice's attempts to recapture the well-fortified city had been unsuccessful. If the crusaders would agree to assist Venice in returning Zara to obedience, then the Venetians would suspend the crusaders' debt until they could acquire it in war booty. The crusade could spend the winter at Zara and depart for Egypt in the spring.

The crusading leaders discussed the Venetian offer. There was no doubt that the recovery of Zara was a just act, but there were other complicating factors. Zara was controlled by King Emeric of Hungary (1196–1204), who had himself taken the crusader's cross in 1200. Although Emeric had no plans to crusade in the near future, it remained that his lands were under the protection of the church. Some worried about the shedding of Christian blood, although fighting Christians on the way to the Holy Land had become rather standard. Richard I and Frederick I had waged protracted wars against Christians during the Third Crusade. With mixed feelings, the leaders accepted the proposal. The alternative, in any case, was the dissolution of the crusade. Even the papal legate, Peter Capuano, advised the crusaders to do what was necessary to keep the army intact.

As the crusaders prepared for their long-delayed departure, their leaders received an intriguing proposal. Alexius Angelus, a young refugee prince of Byzantium, sent envoys to some of the crusader barons asking them to take pity on him. The young man's father, Emperor Isaac II (1185–95), had been blinded and deposed by his own brother in 1195. The usurper, Alexius III (1195–1203), imprisoned Isaac and kept his nephew and namesake on a short leash in Constantinople, but the young Alexius managed to escape his uncle's clutches and fled to the court of Philip of Swabia. He now begged the crusaders to take up his cause and right the wrong perpetrated by his evil uncle. He assured them that the people of Constantinople yearned to welcome him as their ruler if only someone would return him to the imperial city. In return for this act of Christian charity, young Alexius would reward the crusaders handsomely and assist them on their mission to Egypt. There was much to commend this proposal to the barons. Not only would it relieve their poverty, but with the support of the Byzantine Empire, the crusade would have an excellent chance of achieving its goals. They sent envoys to the court of Philip of Swabia to relate their interest in the plan.

In early October, the great fleet, arrayed in the bright colors of the crusading barons, set sail. Accompanying the crusaders was the aged Enrico Dandolo, who took the cross to lead the Venetians on their holy journey. With the assent of the people, he left his son, Ranier Dandolo, as vice-doge during his absence. Given his advanced age, Dandolo surely knew that there was little chance that he would ever return to the lagoons of Venice. The imposing fleet made its way along the Dalmatian coast, receiving oaths of loyalty and material support from Venice's cities there. On November 10, the ships cast anchor at Zara. The crusaders disembarked, pitched their tents, and prepared for a siege.

The people of Zara were not fools; they saw clearly that they could not withstand an attack by so large a force. Two days after the fleet arrived, they sent envoys to discuss terms of surrender. Dandolo received the Zarans and agreed to their terms but then departed to discuss the matter with the crusading barons. While the envoys waited in the doge's tent, the powerful French lord, Simon of Montfort, visited them. Simon had been one of the first barons to take the cross, and he was one of the crusade's staunchest promoters, but he did not like the way things were going lately. To his mind, and those of his followers, the crusade was off course, hijacked by the Venetians, who were using the holy army for their own profane goals. He knew that a letter had just arrived from Pope Innocent III forbidding the crusaders to attack Zara or any Christian city. It was more than he could bear to think that the Venetians would now win a great city that, without French help, they could not take themselves. Simon therefore informed the Zarans of the friendship of the French. If they could defend themselves against the Venetians, they would be safe enough. The Zarans thanked Simon profusely and returned to their city.

When Dandolo and the barons returned to the doge's tent, they found no surrendering Zarans, only Simon and his followers. The peaceful surrender was scuttled. A Cistercian in Simon's entourage, Guy of Vaux-de-Cernay, approached the crusading barons with the papal letter in hand and exclaimed, "I forbid you, on behalf of the Pope of Rome, to attack this city, for those within are Christians and you are crusaders!" To ignore this prohibition, he continued, would mean excommunication. The Franks were astonished and the Venetians outraged. Dandolo turned to the barons and said, "Lords, I had this city at my mercy, and your people have deprived me of it; you have promised to assist me to conquer it, and I summon you to do so."[2]

The crusade leaders were again in a difficult bind. On one hand, they did not wish to incur the penalty of excommunication. They endured the hardships of a crusade for the salvation of their souls, and they did not want to endanger those souls in the process. On the other hand, they had sworn to assist the Venetians if necessary. It was all well and good for the pope to forbid the attack now, but the papal legate had given tacit approval of it a few months earlier when they had struck their bargain with Venice. The barons were also angry with Simon of Montfort. He had become a tiresome malcontent ever since the crossing of Boniface of Montferrat. It seemed to them that he cared for nothing but increasing his own power at the expense of others. They would not let him have his way now. They informed the doge that they would honor their promises by attacking Zara. Simon of Montfort and his followers withdrew from the army to avoid the sin, pitching their tents at a distance.

With great energy, the crusaders attacked the walls of Zara, on which the city inhabitants draped crosses, making clear that it was a Christian city under the protection of the pope. The city succumbed in less than a week. The poverty-stricken crusaders fell on it, taking everything of value and destroying what they could not take. They subsequently divided it among the Franks and Venetians, and both groups prepared for the winter.

With the fall of Zara, the Fourth Crusade was now an excommunicate. Swiftly, the Frankish crusaders sent envoys to Rome to beg forgiveness from the pope. Innocent was pleased to see their remorse and, after strong admonitions, gave absolution to the Franks. The Venetians were another matter. They refused to admit their sin, arguing that the conquest of Zara was within their right to stabilize their domains. The pope formally excommunicated the Venetians—more than half the army—although he gave permission to the Franks to continue to travel with them. When Boniface of Montferrat received the bull of excommunication, he suppressed it.

THE DIVERSION TO CONSTANTINOPLE

On January 1, 1203, envoys from Philip of Swabia arrived in Zara on behalf of young Alexius Angelus. After relating again the story of the treacherous Alexius III, they begged the crusaders to transport the young prince to Constantinople, where the people would welcome him. In return for this service, the young Alexius promised to place the Greek church in obedience to Rome, join the crusade with an army of ten thousand men, permanently maintain five hundred knights in the Holy Land, and pay the crusaders 200,000 silver marks. It was a stunningly attractive offer, and it seemed to come at the perfect time. The crusaders' transportation contract with the Venetians would expire in June, and they had not even paid what they owed for the first year. By helping Alexius to his throne, they could perform a good and chivalrous deed, save themselves from poverty, and strengthen the crusade for its mission in the East. Despite these incentives, the majority of the crusading host wanted nothing to do with the proposal. They had only just received absolution for their attack on Zara, and they were not eager to incur the pope's wrath again. The crusade was already heavily delayed, and the majority were tired of waiting. A detour to Constantinople, they said, was out of the question.

Without the support of the rank and file, a few of the leading barons—Boniface of Montferrat, Baldwin of Flanders, Louis of Blois, and Hugh of Saint Pol—signed a treaty committing the Fourth Crusade to supporting Alexius Angelus in his bid for the throne of Byzantium. The decision was extremely unpopular. Hundreds left the crusade in disgust, making their own way to the Holy Land. Hundreds more washed their hands of the whole mess and went home. Those who remained were by no means unified. Although the rank and file eventually agreed to the diversion to Constantinople, they insisted that they remain only briefly and then make all speed to the Levant.

On April 20, the crusade set sail for the Byzantine island of Corfu, where they waited for the arrival of the young Alexius. Relations with the Greeks of the island were good at first, but that changed when the inhabitants discovered what the crusaders were up to. No sooner had the pretender to the throne arrived at Corfu than the Byzantines attacked the Venetian vessels. In response, the crusaders laid waste to part of the island. The reaction of the Greeks to their "rightful" emperor did not augur well for his reception in the imperial city.

Innocent III knew all about Alexius Angelus and his promises. The young man had already visited the pope to ask for assistance in his bid for the throne. Innocent sent him packing and later informed Boniface of Montferrat that the crusade was to have nothing to do with this scheme. The pope, therefore, was not happy when he learned that his penitent soldiers were once again disobeying his commands. He wrote a strongly worded letter to the crusaders forbidding them to travel to Byzantium:

> Let no one among you rashly convince himself that he may seize or plunder Greek lands on the pretext that they show little obedience to the Apostolic See, or because the emperor of Constantinople deposed his brother, blinded him, and usurped the empire.[3]

Although these actions were unjust, they were not the crimes that the crusaders had sworn to avenge. Rather, their duty was to punish the greater injuries to the crucified Christ.

The crusade fleet sailed through the Aegean and the Sea of Marmara with no resistance. On June 23, it entered the Bosporus, where the crusaders got their first glimpse of the legendary city of Constantine. They were awestruck. Constantinople was simply beyond the ken of the Franks. The ten largest cities in western Europe could have fit comfortably within its walls. Robert of Clari, a simple knight of Picardy and one of the crusaders, wrote:

> For no man on earth, however long he might have lived in the city, could number them [the marvels] or recount them to you. And if anyone should recount to you the hundredth part of the richness and the beauty and the nobility that was found in the abbeys and in the churches and the palaces and in the city, it would seem like a lie and you would not believe it.[4]

Here these hardy knights of the medieval world came face to face with the still-beating heart of antiquity. No man, said Villehardouin, was so brave and daring that he did not shudder at the sight, and with good reason. Constantinople was legendary not only for its opulence but also for its impregnable fortifications. Beyond those, Alexius III had a garrison three times the size of the crusader army. Beyond those, he had foreign mercenary corps, including the elite Varangian Guard. In its long history, Constantinople had shrugged off armies ten times the size of the Fourth Crusade. To the people of the city, the westerners were an annoyance and an oddity, but not a real threat.

Of course, the crusaders had not thought an attack on Constantinople would be necessary. They made camp across the straits and awaited the expected popular uprising that would overthrow the usurper in favor of the true emperor, but it did not happen. After waiting for more than a week, they considered the possibility that the citizens of Constantinople were unaware that the Latin knights came as friends, delivering their exiled lord. Doge Dandolo and Boniface of Montferrat took the young Alexius on the doge's vermilion galley and rowed it near the city walls. There they displayed the young man and shouted their good intentions. The Byzantine people on the walls responded with hoots, howls, vile insults, and missiles. All of this stunned the crusaders. Clearly, they had been misled. No peaceful coup was going to take place after all.

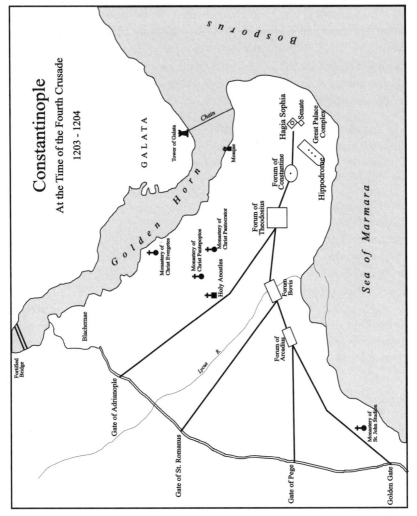

Map 9.   Constantinople at the time of the Fourth Crusade

Figure 3: **Ruins of Constantinople's Sea Walls along the Bosporus.** Photo by the author.

Once again, the crusaders were in a tight spot. They were deep in hostile territory on a fool's errand with no means of escape. Technically, the contract for transportation had expired, and the crusaders had not yet finished paying their bill. They needed the money that young Alexius had promised them. They were also duty-bound to help this victim of treachery whom they had befriended. With enormous courage, they prepared to attack a city of a half million souls. As Villehardouin noted, "never have so many been besieged by so few."

On July 5, the ships crossed the Bosporus and the knights attacked the suburb of Galata. The Byzantine soldiers, though numerous, were inept and cowardly. Galata fell almost immediately. The Venetian galleys then rammed the harbor chain blocking the Golden Horn and occupied the port. Without a navy to speak of, Alexius III was powerless to stop the crusaders. A few days later, the crusaders launched a two-pronged attack on the city's far northwest corner. The knights concentrated their attack on a small section of the land walls, while the Venetians attacked a section of the sea walls. The Frankish forces fought valiantly, but the city's defenders easily repulsed them. The Venetians had more luck, gaining control of a portion of the sea walls and even advancing cautiously into the city itself. As a defensive measure, the Venetians set fire to a number of buildings. The fire was swept by strong winds and devastated a sizable portion of the far northern city before it was contained. The Venetians were soon forced to retreat.

That night, while the crusaders considered the extent of their losses, Alexius III considered the extent of his. Although he was winning militarily, he was losing politically. Many Byzantines were disgusted that their emperor had not led the numerically superior Byzantine forces against the Latins. Others were angry about the damage from the Venetian fire. They did not want further damage to the city simply to save Alexius's reign. Why not accept the young Alexius as emperor? Whether the brother of Isaac II or his son reigned was a matter of trifling importance to Byzantines who had seen far more drastic changes in their lives. Alexius III smelled trouble. He could hear the hushed mumbling and see the averted eyes and strained smiles that suggested a palace coup. That night, he packed as much money as he could carry and fled the city.

The next morning, the crusaders were shocked to receive emissaries from Isaac II. They proclaimed that the usurper had fled in the night and that the people of the city had restored Isaac to the throne. This was welcome and joyous news for the crusaders, but it did have a worrisome wrinkle. It was their understanding that Isaac II was unfit to rule because he was blind. If Isaac was indeed restored, the crusaders could hardly oppose it, but they did want to make certain that he recognized the debt he owed to them. They sent envoys to the imperial court with the treaty they had made with young Alexius and asked Isaac II to ratify it. When the promises of the young man were read to the emperor, he knew immediately that they would be impossible to fulfill. He protested that they were unreasonable, but the envoys insisted that the contract be honored. Finally, Isaac agreed, and Alexius was escorted into Constantinople amid great jubilation. Shortly thereafter, Alexius IV (1203–4) was crowned coemperor. Isaac, old and blind, observed his power waning as his son took control of the Byzantine state.

THE SHORT REIGN OF ALEXIUS IV

With the elevation of Alexius IV, Constantinople's attackers became its tourists. For the first time, the doors of the city were opened to a crusade army. The westerners walked the ancient streets with wide eyes and open mouths. The great forums, columns, statues, and public buildings amazed them. As pilgrims, they sought out the city's plentiful churches and monasteries. Constantinople held more relics than Jerusalem and Rome combined, and the crusaders were eager to see them and acquire their special graces. The soldiers were no longer poor, either. Alexius IV paid half of the money he promised and began making installment payments on the rest. With this infusion of cash, the crusaders paid off their debt to the Venetians with money to spare. Alexius IV moved to keep his other promises as well. He sent a letter of obedience to Innocent III and another letter to the sultan of Egypt telling him to prepare for a great army to sweep Islam from the homelands of Christianity once and for all.

The euphoria of the victory at Constantinople did not last long. Alexius IV found it increasingly difficult to find the money to pay the rest of his debt to the crusaders. After confiscating the wealth of those who supported his uncle, he was still short of funds. Recklessly, he ordered the tombs of emperors opened and the jewelry removed. He even seized ecclesiastical items like chalices and icons, which he destroyed for their precious metals and gems. The citizens of the city watched the sacrilege with horror. It was intolerable to them that the wealth of Byzantium should be stripped from her and handed over to these barbarians from the West. Relations between Byzantines and Latins had been very poor in Constantinople for decades, and the presence of the crusaders only made them worse. Fearing a riot, Alexius IV asked the crusaders to withdraw from the city and camp across the Golden Horn in Galata and Pera. They agreed.

Alexius IV's attempt to settle his debt was making him bitterly unpopular. He feared that if he paid anything further to the Latins, he would lose his throne. On the other hand, if he did not have the military support of the crusaders, he feared a palace coup. Desperate, the young emperor met with the crusade leaders and begged for patience. He would pay every penny he owed them, he insisted, but he needed additional time. If the crusaders would consent to remain in Constantinople over the winter, he guaranteed that he would settle his account with them by the beginning of the sailing season in March 1204. In return, he offered to extend the lease on the Venetian vessels for an additional year at his own expense.

Alexius's proposal was met with a great deal of grumbling among the rank-and-file crusaders. The leaders had assured them that the crusade's stay at Constantinople would be brief. Now they were being asked to remain for the better part of a year. But what was the alternative? It was already too late in the season to depart for the Levant, and they had not yet received the full reward they were promised. The soldiers agreed to winter at Constantinople after their leaders swore to provide vessels to sail east in March, no matter the situation in Byzantium.

Alexius IV made a few token payments to the crusaders, but not much more. In his court, his advisers urged him to send the crusaders away. He had already paid them too much. It was not for these insolent barbarians to dictate to the emperor of Rome. Fearing for his throne, the young emperor accepted this advice. He stopped visiting his old friends in their camp, and soon even the token payments dried up. Matters became even more tense when a small group of westerners set fire to a city mosque and other nearby buildings in August 1203. The small fire was whipped by a high wind into an uncontrollable blaze. The inferno grew rapidly, becoming one of the most destructive urban fires in human history. With great ferocity it tore through the central sections of the city, laying waste to its most populated and wealthy regions. There were few casualties, but the material cost was staggering. For the citizens of Constantinople, the western visitors were no longer just annoying—they were genuinely hated. Fearing reprisals, the Latin residents of the city fled across the water to join the crusading army.

In November 1203, the crusade leaders began to suspect that they would never see the money that Alexius owed them. They sent a delegation to the emperor reminding him of the great service they had rendered and the solemn promises he had made. They called on him to confirm those promises or the crusaders would no longer call him friend and would do all in their power to seize their payment from his domains. When they heard the harsh words of the crusaders, the court attendants erupted in anger. No one had ever dared to defy an emperor in his own court! This is what came of befriending barbarians! Alexius remained silent, frozen between his friends and his countrymen. The envoys left the palace and returned to the crusader camp.

The feudal morality of the western knights was satisfied. Alexius had failed to fulfill his promises to the crusaders, and the crusaders had formally defied him. Because the emperor would not pay what he owed, the knights felt justified in raiding his lands to "pay ourselves." The emperor dispatched troops to defend various crusader targets, with mixed results. There was a strong sentiment in Constantinople that the emperor should lead the imperial army against the crusaders and crush them once and for all. Alexius could not bring himself to do that, although he frequently promised to do so. In reality, he had no wish to destroy the crusaders because he might need them again. He also knew that the crusade would not remain in Byzantium after March, when the rank and file would demand transport to the East. If he could ride the storm until then, all would be well.

But the young emperor was not the equal of the storm. The population of Constantinople was bubbling over in its rage against the crusaders. They were tired of Alexius's empty promises and lame excuses. They wanted action. At last, the frustration broke out in a mass demonstration that centered on the great church of Hagia Sophia. The mobs demanded a new emperor and refused to let the members of the Senate leave until they had chosen one. No one wanted the job. It was plain that a rival emperor would have a difficult time removing Alexius IV from the palace, particularly if he called on his old friends, the crusaders. At last, the mobs settled on a young nobleman, Nicholas Canabus, who was captured and forcibly crowned. He never left Hagia Sophia. His motley collection of followers abandoned him at the first hint of opposition, and he was later executed by Alexius V Ducas Mourtzouphlus, whose rise to the imperial throne was the next act in this unfolding tragedy.

When Alexius IV heard of the uprising, he panicked. Quickly, he called his trusted lieutenant, Mourtzouphlus, and sent him to the crusader camp to retrieve Boniface of Montferrat. Mourtzouphlus was a cagey character, the veteran of several palace coups. He had already been defeated in battle by Boniface and was therefore not pleased to hear that the crusade leader would be restored to his old position in the court. He obeyed the emperor, bringing the marquis to the palace, then disappeared to plan his own course of action.

The young emperor pleaded with Boniface for forgiveness, blaming the whole matter on his counselors and his people. He renewed his promise to pay the crusaders what he owed and invited them to occupy an imperial palace as collateral. Boniface accepted the apology and returned to the crusader camp to muster a contingent to garrison the palace.

Mourtzouphlus was quicker. With well-placed bribes and political skill, he convinced the Varangian Guard to neglect their duties to the emperor for one night. Very late, Mourtzouphlus rushed into the emperor's chamber and woke him, saying that there was a large and angry crowd outside the palace. Alexius pleaded with his servant to save him. Mourtzouphlus obligingly covered the emperor with a blanket and spirited him away down a secret stairway—at the bottom of which was a jail cell. With the young man locked up, Mourtzouphlus declared himself the new emperor of Constantinople. Isaac II, who had drifted into senility, conveniently died at about the same time.

THE WAR WITH MOURTZOUPHLUS

Mourtzouphlus was crowned Alexius V (1204) on February 5, 1204. Although crafty, he was a courageous soldier and an able commander. With great energy, he oversaw every aspect of defensive operations on the city's harbor walls. He did all that he could to put a stop to the crusader raids on the countryside, but his efforts were hamstrung by the poor quality of the imperial troops. No matter their numerical superiority, the Greek soldiers proved themselves utterly incapable of withstanding an attack from the Frankish knights. At the first hint of difficulty, they fled. Mourtzouphlus learned this at first hand when he ambushed a crusader raiding party with a very large army of mounted soldiers. With bravery and zeal, the Franks turned a hopeless situation into a spectacular victory. In the skirmish, the emperor lost the precious icon of the Virgin Mary that Byzantine armies had carried into battle for centuries.

A few days later, Mourtzouphlus met with Enrico Dandolo to discuss a peaceful end to the problem. From the Frankish crusaders' point of view, Mourtzouphlus was a disloyal vassal, a felon who had rebelled against his lord. Dandolo informed the emperor that the crusaders did not recognize his authority. They demanded that he release Alexius IV and inform him that he should pay the crusaders what they were promised. Mourtzouphlus, of course, refused. Realizing that the crusaders' deal with Alexius was the moral underpinning for their attacks on Byzantium, he ordered the young man strangled the following day.

The death of Alexius IV was greeted with cries of good riddance from the crusading rank and file. They were tired of the whole tawdry affair at Constantinople. For two years, they had struggled with little and were no closer to completing their vows. March was only a few weeks away. When it came, they could finally shake the dust of Byzantium from their feet. For the crusade leaders, however, the news of Alexius's death was much more troubling. The young man owed them money. While he was emperor, they were justified in raiding his domains to recapture it, but their agreement was with him and his father, not with Mourtzouphlus or the people of Byzantium. Their reason for remaining at Constantinople disappeared with the death of Alexius. In March, the rank and file would demand transport to the Holy Land, and the leaders would be bound by oath to deliver—but they could not. There was no money to pay the Venetian vessels, which Alexius IV had contracted but never paid for. Their food supply was also low because they had stripped the countryside bare for miles around. How were they to move an army so far without transportation or provisions? Boniface of Montferrat clearly did not wish to abandon Constantinople to the hated Mourtzouphlus. Like his brothers before him, Boniface had been close to the allure of imperial power. He did not relish leaving it behind to lead a poverty-stricken army across the sea.

The bishops and abbots of the Fourth Crusade gave the leaders the solution they needed. After examining the situation, they decreed that Mourtzouphlus was a murderer and therefore had no right to rule Constantinople. By accepting him as their leader, they continued, the people of Byzantium were abettors of murder. They were also grieved to see that the Greek church remained disobedient to Rome. For these reasons, they concluded, a war against Constantinople was right and just, and all who died in such a war would share in the crusading indulgence of the pope. In other words, the prelates of the crusade redefined an attack on Constantinople as a legitimate function of the crusade. The rank and file no longer had reason or right to demand transport to Palestine, for their holy work was in Byzantium itself.

The crusaders boarded their vessels and prepared for the attack on Constantinople's harbor walls. Because the Golden Horn was meant to be a secure harbor, the city's fortifications there were the weakest; nevertheless, they were still monumental, and Mourtzouphlus had strengthened them with the addition of wooden towers. The Venetians rigged flying bridges on the top of their ships' masts so that the soldiers could fight their way onto the walls. The attack came on April 8, 1204. Despite brave efforts, the crusaders were never able to bring sufficient ships to the walls to constitute an effective threat. Late in the day, a strong wind blew the vessels away from Constantinople. To crusaders and Greeks alike, it seemed like the hand of God pushing back the attackers.

The crusaders suffered significant casualties in the attack, while the Byzantines had almost none. Throughout the camp, a wave of fear gripped the soldiers' hearts. Despite the assurances of their clergy, it seemed clear that it was not God's will for his army to wage war on the greatest Christian city in the world. Most refused to have anything further to do with the attack and began to state openly that they wanted to leave Byzantium.

Even among the leaders, there was a strong desire to depart. Boniface of Montferrat and Enrico Dandolo convinced the others to try once more. Dandolo suggested that the vessels be tied together in pairs so that a greater force could be brought to bear on concentrated points along the wall.

On Sunday, April 11, the host was called to hear Mass. The clergy gave fiery sermons on the righteousness of their war against Constantinople. The Greeks, they reminded the army, had murdered their lord and were therefore "worse than Jews." They had also removed themselves from obedience to Rome and considered anyone who followed the pope to be "dogs." These sermons sought to de-Christianize the Byzantines and personalize the struggle for the common soldier. The clergy then called on all the crusaders, including the excommunicated Venetians, to take communion and make a confession, so that they would be ready to face the enemies of Christ. The rank-and-file crusaders had no idea that the verdict of their bishops contradicted the commands of the pope. The crusade again crystallized around the episcopal invention.

The crusading army boarded its vessels and attacked Constantinople again on April 12, 1204. The battle raged most of the day with the crusaders gaining very little. By the early afternoon, they had captured a few towers on the harbor walls, but they were so surrounded by Byzantine forces that they dared not advance farther. A small group of about ten knights and sixty sergeants led by Peter of Amiens landed on a narrow strip of ground outside the wall and near the shore. There they discovered a postern gate that the defenders had walled up. They fell upon it zealously with whatever implements they had on hand. It was hard going and dangerous, for from above the Greeks rained down on them immense stones and boiling pitch, which they deflected with their shields. At last, they succeeded in making a small hole. Peering through, they saw a huge crowd of soldiers inside. Surely, it was suicide to enter. One man, an armed priest named Alleumes of Clari, insisted on the honor of being the first to enter Constantinople. No amount of pleading from his comrades would dissuade him. His brother, Robert of Clari, was particularly upset and even tried to prevent him from crawling through the hole by grabbing his legs. It was no use. Alleumes scrambled through to the other side, where he was faced with an armed multitude.

Then an amazing thing happened. With enormous confidence, Alleumes drew his sword and ran toward the Greek troops. They scattered. Once again, the poorly trained Byzantine troops proved themselves unwilling to fight unless the danger to themselves was minuscule.

Because most of them were provincials, they saw no reason to risk their lives for the sake of the capital. Alleumes called to his companions, who now crawled through the hole, drew their swords, and kept their backs to the wall. When Greek troops at other locations saw the flight of those stationed near the walled gate, they panicked and abandoned their positions along the walls. Soon there was a snowball effect as the imperial army abandoned the length of the fortifications in a mad dash to escape the city—all because of the entry of fewer than a hundred crusaders. Mourtzouphlus, who watched the debacle with horror, spurred his horse and single-handedly charged the small party. When he saw that they would not retreat, he stopped and returned to his command station. With no one to stop them, Alleumes and his comrades opened the city gates, and the entire crusading army swarmed in.

That evening, the crusaders camped in the open region in the north city that had been burned by the Venetians nine months earlier. Strict orders were given to the host that no one was to venture farther into the city itself. In the winding streets and back alleys of the megalopolis, the mobs could pick off crusaders easily. They resolved to call for the surrender of the city on the morrow. If that was refused, they would begin burning the place down.

With the imperial army in full retreat, Mourtzouphlus could rely only on the Varangian Guard. It was not enough. Desperately, he rode through the streets exhorting the people of Constantinople to rise up and defend their city from the invading westerners. No one would listen. From their perspective, it was not their city that was at stake, but Mourtzouphlus's crown. They would not suffer further damage to the capital to save his reign. Instead, they made plans to offer the city peacefully to Boniface of Montferrat, who they assumed would be the new emperor. Once he had the imperial throne, they expected that Boniface would restrain his army, since it was not in his interest to have his city destroyed. At least that is the way it had worked in all the other armed coups in Constantinople's long history. Without the support of the people or the army, Mourtzouphlus fled the city.

THE SACK OF CONSTANTINOPLE

On the morning of April 13, Boniface received an honor delegation of dignitaries and clergy who offered the city to him. The triumphal procession was prepared. The streets were lined with citizens ready to acclaim their new emperor on his way to Hagia Sophia, where he would receive the diadem. Boniface wanted nothing more than to accept this offer, but he could not. A few weeks earlier, the crusade leaders had signed a treaty stating that if the city fell to them, the emperor would be elected by a council of Franks and Venetians after the city's booty was distributed. Although Boniface hoped to win that election, in the meantime it was in his interest, and in the interest of every crusader, to pick Byzantium clean.

The army of Christ fell upon the Queen of Cities with startling ferocity. The crusading host and the Latin refugees merged into a hideous mob driven by greed, lust, and hatred. Oaths sworn on the Gospels to leave women and ecclesiastical buildings unmolested were forgotten in the frenzied anarchy. The crusaders streamed down the opulent avenues, where the people of the city stood with their precious icons to welcome the new emperor. They were the first to have their goods stripped from them. The soldiers broke into the palaces of Constantinople's elite, confiscated everything, and expelled the owners. With nowhere to live, these bands of ragged lords streamed out of Constantinople, leaving it to its Latin conquerors. In the holy sanctuaries, the Latins stripped the altars of all precious furnishings, smashed icons for the sake of their silver or gems, and defiled the consecrated Eucharist and Precious Blood. Radiant Hagia Sophia was stripped of everything of value. The priceless altar fashioned from precious metals, gems, and marble was smashed into pieces and divided among the looters. A French prostitute was put on the throne of the patriarch, where she provided entertainment for the looters with her bawdy songs and high-kicking dances.

Equally sought after in the churches and monasteries were Constantinople's hoards of relics. Thousands of items were shipped back to the West. A few of the city's priceless works of ancient art were also sent home—but only a few. These included the four magnificent bronze horses that Enrico Dandolo sent back to Venice, where they would become the new symbol of Venetian prosperity and pride. Most of the artworks simply were destroyed. Hundreds of ancient bronze masterpieces were melted down for coin. Thousands of Byzantines took what little they still had and abandoned the ancient city of New Rome.

The sack of Constantinople ranks as one of the most profitable and shameful in history. Although a sack of a city that resisted capture was acceptable in the medieval moral code, it is clear that the crusaders did much more than just plunder. Despite their oaths and the threat of excommunication, they ruthlessly and systematically violated Byzantium's holy sanctuaries, destroying, defiling, or stealing all they could lay hands on. Many also dishonored their vows to leave the women of Byzantium unmolested. When Innocent III heard of the conduct of his pilgrims, he was filled with shame. He wrote to his legate:

> For they who are supposed to serve Christ rather than themselves, who should have used their swords against the infidel, have bathed those swords in the blood of Christians. They have not spared religion, nor age, nor sex, and have committed adultery and fornication in public, exposing matrons and even nuns to the filthiness of their troops.[5]

Nicetas Choniates, a Byzantine senator who witnessed the events, contrasted the sack of Constantinople with the fall of Jerusalem to Saladin, judging that Byzantium would have fared better had it been conquered by the infidel. He lashed out at the crusaders, who had sworn to deliver Jerusalem, promised to kill no Christians, and even proclaimed that they would refrain from sex until they had arrived in the Holy Land.

> In truth they were exposed as frauds. Seeking to avenge the Holy Sepulcher, they raged openly against Christ and sinned by overturning the Cross with the cross they bore on their backs, not even shuddering to trample on it for the sake of a little gold and silver.[6]

The Byzantines' deep sense of betrayal and bitter anger toward the Latins became the legacies of 1204 that would not die with the generation that experienced the events. They would animate centuries of tragic history and, for many, still live today.

In May, the representatives of the Frankish and Venetian crusaders met to elect an emperor of Constantinople. They chose Baldwin of Flanders. He was crowned in Hagia Sophia and escorted to the Great Palace, where the Flemish knight took his place on the throne of the Caesars. The new patriarch of Constantinople, Thomas Morosini, was a Venetian priest. Faced with a *fait accompli,* Innocent III absolved the crusaders and welcomed Constantinople back into the Catholic fold. The Byzantine Empire was divided among the emperor, the Franks, and the Venetians. Thus was constituted the Latin Empire of Constantinople, a new feudal state built on the ruins of the Byzantine Empire. The candle of Byzantine civilization remained lit in Nicaea, where a state in exile was formed. In 1261, the sickly Latin Empire fell to the forces of Nicaea, and the Byzantine Empire was restored, but Constantinople would never be the same. The Queen of Cities had become poor, dilapidated, and largely abandoned.

The Fourth Crusade was a disappointment to the people of the crusader states, who had counted on its help to expand Christian power and perhaps reconquer Jerusalem. It was also a disappointment to the pope, who had watched helplessly as it spun out of control. He still hoped the crusade would press on to the Holy Land after consolidating its Byzantine conquests, but that was not to be. The crusaders remained in Byzantium for a year to defend the new empire and then took their riches and went home. They received heroes' welcomes. For most Europeans, the outcome of the Fourth Crusade was God's vengeance on the Greeks for their treacherous betrayal of the Holy Land. The favor of Christ now rested with his brave soldiers from the West, and it was therefore only right that he should bestow on them the empire of the East.

The belief that conquest of Byzantium would assist in the conquest of the Holy Land was a mirage. The Latin Empire was so weak that it teetered constantly on the brink of destruction. It never freed itself from its own troubles long enough to consider the condition of Jerusalem. In truth, the Latin Empire weakened the crusader states, for it siphoned off much of Europe's crusading energy to Greece.

NOTES

1. Donald E. Queller and Thomas F. Madden, *The Fourth Crusade: The Conquest of Constantinople*, 2d ed. (Philadelphia: University of Pennsylvania Press, 1997), 224.

2. Ibid., 75.

3. Ibid., 102.

4. Robert of Clari, *The Conquest of Constantinople*, trans. Edgar Holmes McNeal (New York: Columbia University Press, 1936), 112.

5. Queller and Madden, *The Fourth Crusade*, 198.

6. *O City of Byzantium, Annales of Niketas Choniates*, trans. Harry J. Magoulias (Detroit: Wayne State University Press, 1984), 316.

6

CRUSADING AT HOME

CRUSADES IN EUROPE

The enemies of Christianity were not confined to the Levant; they could be within Europe itself. The idea of crusading at home was an old one. Many of the foundational concepts of Christian wars of faith were forged in Spain, where popes had urged soldiers to turn back Muslim conquests for centuries. During the early ninth century, Charlemagne (768–814) waged wars of conversion repeatedly in Saxony. In the strictest sense of the word, these were not crusades, because they had associated with them no crusading vow, indulgence, or any notion of pilgrimage. The subsequent introduction of the crusade into European thought changed the way people thought of religious wars. Popes generally equated the *reconquista* with the eastern crusades, urging Spanish Christians to fight Muslims at home rather than sailing to the Holy Land. Crusade indulgences were forthcoming for those who heeded this advice. By the time of the Second Crusade, the definition of a crusade had expanded to include various wars in defense of the faith at home.

Few popes took the crusade to heart as fervently as Innocent III. He believed that the restoration of Jerusalem was vital for the health of Christendom, and it therefore became his most cherished goal. His hopes were dashed when the Fourth Crusade veered off course, presenting him with an obedient patriarch of Constantinople, but no resanctified Holy Sepulcher. Despite the disappointment, Innocent remained committed to the greater goal. He had other problems, however, that required attention. Some of these were serious threats to the faith, and Innocent made judicious use of the crusade to deal with them. During his pontificate, he had more than one occasion to call a crusade against a domestic enemy.

When Innocent III took the throne of St. Peter, there was already a crusade under way in the Baltic. On October 5, 1199, he renewed the call to defend the church of Livonia, offering indulgences for those willing to take up the cause. Closer to home, the pope proclaimed a crusade against Markward of Anweiler, an imperial official who usurped the rights of the pope by retaining power in southern Italy after the death of Henry VI. When Markward invaded Sicily in November 1199, Innocent described him as worse than an infidel. This "political crusade" formed alongside the Fourth Crusade. In a fit of anger, Innocent even once threatened to divert the entire Fourth Crusade against Markward, although this was probably only a bluff. The crusade against Markward did attract the powerful Count Walter of Brienne, as well as many other knights who decided to join Walter rather than rendezvous with the troubled enterprise in Venice. The crusaders of the Fourth Crusade kept close watch on this crusade. At Zara, many of the crusade's defectors crossed the Adriatic to complete their vows with Walter of Brienne. Many more threatened to do so. Although he did not intend it, the crusade against Markward had a corrosive effect on Innocent's crusade to the East.

The pope also remained concerned about the Muslims of Spain. Like his predecessors, he routinely commuted the crusading vows of knights who agreed to fight in Spain. When Caliph Muhammad an-Nasir captured Salvatierra in September 1210, Innocent responded with a general call for a crusade in Spain. By 1212, a large army was assembled, led by King Alfonso VIII of Castille (1158–1214) and King Peter II of Aragon (1196–1213). On July 17, 1212, the crusading army dealt a serious defeat to the Muslims at the Battle of Las Navas de Tolosa. The spectacular victory was hailed across Europe. It marked a turning point in the long history of the *reconquista,* placing the Muslims squarely on the defensive.

THE ALBIGENSIAN (CATHAR) HERESY

In the heart of Europe, a much more serious threat faced the church—heresy. In the medieval world, heresy did not represent benign religious diversity. Far from it. It was seen as an insidious and cancerous threat to the well-being of Christendom and the salvation of the faithful. Christ's

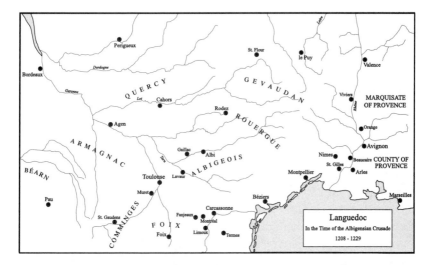

Map 10.   Languedoc at the time of the Albigensian Crusade

admonition to St. Peter still bound his successors: "Feed my sheep" (John 21:17). As the shepherds of Christ's flock, the pope and bishops kept a sharp eye out for those who would lead the members astray. Heretics were not merely lost sheep, doomed to spend eternity in Hell; they actively sought to lead others along their path to perdition. They struck at the heart of the church's reason for existence: to save souls. Because it threatened the Body of Christ from within, heresy was held to be far more dangerous than faraway Muslims.

In Languedoc, near the city of Albi in the south of France, a very strong and ancient heresy had taken root and flourished. Catharism—also known as Albigensianism—was a heresy with a pedigree stretching back to the first centuries of Christianity. There were at least two varieties of the heresy, but both were neo-Manicheistic and neo-Gnostic. The Cathari believed that the universe is a battleground between a good god and an evil god. The spiritual world is the work of goodness, while the material world is inherently evil. The goal of all living creatures, therefore, is to free themselves from the bonds of matter, thus allowing them to rejoin God and thwart the designs of the evil one. The breaking of those material shackles, they believed, could be accomplished only through the *consolamentum,* a ritual administered by the Catharist church.

The *consolamentum* was both baptism and ordination. Like baptism, it cleansed the recipient of all sin and prepared him or her for entrance into heaven. Like ordination, it allowed the recipient, now called a "Perfect," to perform the rituals of the faith. Once cleansed, a Perfect had to remain sinless, free from the stain of the material world. Perfects practiced great austerity, attempting to reduce their body mass by rigorous fasting. Sex was perceived as a device of Satan, used to entrap more souls into the prison of material bodies; therefore, Perfects refrained from sex and refused to eat meat or eggs, both products of sexual union.

The vast majority of Cathari were not Perfects. They were "Believers," those who accepted the Albigensian faith but had not yet received the *consolamentum*. Although they were enjoined to avoid sex and meat, there was no requirement to do so—and few did. This was not only more convenient but also provided a certain amount of deniability if that became necessary. As one Believer told the authorities, "I am not a heretic, for I have a wife and I sleep with her. I have sons, I eat meat, and I lie and swear, and I am a faithful Christian."[1] Most Believers did not undergo the *consolamentum* until they were very old or nearing death. In this way, they could dramatically spurn the material world after enjoying a lifetime of its fruits. The Cathari believed that those who did not receive the *consolamentum* in this life could do so in their next incarnation.

The Cathari accepted Christ as God, but not man. On earth, he was a phantom who appeared corporeal but remained a spirit. During his life, he had preached the message of spiritual release, but after his return to heaven the message was warped beyond recognition by Satan's latest creation: the Catholic church. The church, the Cathari contended, perverted Christ's words, blasphemously convincing the world that the Savior had become flesh. The idea that Christ was materially present in the Eucharist was thoroughly repugnant to the Cathari. Likewise, they maintained that purgatory was a fiction and the resurrection of the body a cruel joke. They insisted that marriage was among the most destructive human institutions, for it bound earthly bodies together to enslave more souls in a material shell. Motherhood was not an honorable status but a mark of shame. The Cathari believed that the pope and bishops were active agents of the evil one, damning the world in the name of the Lord.

Catharism found fertile ground for expansion in Languedoc. Throughout Christendom, the church relied on secular authorities to punish heretics who refused reconciliation to the faith. In Languedoc, the secular powers were highly independent and politically fractious. The most powerful lord in the region was the count of Toulouse, who was legally bound to the king of France but also held lands from the kings of England and Aragon as well as the German emperor. The result was a large fief that lacked political order. Counts of Toulouse tried for decades to assert their control over the region, but with little success. Their attempts at combating the heresy in their lands also failed, for the same reason. Indeed, rebellious vassals were often themselves Cathari leaders. The state of the church in Languedoc did not help matters. Bishops and abbots (who were themselves powerful lords) resented interference from the counts of Toulouse. The lavish lifestyle of these prelates contrasted sharply with the asceticism of the Perfects, leading many of the pious to believe in the holiness of the latter.

Although Cathari could be found in almost every social class, there were a large number of them among the nobility. Even bishops and abbots could point to Cathari in their own families. The religion had much to commend itself to the aristocracy. Although politically chaotic, the south of France was quite wealthy in the twelfth century. This wealth brought to the noble courts advanced education, cosmopolitan tastes, and cultural elitism. For this new class of sophisticates, Albigensianism was something new, a means of distinguishing oneself from the unlettered and ignorant. The fact that the heresy condemned the kind of lavish lifestyle found in court culture only made it more intriguing. Often in human history, intellectual and social elites embrace beliefs that contradict their own status and seemingly threaten their own comfortable way of life. Romanticism and Anarchism in the nineteenth century and Marxism in twentieth-century western countries are recent examples of the phenomenon. Like these modern beliefs, Albigensianism described a radically different universe that had no danger of becoming a reality soon. In other words, it allowed elites to embrace asceticism without the necessity of practicing it.

Attempts to Combat the Heresy

Because of the fragmented and particularistic nature of power in Languedoc, the counts of Toulouse made little progress in their efforts to contain and eliminate Albigensianism. These efforts ceased altogether after 1194, when Count Raymond VI of Toulouse succeeded his father.

The new count was the product of a court culture that embraced the vibrancy of the heresy and scoffed at the Catholic rabble who could not see the truth. Although he could not openly embrace Albigensianism, Raymond was by no means its enemy. His attitude did not sit well with Innocent III, who was determined to wipe out the heresy once and for all. Immediately upon his accession, the pope sent a string of legates to southern France with broad powers to reform the local church, preach the Gospel, and engage in public disputations with the heretics. Likewise, he urged Bishop Diego of Osma and his companion St. Dominic to preach in Languedoc. The new mendicant order later founded by Dominic was a dramatic counter to the Perfects. Like the Perfects, the Dominicans embraced poverty, but the message they proclaimed was orthodoxy. Unlike the wealthy prelates of Languedoc, the Dominicans actually lived the Gospel that they preached.

Although it had some marginal effect, Albigensianism was too entrenched simply to be preached out of southern France. Anywhere else, the heretics would have been handed over to the secular authorities, but in Languedoc they had already converted a good part of the nobility and won the favor of many of the rest. Raymond of Toulouse was thoroughly opposed to taking any action against them. In desperation, Innocent III turned to Raymond's lord, King Philip Augustus of France. The pope urged Philip repeatedly to bring Raymond into line or remove him with arms. By 1204, Innocent was even offering to bless a campaign against the heretics of the south with a crusade indulgence. Philip was unmoved, too busy with his wars against John of England to concern himself with the state of souls in Languedoc.

Papal attempts to reform the church in Languedoc and combat the heresy not only were ineffectual but also engendered bitter resentment. By 1206, Innocent's legate, Peter of Castelnau, was so thoroughly hated by orthodox and heretics alike that he left the region for six months to foil plans for his own assassination.

In 1207, Innocent's patience with Raymond of Toulouse was at an end. He excommunicated the count and placed his lands under interdict. In January 1208, Raymond met Peter of Castelnau to secure an absolution. It was not a civil discussion. During the course of the meeting, Raymond became so enraged that he expelled the legate, warning him that he would be watching him wherever he went. It was a clear threat, the kind that Peter was becoming used to. The next morning, January 14, 1208,

Peter was assassinated near Arles. The assassin was never caught, but Raymond was naturally suspected of being behind it.

Innocent was furious when he heard of the death of his legate. He had no doubt that Raymond was responsible; therefore, he renewed his excommunication of the count. For his part, Raymond officially denied any knowledge or involvement in the murder, but he was obviously pleased that it had happened and made no real effort to apprehend the assailant. For Raymond, the matter was a source of minor amusement; for Innocent, it was the final straw.

THE ALBIGENSIAN CRUSADE

On March 10, 1208, Innocent III wrote a letter addressed to the kings, prelates, nobles, and commoners of France. In it, he denounced Raymond of Toulouse as a murderer and a heretic. He urged the French, for the sake of the faith, to march against the heretics and supporters of heresy in Languedoc and take their lands from them. Two weeks later, on March 28, Innocent wrote to his legates in France, officially defining the campaign as a crusade, with all indulgences and privileges normally associated with a crusade to the East. Of course, a march to Languedoc was by no means a pilgrimage; therefore, the pope declared that completion of the crusader's vow in this instance required only forty days of military service, the customary amount of military service a vassal owed each year to his feudal lord. Preachers fanned out across northern France. The response was tremendous. Not only was this a chance to fight for the cause of Christ, but a crusader could do his duty close to home and in the space of a single campaigning season. Philip Augustus did not share his nobility's enthusiasm for the crusade. He did not join it himself, and he discouraged others so that they could remain with him in his fight against King John of England.

As thousands of knights from across France mustered for the invasion of Languedoc, Raymond of Toulouse reconsidered his position. A large and angry feudal army was infinitely more persuasive to the count than a shrill and annoying papal legate. He contacted the pope, begging for absolution from his grave sins. He agreed to all charges against him, including supporting heretics, violating feast days, and trampling on the rights of the clergy. On June 18, 1209, he went to the abbey church of

St. Gilles, where he promised to perform penitential services, was publicly flogged, and absolved. There was, of course, still the matter of the crusade army, which Raymond naturally feared. What he could not defeat, he joined. With papal permission, Raymond rode out to meet the crusaders wearing the cross of a pilgrim. By taking part in the crusade, he planned to make certain that it did not veer toward his own lands.

The crusaders chose as their first goal one of the regions most densely populated with Cathari, the lands of the Trencavel family. The lord, Raymond Roger, a vassal of Count Raymond of Toulouse, was viscount of Béziers and Carcassonne. He had refused to join the crusade, for he believed that his solid fortifications would outlast so large an army's ability to remain in the field. The crusaders first laid siege to Béziers, while Raymond Roger traveled to Carcassonne to supervise its defense. The people of Béziers shared the confidence of their leader. Indeed, they were too confident. Rather than remain behind their walls, the citizens led a sortie against the army. During the retreat, some crusader foot soldiers were able to enter the city and capture it. The subsequent carnage and destruction were staggering. So shocked were the Albigeois by the brutality of the sack of Béziers that the towns from there to Carcassonne opened their gates to the crusaders rather than risk the same fate. It was left for Raymond Roger to make his stand at Carcassonne. The siege dragged on for two weeks in the summer heat. Finally, on August 15, 1209, Raymond Roger asked for terms of surrender. The people of the city were allowed to leave unmolested but with no possessions. In return, Raymond Roger gave himself up. He died a few months later, apparently from dysentery, although foul play was suspected.

The crusade was off to a good start. Within a few short months, it had conquered the heart of heretic country, but much remained to be done. Who would do it? Having served their forty days, the vast majority of the crusaders prepared to return home. What was needed was someone to take ownership of the conquered lands, defend them, and prosecute the crusade again in the spring, when new recruits arrived. The Trencavel lands were offered to various French barons, but all refused them. At last, the crusaders and papal legates settled on Simon, the lord of Montfort and earl of Leicester. Simon was a skilled tactician and pious soldier, but he was also self-centered, rash, and volatile. He was one of the French barons who had sailed with the Fourth Crusade when it left Venice in 1202, but he subsequently abandoned the enterprise when it attacked Christian Zara. Rather than continue to Constantinople, Simon and his retinue washed their hands of the whole affair and made their way to Palestine, where they fought Muslims but achieved nothing. When he returned to Europe with a coat of radiant self-righteousness, he was disgusted to learn that the crusade he had abandoned was celebrated and honored for its dramatic conquest of Byzantium.

As leader of the Albigensian Crusade, Simon soon learned its greatest weakness: the short enlistment of the crusaders. With blessings and good wishes, the army vanished, leaving him and his men to defend the conquests. It was impossible. Most of the towns and castles that had opened their gates now closed them. King Peter of Aragon, who was overlord of Carcassonne, refused Simon's homage for the city. In the spring, the situation reversed itself. Simon's wife arrived with reinforcements ready to perform their forty days of service. This annual drastic fluctuation in crusader strength was a fact of life for the Albigensian Crusade, given the nature of the papal indulgence. It meant that each spring and summer, Simon could make important gains and consolidate victories, but during the fall and winter he would have to hold on to his conquests with only a skeleton force.

Count Raymond VI returned to Toulouse after the conquest of Carcassonne. He watched with pleasure as Simon's conquests evaporated with the departure of the crusade army. Perhaps, he thought, the Albigensian Crusade was not so grave a threat after all. Raymond resumed his prior attitude toward the church and began putting off demands that he fulfill his penitential promises made in 1209. In 1211, he flatly refused to make good on his promises; therefore, his excommunication and the interdict on his lands were renewed. Raymond had again become the object of the crusade, but Simon did not directly attack heavily defended Toulouse. Instead, he slowly captured the areas around the city, including Comminges, Foix, and Béarn, hoping to encircle Toulouse before launching a major attack on it.

King Peter of Aragon had remained aloof from the Albigensian Crusade, despite the fact that some of the lands in question were held by his vassals. As Simon led his forces to surround Toulouse, Peter at last acceded to Raymond's requests to get involved. In the spring of 1212, he visited Toulouse and, amid great cheers, took it under his protection. He then returned to Spain, where he defeated the Muslims at Las Navas de Tolosa, thus becoming the celebrated savior of Christendom. This victory brought him not only fame but also political currency to expend in the defense of Toulouse. At once, he sent envoys to Rome to complain about the course of the Albigensian Crusade. Simon of Montfort had gone too far, Peter argued. It was one thing to capture the lands in which heresy thrived, but Simon's strategy of surrounding Toulouse meant that he was conquering Christian lands held by Catholic lords.

Innocent put great stock in the words of Peter, and he was in any case eager to phase out the crusade indulgence for those going to Languedoc so that he could proclaim a new crusade to win Jerusalem. On January 15, 1213, Innocent wrote to Simon, scolding him for his attacks against Christians. On the same day, he wrote to his legate, "Foxes were destroying the vineyard of the Lord in Provence; they have now been captured." Because the primary objectives of the crusade had been met, the pope continued, he was removing most of the crusading indulgence for the campaign. He ordered Simon and the papal legates to hold a council of clergy and nobility to hear Peter's proposals and report back to him with their recommendations.

The Council of Lavaur was already planned, so it simply adopted Innocent's agenda. Peter did not attend the council, but he was allowed to make his observations in writing. He insisted that the lands of the counts of Comminges and Foix and the viscount of Béarn be returned to them, for they were Christian lords and therefore not legitimate targets of the crusade. As for Raymond, Peter affirmed that the count of Toulouse stood ready to make amends and receive absolution, after which Simon should return lands taken from him. If the council was unwilling to accept this, then Raymond would go on crusade to the East or Spain, if his lands could be put into trust for his son, who was innocent of all heresy. Peter himself offered to serve as trustee. The council listened to Peter's recommendations but rejected them all. The clergy of the council refused to absolve Raymond under any circumstances. They insisted that Comminges, Foix, and Béarn were infected with heresy and that their lords were abettors of that heresy. Not one square inch would be returned to them. In defiance of the council's decision, Peter took Comminges, Foix, and Béarn under his protection.

The next battle was one of paper. While Peter appealed his case to Rome, the clergy in Languedoc showered the papal court with letters and testimonies to support their position. Raymond of Toulouse, they maintained, had to be crushed if Albigensianism was ever to be removed from the region. Innocent was convinced by the clergy. He wrote to Peter, rebuking him for falsely informing him of the conditions in Languedoc. In a general letter, he demanded that the lords of Comminges, Foix, and Béarn acquire absolution, and he urged Peter and Simon to make peace between themselves for the good of Christendom.

That was not to be. Both sides were prepared for war. Peter was threatened with excommunication, but it was a hollow threat—the hero of Las Navas de Tolosa could not be excommunicated. The two armies met on September 12, 1213, at the Battle of Muret. Although greatly outnumbered, Simon decisively defeated Peter's forces. "On that day," poet Guillaume le Breton later wrote, "the power and virtue of the French shone forth clearly; they sent 17,000 men to the swamps of hell."[2] Peter himself was among those killed. Simon's victory was total. The Albigensian Crusade had succeeded not only in wiping out all opposition to its progress but also in killing one of the most successful defenders of Christendom.

THE FOURTH LATERAN COUNCIL

In the wake of Muret, Simon quickly went from victory to victory in Raymond's lands, conquering almost everything. All that he lacked was papal confirmation of his conquests. Innocent referred the question to the Fourth Lateran Council, which met in November 1215. After a vigorous but probably pointless debate, the council ruled that Raymond VI of Toulouse was guilty of aiding and abetting heretics. He was deprived of his lands but allowed an annual stipend. All conquered lands were assigned to Simon of Montfort. All unconquered lands, which consisted only of Provence, were to be held by the church until Raymond's son, Raymond VII, came of age. The next year, Simon received formal investment of the lands from Philip Augustus.

The Fourth Lateran Council confirmed Simon's conquests but it also turned off the last trickle of recruits to the Albigensian Crusades. At the council, Innocent III declared a new crusade to the East, the Fifth Crusade. As a result, Simon was forced to rely on mercenaries to make good his claims. Determined to control his prize, he became ruthless in his drive to impose rigorous feudal order in a region that never knew it. He compelled all citizens of Toulouse to take loyalty oaths to him, then ordered the destruction of their city walls. Always unpopular, he now incurred, with his harsh rule, genuine hate among many.

REBELLION IN THE SOUTH

Raymond and his son arrived in Provence to great applause. The younger Raymond was nineteen years old, courageous, bold, serious, and accomplished in battle. In other words, he was nothing like his father. In Provence, father and son heard often about Simon's rule and the general longing for the return of the family of St. Gilles. They began to consider the possibility of recapturing their lands.

Raymond VI went to Aragon to hire mercenaries and drum up support. Meanwhile, Raymond VII came upon an intriguing opportunity. The citizens of Beaucaire, on the west bank of the Rhône, sent word that they would open their gates to him. The young Raymond had an attachment to the city, the place of his birth, and he saw that its capture would pose a difficult problem for Simon of Montfort. The archbishop of Arles had recently given Beaucaire to Simon; nevertheless, it could be argued that it was properly part of the Provençal lands that were to be held in trust for Raymond. It did not take long for the young man to take the citizens up on their offer. When the gates were opened, Simon's garrison fled to a fortification north of the city. Raymond followed them and laid siege to the castle. Simon's brother, Guy, and his son, Amalric, brought troops to break the siege, but with no success. Soon Simon himself arrived, but he was unable to save the castle. In August 1216, after a three-month siege, the garrison was starved into surrender.

The victory at Beaucaire, though small, had great symbolic impact. In the defeat of Simon, many in Languedoc saw the rise of the young Raymond of Toulouse, who, they hoped, would reclaim his patrimony and drive out the hated northerners. Inspired enthusiasm and hope in the hearts of the vanquished never bode well for a conqueror. Simon rightly feared that his defeat at Beaucaire would lead to rebellions across the region. The elder Raymond was already in the city of Toulouse, where most of the citizens swore allegiance to their old lord. Simon moved quickly to nip this insurrection in the bud. Toulouse lacked fortifications, but the citizens built makeshift defenses with amazing speed. In characteristic style, the elder Raymond fled the city before Simon arrived, leaving his supporters to defend themselves as best they could. They did so bravely, but in the end Simon took the city. Punishments meted out to the rebels were brutal. Aside from mass executions, Simon exacted other harsh penalties including an enormous indemnity payment of thirty thousand marks.

The victory at Beaucaire lifted the hopes of the southerners. The courageous rebellion and crushing defeat at Toulouse enflamed their anger. The treatment of the citizens of Toulouse had nothing to do with heresy; it was merely an exercise in raw power. Even his own supporters began to view Simon not as a pious crusader but a ruthless tyrant. Those who had supported the crusade against the Cathari turned their heads in disgust at the rivers of Christian blood spilled at Toulouse.

The elder Raymond returned to Aragon, where he continued to raise a mercenary army. Despite their grave punishments, the people of Toulouse remained doggedly opposed to Simon. In the summer of 1217, they sent word that they were again ready to accept Raymond as their lord if he would journey there with an army. He wasted no time. With his Spanish troops, he crossed the Pyrenees. Along the way to Toulouse, the nobles of the region rallied to Raymond's banner, thus enlarging his forces. Some of these men were heretics or supporters of heresy, but many more were good Christians who despised Simon and favored the restoration of the family of St. Gilles.

On September 13, 1217, Raymond's forces entered unfortified Toulouse under cover of fog. Simon's garrison fled to a nearby fortification, Château Narbonnais. Once again, the citizens of Toulouse set to work building earthwork and timber fortifications. "Everyone began to rebuild the walls," wrote a chronicler. "Knights and burgesses, ladies and squires, boys and girls, great and small carried up the hewn stones singing ballads and songs."[3] When Simon heard of the rebellion, he swiftly called for troops from his new lands to assist him in the siege of the city. Most had already defected to the rebel side. The lines were now clearly drawn. Toulouse became the centerpiece of an effort to resist and remove Simon and the northerners once and for all. Here, it seemed, the fate of Languedoc would be decided.

It was clear to all that the advantage of momentum had shifted to the southerners. Despite a number of attacks on the city, Simon was unable to take it. Pope Honorius III (1216–27) sent various letters demanding an end to the rebellion and calling on other crusaders to assist

Simon in his efforts. Nothing came of these exhortations. The siege dragged on through the winter of 1217/1218 with plenty of action, none of it decisive. The crusaders made an attempt to improve their position in the summer, but without success. On June 25, 1218, during one such offensive, a rock propelled from a mangonel in the city struck Simon of Montfort squarely on the head, killing him instantly. The defenders joyously cheered this piece of extraordinary good luck.

With the death of Simon, the siege was over. Simon's son, Amalric, withdrew from the city, making his way back to Carcassonne. The victory at Toulouse and the death of Simon gave heart to the last holdouts against rebellion. Defections were widespread. Even the appearance of Prince Louis, the heir to the French throne, could not reverse the disaster. By 1220, Amalric held only a small core of lands in the lower Languedoc around Carcassonne. In essence, he controlled the lands that his father had conquered in the first two years of the crusade.

In August 1222, Raymond VI died, but that was no help to Amalric. Raymond VII was a far more able leader than his father. He already had won the earnest respect of both the nobility and the common people for his liberation of the Languedoc region. For his part, Amalric's resources were exhausted. He attempted to give his lands to Philip Augustus, but the king continued to refuse to become involved in the matter.

THE END OF THE ALBIGENSIAN CRUSADE

The indifference of the French crown changed dramatically when Philip died and Louis VIII was crowned in 1223. Having already crusaded twice in the south, Louis was now eager to put the resources of the kingdom behind the effort. The change in attitude of the French royalty could not have come at a better time for Amalric, who was at the end of his rope. On November 30, 1225, the Council of Bourges was held to hear the arguments of Raymond and Amalric concerning the ownership of lands. Louis had already made it clear that he would enforce the decisions of this council. Raymond pledged to pursue all heretics in his domains and obey all directives of the church if his father's lands were restored to him. Amalric countered that the church had already distributed those lands to his father in 1215, and he had done homage for them to the king. After short deliberations, the council declared Raymond a heretic, excommunicated him, and pronounced his lands forfeit. Clergy were then dispatched across France to recruit men for a crusade led by the king himself.

With royal sponsorship, recruitment for the crusade went very well. Soon Louis had an imposing force ready to invade the south. There was little doubt that he could crush the rebellion in Languedoc, so most of the rebels hurried to make their own peace with the church. Raymond watched his supporters abandon him one by one. Louis first marched to Avignon, which he invested for three months. On September 9, 1226, the city capitulated. The king then made plans to invade the heartland of the region, but, on November 8, 1226, he died. His son, Louis IX (1226–70), who would one day be the most famous of crusaders, was only twelve years old. Louis's widow, Blanche of Castille, took charge of the regent government.

The death of the king gave Raymond some breathing room and even allowed him to reclaim some lost ground, but his situation remained untenable. How long could he sustain a war against the crown? In the end, he would surely lose. Reluctantly, he went to the peace table to make what deal he could. The Peace of Paris, a lengthy and very detailed document signed on April 12, 1229, ended the Albigensian Crusade. As a result of the agreement, Raymond was absolved and reconciled to the church. In return, he agreed to pay to the crown a large war indemnity and to give his daughter Joan in marriage to Alphonse of Poitiers, a brother of Louis IX. Raymond retained control of Toulouse, Foix, and other lands he currently held in Languedoc while he lived, but they were to pass to Alphonse of Poitiers or his heirs by Joan after his death. Under no circumstances could they be inherited by Raymond's own heirs. In that way, the long history of the house of St. Gilles came to an end, signed away by Raymond to bring peace to the troubled region.

The winner of the Albigensian Crusade was the Capetian monarchy of France. Although a latecomer to the effort, the crown brought all the rich lands of Toulouse into the patrimony of the royal family. The loser, obviously, was the house of St. Gilles. Raymond made subsequent attempts to regain inheritance rights for his family, but none were remotely successful. As for the Cathar heresy, it remained firmly entrenched in Languedoc. Two decades of bloodshed deprived it of its support among the nobility, but not of its fundamental appeal. Shortly after the Peace of Paris, a council was held in Toulouse to organize an inquisition to root out and destroy the heresy. This proved a far more effective tool than large crusading armies. Thanks to the work of the Dominican inquisitors, Albigensianism was virtually extinct in Languedoc within a century.

THE CHILDREN'S CRUSADE

During the course of the wars against the Albigensians, crusade preaching became a constant fact of life in northern France and parts of Germany. The constant drumbeat of enthusiastic sermons added to an atmosphere already supercharged with popular piety, anticlericalism, and profound anxiety about the state of Jerusalem. In a world in which religious enthusiasm was common and respected, these tensions often manifested themselves in bizarre and startling ways. One such set of events is commonly called the Children's Crusade.

This Children's Crusade was not an army of children, and it was not a crusade. Indeed, it is not even one thing, but a blanket term used to describe a variety of popular uprisings and processions. At its core was the long-held medieval belief in holy poverty—that the poor of Christ could achieve things by their pious righteousness that church prelates and secular lords could not. These were the kinds of ideas that gave birth to and propelled the "People's Crusade" in the wake of the preaching of the First Crusade. Since then, Christians had become disillusioned by the failure of powerful crusades to achieve their stated goals. Perhaps, they reasoned, it was the weak and humble that Christ was calling to victory in the Holy Land. Had he not preached, "Blessed are the meek, for they shall inherit the earth" (Matt. 5:5)?

Because it was a popular movement, the Children's Crusade is difficult to trace. Unlike most crusades, there was no participant who wrote a memoir of the event. What we can glean comes from the reports of outsiders, primarily monastic chroniclers who watched it all go by. It is difficult, therefore, to say precisely how it began, or for that matter how it ended. What is clear is that in early 1212, a young man named Nicholas from Cologne either initiated or quickly became the focus of a popular movement that swept through the Rhineland. Nicholas had in mind to go to Jerusalem and rescue the Holy City from the Muslims. Under divine instruction, he began walking south to the sea, which he believed would open up before him, allowing him to walk to Palestine. Tens, then hundreds, then thousands joined him in his march.

As Nicholas and his followers marched from town to town, they spread their enthusiasm. Children, adolescents, women, the elderly, the poor, parish clergy, and the occasional thief joined the movement in throngs. Wherever they went, they were hailed as heroes. They received gifts, food, money, and prayers from their abundant well-wishers. When clergy members expressed reservations or skepticism about the "crusade," they were ridiculed and accused of jealousy. Had not the church-sponsored crusades failed repeatedly to reclaim the Holy Sepulcher? Were the prelates so blind that they could not see the hand of God in this extraordinary pilgrimage of the poor and the weak?

The throngs continued south, picking up many and shedding some as they went. In July 1212, they began crossing the Alps into Italy. The heat was stifling, causing many to give up and return home, but others pressed on.

Word of these wonders spread across Europe, sparking in some places smaller imitations of the event. The largest of these echoes occurred in Cloyes, a small town in France near Vendôme. Stephen, a twelve-year-old shepherd boy, had a vision in which Jesus, dressed as a pilgrim, asked him for bread. When Stephen gave it to him, Jesus handed over a letter for the king of France. Letters from heaven were a fairly common occurrence in the Middle Ages, but they rarely came from the hand of Christ himself. Stephen began his trek to Paris and was quickly joined by his fellow shepherds, then other bands of children, then lesser clergy, then the same kind of poor who were enlisting in Nicholas's pilgrimage in Germany. As they marched through the towns, they sang "Lord God, exalt Christianity! Lord God, restore to us the True Cross!" At last, they reached Paris, where Stephen delivered his missive to Philip Augustus. The contents are unknown, but the letter probably urged the king to lead another crusade to the East to rescue the True Cross and restore Jerusalem. Philip thanked Stephen for the letter, and that was the end of it. Unlike the Germans, the French participants saw themselves as messengers, not crusaders. With their message delivered, most of them returned home. A few of the able-bodied enlisted in the Albigensian Crusade.

By the beginning of August, the Rhenish multitudes were in Lombardy. From there, the movement broke apart as different groups made their separate ways to various ports. Nicholas and his band of followers arrived in Genoa on August 25. To their great disappointment, the sea did not open for them, nor did it allow them to walk across its waves. Some pushed on, hoping for better luck at other ports. According to one story, a large band of these "crusaders" arrived in Marseilles, where two unscrupulous men offered them free transportation to the Holy Land. When the vessels landed in Alexandria, the passengers were sold on the Egyptian slave markets. Others apparently went to Rome, where Innocent III praised their zeal but released them from their vows—which were not valid in any case. The fate of Nicholas is unclear. One story has it that he embarked on the Fifth Crusade, where he fulfilled his vow before returning home. Another states that he died in Italy.

Thus, the Children's Crusade came to a humiliating end. Most of its participants turned back home, but they had a difficult journey ahead. They were now reviled and ridiculed by the same people who had previously acclaimed and assisted them. Food was a problem, because they could no longer count on gifts. Many simply could not make the journey and therefore settled wherever they found themselves. Centuries later, a few of Genoa's leading families would claim descent from these wayward pilgrims.

THE TEUTONIC KNIGHTS
AND THE BALTIC CRUSADES

The Teutonic Knights, a German military order founded during the Third Crusade, retained their presence in the Near East. By the thirteenth century, however, the knights had begun to shift their focus to holy war in Europe. The grand master, Hermann von Salza (1210–39), was instrumental in focusing the order's energies on eastern Europe. In 1211, King Andrew II of Hungary invited the Teutonic Knights to protect his eastern border against the pagan Cumans by colonizing Transylvania and converting the people to Christianity. The knights were successful, but their power in the region grew too rapidly, startling the king and causing him to expel them in 1225. Just then, a similar situation arose in the Baltic region, where the Polish duke, Conrad of Mazovia, needed assistance against the pagan Prussians and was willing to grant lands to get it. Hermann von Salza was eager to assist Conrad, but he did not want to settle the knights in a region that would later be taken from them. To forestall that, in 1226 the knights received a charter from Emperor Frederick II granting them all lands promised by Conrad as well as those they could conquer from the Prussians. Subsequently, Pope Gregory IX decreed that all current and future conquests of the order in the Baltic region were the property of the Holy See, to be held in perpetuity by the Teutonic Knights.

In 1233, the Teutonic Knights and an army of German crusaders invaded Prussia. Over the next fifty years, the order conquered the entire region. Livonia was added to these conquests when the Order of the Brothers of the Sword, which crusaded in that area, was merged into the Teutonic Knights in 1237. The order oversaw the building up of Prussia and the importation of German peasants to work the land. Soon, the region became a prosperous state. The Teutonic Knights and their lands would play important parts in European history for centuries, long after their removal from the Holy Land.

Crusading at home was a regular phenomenon that reached a fevered pitch during the pontificate of Innocent III but continued for centuries. The Children's Crusade was not the pope's fault, merely a by-product of constant crusade preaching and the repeated failures of the crusades. Like Innocent's Fourth Crusade, the Albigensian Crusade had far-reaching consequences, but it failed utterly to achieve its projected goal. It is ironic that despite his successful pontificate, Innocent III failed where he most ardently wanted to succeed: in his crusades.

NOTES

1. Quoted in Carol Lansing's epilogue to Joseph R. Strayer, *The Albigensian Crusades* (Ann Arbor: University of Michigan Press, 1992), 223–24.

2. Quoted in Strayer, 95.

3. Ibid., 112.

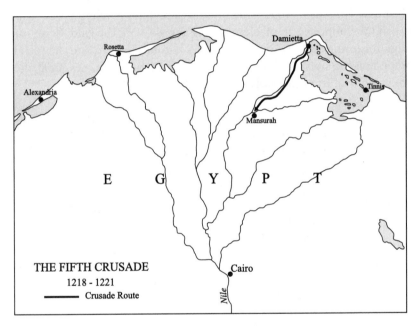

Map 11.   The Fifth Crusade, 1218–1221

7

THE FIFTH CRUSADE AND THE CRUSADE OF FREDERICK II

Episodes like the Children's Crusade make clear that, despite repeated failures, Christians in Europe still had a strong desire to recapture Jerusalem and rescue the True Cross. Pope Innocent III shared that desire—indeed, nothing was closer to his heart. Almost immediately after the disintegration of the Fourth Crusade at Constantinople in 1204, Innocent began planning for another campaign to the East. The Albigensian Crusade delayed those plans, but by early 1213 the pope was convinced that the primary objectives of the war against the heretics had been met. He removed most of the indulgences associated with that crusade, making it less attractive to pious soldiers.

THE FIFTH CRUSADE

The shape of Innocent's new crusade to the East was revealed in *Quia maior,* the encyclical that he sent to the people of Christendom in April and May 1213. This impressive document represents the full maturation of the crusading idea and would become the model for all subsequent crusade bulls. In it, Innocent called all the faithful, irrespective of social or economic status, to heed the call of the church and come to the aid of the crucified Christ. For too long, he proclaimed, the infidel had held the Holy City. Even now, the Muslims were preparing to wipe out the last remnants of the crusader states. Innocent reported that they had built a fortress on Mt. Tabor, the site of the Transfiguration of the Lord, from which they planned to launch their final attack. Now was the time for action. The opportunity to crusade should not be squandered. It was a rare gift of grace, a blessed avenue toward eternal salvation.

Innocent sought nothing less than to harness the full economic, military, and spiritual might of western Europe against the Muslim conquerors of Jerusalem. No Christian was too great or too small to take part in the effort. Those who could not physically travel to the East were enjoined to wage spiritual warfare through fasting and prayer. Monthly processions of holy relics were instituted throughout Europe, and a new prayer was added to the rite of the Mass, beseeching God to take pity on the land of his Son.

The pope was determined that this new enterprise would not follow the example of the Fourth Crusade, tragically spinning out of control. Unlike any before it, the Fifth Crusade was designed to be an enterprise fully administered and managed by the church. Toward that end, the pope commissioned a new corps of crusade preachers, each one trained in the approved texts. With preaching manuals in hand, these clerics were dispatched to strategically selected regions to raise up the faithful for the holy cause.

Among the preachers was Robert of Courçon, papal legate to France. Robert traveled across the countryside distributing crosses to everyone, regardless of station. Most, of course, were unfit for military service and could offer no tangible benefit to the crusade, but the enthusiasm among the old, infirm, and poor was indeed impressive. Another preacher, Oliver of Paderborn, had better luck in northwest Germany, Flanders, and Holland. Oliver, who was master of the cathedral school in Cologne, put his rhetorical skills in the service of the crusade. Wherever he went, crowds gathered to hear his words, see the miracles, and take the cross. In time, he assembled a very large army, which he then led on the crusade himself. Years later, after his return to Europe, he wrote the *Historia Damiatina,* a valuable eyewitness account of the Fifth Crusade.

The new crusade was among the most important items of business for the Fourth Lateran Council, which opened on November 11, 1215. There the blueprints for the campaign were drafted. The crusaders were to assemble in Brindisi and Messina on June 1, 1217, the day on which the truce with the Muslims in the Holy Land expired. There the pope would personally bless the fleets, sending them on to their holy task. To ensure that they had all that was required, the pope promised to pay thirty thousand pounds of silver himself and imposed a 5 percent tax on Europe's clergy for the next three years. All transport vessels were ordered to abandon their trade with the East and prepare themselves to carry the great crusading army.

Quia maior and the subsequent decrees of the council expanded and regularized the rights and privileges of the crusader. In addition to the crusading indulgence, participants were given immunities from all taxation and penalties for usury. Their personal debts were suspended and their lands placed under the protection of the church. Clergy who crusaded could continue to receive their benefices while absent for up to three years. It was also decreed that those who paid to outfit and supply a crusader could share in the crusading indulgence. This not only increased the number of those able to make the journey but also extended to women, the elderly, and the sick spiritual benefits previously available only to fighting men. No one could see it then, but in this provision was planted the seed that in three centuries' time would grow into the weed of abuses that led to the Protestant Reformation.

Europe was once again energized by pious crusading zeal. Aside from the multitude of the poor, who served in humble prayer, many thousands of fighting men eagerly donned the cross of Christ. Only in France, the heartland of the crusades, was the response poor. Many French had already acquired their indulgences through forty days of service in the Albigensian Crusade, which continued to sputter along even after the Fourth Lateran Council. Enthusiasm similar to that inspired by Oliver of Paderborn in Germany stirred the knights of Austria, who vowed to follow their crusading lord, Duke Leopold VI. The new crusade was also popular in Hungary. King Bela III (1173–96) had taken the cross many years earlier but died with his vow unfilled. When his two sons, Andrew and Emeric, locked horns in a fierce civil war, they both assumed the cross to gain papal favor. Emeric I (1196–1204) won the war, but despite repeated warnings from the pope, he never crusaded. He did make much of his crusader status when the Fourth Crusade took the city of Zara from him, but usually he tried to avoid drawing attention to his vow. Shortly after Emeric's death in 1204, Andrew II (1205–35) took the throne, but he also stalled and made excuses to avoid a crusade. With Innocent's patience at an end, Andrew at last prepared to complete his vow two decades after he had taken it.

The most powerful monarch to heed the church's call was young Frederick II (1212–50). The orphan son of Emperor Henry VI and

Constance of Sicily, Frederick was heir to two kingdoms: Norman Sicily and the German Empire. His guardian, Innocent III, allowed him to take the crown of Sicily but kept him from power in Germany until the pope fell out with his own candidate, Otto of Brunswick. In July 1215, Frederick was crowned king of the Germans in Aachen. During the ceremony, the new monarch surprised everyone by proclaiming that he would use his many blessings for the cause of the Holy Land. With intense emotion, he took the vow of the cross and urged all the nobility of Germany to do the same. Because Frederick was still engaged in a civil war with Otto of Brunswick, there was no way for him to make good on his promise until he acquired his kingdom in fact as well as in theory.

Innocent worked feverishly, overseeing every aspect of crusade preparations. In the midst of this activity, on July 16, 1216, he died. His successor, Honorius III (1216–27), was elderly but still vigorous and thoroughly committed to the crusade. He earnestly believed that Jerusalem would be restored during his pontificate and went about his duties with that calm resolve. Although he was an effective leader, Honorius was handed a complex enterprise that even his predecessor had had difficulty controlling.

Very few crusaders traveled to the southern Italian ports designated by the pope. The Hungarian and Austrian forces converged on Spalato in August 1217. Leopold and his forces sailed immediately, but the Hungarian armies were so large that King Andrew had to send to Venice for additional vessels. Shortly thereafter, the Hungarian crusaders also departed.

Conditions for a crusade in the Levant were not unfavorable. After Saladin's death, his lands were divided between his brother, al-Adil, and his two sons. By 1200, al-Adil had succeeded in pushing aside his nephews, gaining overlordship of the entire Ayyubid Empire. For administrative purposes, he put the three main areas of the empire under the control of his three sons. The eldest, al-Kamil, took Egypt; al-Mu'uazzam ruled Syria and Palestine; and al-Ashraf governed upper Mesopotamia. None of this occurred without resentment and rebellion, so al-Adil was more than willing to maintain peace with the Christians while he dealt with his own internal problems.

The Austrian and Hungarian crusaders landed at Acre, where they were joined by smaller armies led by Prince Bohemund IV of Antioch and King Hugh of Cyprus. John of Brienne, titular king of Jerusalem, also joined them. Altogether, it was a considerable force. The question was what to do with it. A council of war was called and various plans proposed. Since the Third Crusade, it was generally held that the only way to capture and hold Jerusalem was to conquer Egypt, the source of Muslim power in the region. Richard I had argued unsuccessfully for this plan in 1192, and the planners of the Fourth Crusade had adopted it in 1201. Many, including King John, thought that it was now time to put it into effect, but there were too many leaders with no clear consensus. Frederick II was expected soon, and many thought they should wait for him before launching any major offensive. To occupy themselves in the interim, the crusaders undertook various minor campaigns against the Muslims in late 1217, none with any lasting effect. These included an unsuccessful assault on the new fortress at Mt. Tabor, which Innocent III had described in *Quia maior*.

Having traveled to the Levant and participated in one minor campaign, Andrew of Hungary proclaimed his long-delayed vow fulfilled. Despite the patriarch of Jerusalem's threats of excommunication, Andrew began his march home in January 1218. With him went Hugh of Cyprus and Bohemund of Antioch. The departure of the armies of Hungary was a severe blow to the crusade, which was left with an army too small to undertake any effective operations. All that was left was to wait for reinforcements while keeping the soldiers busy rebuilding fortifications and performing other odd jobs.

The crusade's numbers were replenished in the spring with the arrival of Oliver of Paderborn and his army of Frisians and Germans. A large number of Italian crusaders with sizable fleets also arrived to join the enterprise, but Frederick II was nowhere to be seen. Reassurances of his impending arrival continued to flow from Europe, but the crusaders decided to strike while they had sufficient numbers to do so. In council, the plan to attack Egypt was approved. The first target was Damietta, an important and prosperous port at a strategic point on the Nile Delta. With Damietta as a base, the crusaders could launch an attack on Cairo itself.

The Siege of Damietta

The crusader fleets arrived at Damietta on May 27, 1218. They made a fortified camp on the west bank of the Nile, just opposite the city. Damietta was heavily fortified with triple land and sea walls. The crusaders quickly realized that the only way of taking the city was to cut it off from supplies and starve out the inhabitants. Nothing could be accomplished, though, until they had command of the Nile, and for that they would have to take the chain tower. The latter was an impressive fortification built on an island in the middle of the Nile, from which massive harbor chains stretched across, blocking access. The tower itself was connected to the city by means of a pontoon bridge. Throughout the summer, the crusaders made numerous attempts to capture the tower, but all failed. At last, it was the bookish master of Cologne, Oliver of Paderborn, who saved the day. He designed a new siege engine constructed from two cogs bound together with four stout masts mounted on them. On top of the masts, Oliver directed the building of a wooden fortress with a rotating scaling ladder operated by a complex pulley system. On August 24, a company of brave crusaders entered the monstrosity and approached the tower. Fighting was fierce, but at last the soldiers were able to attach their ladder and capture the tower. The rest of the army looked on with joy as they saw the standard of the sultan removed and a cross put in its place. The clergy, who had been praying fervently along the banks, lifted their voices to heaven, singing the *Te Deum.*

The crusaders' arrival on the Nile took al-Kamil completely by surprise. He scrambled to Damietta and set up camp on the south side of the city and along the east bank of the Nile. The fall of the tower was a great shock to al-Kamil but an even greater one to his father, al-Adil, who died when he heard the news. Al-Kamil immediately ordered the Nile blocked with sunken vessels, thus preventing the crusaders from surrounding the city along its sea walls. This measure forced the crusaders to spend much of the winter dredging an abandoned canal, through which their vessels could pass.

Shortly after the fall of the tower, new recruits arrived from Italy, France, England, and Spain, but these additions were offset by the departure of others. Indeed, as James M. Powell has shown, the history of the Fifth Crusade is one of a fluid army defined by the constant arrivals and departures of soldiers. In part, this was the logical outcome of the new formulation of a crusade as a papally sanctioned war against the enemies of the faith, rather than an armed pilgrimage to the land of Christ.

As had occurred in the Albigensian Crusade, the completion of one's vow was now defined as a period of military service, not necessarily the attainment of a stated goal.

As in all crusades, the notion of a chain of command among the Christians at Damietta was troublesome at best. In the continued absence of Frederick II, the barons elected John of Brienne commander in chief. The power structure of the crusade began to shift after the September arrival of the Portuguese cardinal legate, Pelagius of Albano. The cardinal had a strong personality, to say the least. He was self-assured, imperious, and rash. He shared Innocent's view that the crusade should proceed under the control of the church, although it is not clear that he initially envisioned commanding the enterprise himself. He found a crusade army in desperate need of a strong commander. Split along factional and national lines, the soldiers were almost as much at war with themselves as with the enemy. In his attempts to mediate these disputes, Pelagius became the focus of his own faction. Some supported him; others supported John of Brienne.

The crusaders had important internal problems, but those of al-Kamil were worse. With the death of his father, dissident factions, seething at the increase in taxes and military levies, staged a coup against the sultan. In a panic, he fled, and his army broke apart. It was a stroke of good luck for the crusaders. On February 5, 1219, they took al-Kamil's abandoned camp without a fight. Not only did they find a rich haul of booty, but they also were able to encircle Damietta, cutting it off from all aid or supplies.

Before the coup, al-Kamil had sent repeated messages to his two brothers to come to his aid in Egypt. Al-Ashraf was occupied in Mesopotamia, but al-Mu'uazzam responded to the call. With his help, al-Kamil put down the rebellion and established control of Egypt once more, but there was still the problem of the crusade. Al-Kamil knew well that unless the siege of Damietta was broken, the city eventually would fall. Once the Christians owned Damietta, it would be very difficult to dislodge them. Like the crusaders, al-Kamil expected the arrival of Frederick II with his mighty armies, and he did not want the emperor to have Damietta as a secure base for his conquest of Egypt. In the meantime, the continued presence of the Christians in Egypt was destabilizing to the sultan's already shaky hold on power.

Al-Kamil decided that it was time to make a deal. He sent envoys to the crusaders with an attractive offer. In return for their immediate evacuation of Egypt, he would hand over to them the entire kingdom of Jerusalem, with the exception of the fortresses of Kerak and Krak de Montréal in the Transjordan. For those, he would render an annual lease payment of fifteen thousand bezants. In addition, he would grant a thirty-year truce to the Christians of the restored kingdom. In other words, al-Kamil offered to wipe away all of Saladin's conquests in Palestine in return for the crusaders lifting one siege in Egypt. In council, King John argued strenuously in favor of accepting the offer. This was the crusaders' chance to restore to Christian control not only Jerusalem but also its kingdom. Was that not the reason they had attacked Egypt in the first place? Was the restoration of Jerusalem not the purpose of the crusade? The Templars and Hospitallers opposed the bargain. They pointed out that truces were easily broken and that Jerusalem would be difficult to defend without the fortresses of the Transjordan. Pelagius agreed. Negotiations continued but did not progress. Al-Kamil could not allow the Christians to control the Transjordan, the only secure line of communication between the two halves of the Ayyubid Empire. Certain that the crusaders would eventually make a deal, al-Mu'uazzam destroyed the walls of Jerusalem in March 1219.

During the spring and summer of 1219, the crusaders maintained the siege of Damietta while al-Kamil stepped up his attacks on them. They responded with counterattacks, but nothing was accomplished. In May, the valiant Duke Leopold departed for home, having served a year and a half on the crusade. In August, St. Francis of Assisi arrived in the crusaders' camp. This humble man of peace had journeyed across the Mediterranean to end the crusade by converting the sultan to Christianity. Pelagius initially refused to give Francis permission to go to al-Kamil's camp, but after repeated requests he relented. The Muslims mistook Francis for an envoy sent to discuss peace. When he was brought into the tent of the sultan, Francis spoke not of terms but of the errors of Islam. The attendants were outraged and prepared to kill him where he stood, but al-Kamil forbade it. The sultan was intrigued by Francis, but he was clearly not interested in converting. After a polite conversation, he sent Francis back to the crusader camp.

As conditions in Damietta worsened, al-Kamil again contacted the crusaders and sweetened his deal. In addition to the kingdom of Jerusalem, he offered to hand over the True Cross taken by Saladin at the Battle of Hattin thirty years earlier. He also promised to rebuild the walls of Jerusalem at his own expense. Again John of Brienne urged the acceptance of the offer, and again Pelagius and the military orders turned it down. The addition of the True Cross, they argued, did not make up for the subtraction of the Transjordan. They also doubted that al-Kamil had the True Cross. Saladin had not been able to find it when he needed it to ransom captives in 1191.

By October 1219, the blockade of Damietta had devastated the city. On the night of November 4, crusader sentries noticed that one of the city towers was unmanned. Quickly, they climbed the tower and found the fortifications largely abandoned. Without a fight, the city was taken. What they found inside horrified them. Damietta had become a city of the dead. Of the original sixty thousand inhabitants, only about ten thousand were still alive, and most of those were very ill. Dead bodies lay everywhere. Oliver of Paderborn recounted:

> As we were entering it [Damietta], there met us an intolerable odor, a wretched sight. The dead killed the living. Man and wife, father and son, master and slave, killed each other by their odor. Not only were the streets full of the dead, but in the houses, in the bedrooms, and on the beds lay the corpses. When a husband had perished, a woman, powerless to rise and lacking the help of one to support her, died, not being able to bear the odor; a son near his father or vice versa, a handmaid beside her mistress or vice versa, wasted away with illness and lay dead. Little ones asked for bread and there was none to break it for them, infants hanging at the breasts of their mothers opened their mouths in the embrace of one dead.[1]

Most of the surviving citizens were allowed to ransom themselves or go into voluntary exile. The crusaders cared for and baptized the many orphaned children, although most of them soon died of their sickness.

It took the soldiers some weeks to clean up the city. Although food was scarce in the besieged town, wealth was not, so the crusaders had a rich haul to distribute—a source of inevitable conflict. Internal factionalism among the crusaders rose to a fevered pitch, even erupting in armed conflicts. At last, Pelagius ordered national groups to occupy separate areas of the city to reduce the level of violence. After settling down in

Damietta, the crusaders took the nearby town of Tinnis without a fight on November 23.

After the fall of Damietta, al-Kamil retreated upriver to Mansurah, where he constructed a fortified camp to block access to Cairo. He ordered al-Mu'uazzam to return to Syria and attack the crusader states there, hoping to put additional pressure on the crusaders to make a deal.

The Crusade Stalls

In Damietta, the life of the crusaders changed from spartan to hedonistic. The clergy complained that the soldiers of Christ were now too occupied in the brothels and gambling houses to concern themselves with crusading. It is true that the crusade stalled, doing nothing throughout the year 1220, but that was caused more by uncertainty in leadership than by moral decay among the rank and file. Early in the year, John of Brienne returned to Acre. He had a claim in Armenia to settle and also was needed for the defense of his kingdom against al-Mu'uazzam. Theoretically, this left Pelagius as the sole commander of the crusade; in actuality, many of the soldiers refused to be led by a priest. Inaction at Damietta was also fueled by the continued expectation of the arrival of Frederick II. On November 22, 1220, he was crowned Holy Roman Emperor, and in a splendid ceremony he renewed his crusading vow, promising to send part of his forces in the spring and depart himself in August. He sent word to the crusaders that they should await his arrival before pressing onward.

By the spring of 1221, al-Kamil had been able to turn his makeshift defenses at Mansurah into a formidable stronghold against invasion. He again sent envoys to the crusaders, offering the kingdom of Jerusalem for their withdrawal, and again they refused unless he included the Transjordan.

In May, the first armies of Frederick II arrived, under the command of Duke Louis of Bavaria, a famous and respected German baron. As the emperor's man, he won the support of those who would not follow Pelagius. The cardinal legate had for some time favored a plan to capture Cairo, and thereby Egypt itself, but he could not gain sufficient support among the crusaders. Louis had received strict orders from Frederick to oppose any such plan, but he was moved by the obviously corrosive effect that a year of comfortable idleness and rancorous factionalism had had on the crusade army. He agreed with Pelagius that the men needed a new campaign and suggested a compromise. Rather than a full-scale invasion of Egypt, he proposed an attack on the sultan's position at Mansurah with a portion of the crusader army and fleet. The capture of the fortified camp was a limited goal that would not jeopardize the crusaders' control of Damietta and could provide Frederick with a strong base from which to capture Cairo when he arrived. With the support of Pelagius and Louis, all the various factions in the army agreed to the plan. At the end of June, the advance forces joyously marched out of Damietta. They prepared their weapons and machines at their old campsite across the Nile.

The pope had earlier written to John of Brienne, scolding him for his departure from Damietta and ordering him to return immediately with his forces. John arrived on July 7, a few days after the crusaders had decided to march on Mansurah. The king strongly opposed the plan, urging the crusaders to remain in Damietta until Frederick II arrived. When John asked the council to reconsider, Pelagius dismissed him as a malcontent, more interested in his own gains in Palestine than the good of the crusade in Egypt. Henceforth, Pelagius decreed, anyone who opposed the southern march risked excommunication.

At some point in July, al-Kamil again made his offer, which Pelagius opposed and John favored. Louis of Bavaria had no choice but to agree with Pelagius, because the emperor had forbidden him to accept a peace before he could personally take command of the crusade.

The Loss of Damietta

On July 17, 1221, the crusaders bade farewell to their comrades in Damietta and began their march. Theirs was a considerable force, led by all the prominent leaders and constituting half or more of the crusade's total strength. One week later, on July 24, they arrived near Mansurah. Pelagius ordered the crusaders to camp at a wedge of land formed by the Nile and one of its tributaries. It was a foolish choice, one that demonstrated an utter lack of familiarity with the Nile's hydrography. King John tried to inform Pelagius of the danger, but the legate would no longer listen to him. The other soldiers, sure of their imminent victory, threatened to kill John if he did not stop his incessant doomsaying.

Sometime early in 1221, al-Ashraf, having settled his problems in Mesopotamia, was ready to assist his brother in Egypt. By early August, the three brothers were united and ready for battle. Their combined forces considerably outnumbered the crusaders. Oblivious to the arrival of the new armies, the crusaders at Mansurah allowed themselves to become surrounded, cut off from retreat or supply from Damietta. Their position changed from besiegers to besieged. Very quickly, provisions ran low. Finally, on August 26, Pelagius ordered the crusaders to march north and cut their way out of the noose, but on the road to Damietta, they did not encounter the troops they expected. Instead, al-Kamil took advantage of the rising river, opening the sluices and flooding their route. The army was hopelessly bogged down. Too late, Pelagius begged John to take command of the crusade and save them from destruction. There was little to do. Resolved to die fighting rather than in a flood, John formed battle lines against the enemy, but the sultan refused to risk his soldiers while the Nile was winning the war for him. There was no choice but to sue for peace.

Al-Kamil's brothers favored extermination of the crusade army. The sultan did not. Damietta was still well garrisoned by crusaders. If he massacred the Christian army, he would have to lay siege to Damietta, and that would take time, which al-Kamil did not have. It was vital to remove the crusaders from Egypt before Frederick II arrived. The deaths of the crusaders would stir passions in Europe and cause Christian knights to flock to the emperor, allowing him to land at Damietta with an awesome force. It would be much better to make a deal.

When the crusader representatives arrived in the sultan's tent, they were surprised to be treated with every kindness and courtesy. Immediately, al-Kamil ordered food to be sent to the afflicted army. His terms of surrender were simple: In exchange for their lives, the crusaders were to hand over Damietta and evacuate Egypt. He would grant an eight-year truce between Muslims and Christians with an exemption for a crowned head of Europe on crusade. As a fig leaf for the crusaders, al-Kamil also agreed to return the True Cross. It was their only victory, and Oliver of Paderborn embraced it: "Let all posterity know that in view of the critical point of our necessity, we made an excellent bargain, when the Wood of our redemption was restored to us in exchange for one city which Christianity could not hold for long."[2]

Word was sent to Damietta of the crusaders' defeat and the necessity of returning the hard-won city to the Muslims. Additional German troops had just arrived, and the leaders were appalled that Frederick's orders to remain at Damietta were not obeyed. They insisted that no deal should be honored until the emperor arrived. The Italians and Normans agreed, swearing that they would not hand over the city. The French and the military orders were on the other side, declaring that they must redeem the lives of their comrades. Fighting between the two factions broke out in the streets of Damietta. Only when John of Brienne sent word that he would forfeit Acre if the crusaders would not relinquish Damietta did the dispute end. The Christians prepared to evacuate the city.

On September 8, 1221, al-Kamil entered Damietta in triumph and the crusaders went home. The Fifth Crusade repeatedly had been on the brink of fantastic success, yet it ended in humiliating failure. The one apparent minor victory, the return of the True Cross, never occurred. The Templars, it appears, were right: Al-Kamil did not have it.

THE CRUSADE OF FREDERICK II

News of the crusaders' crushing defeat stunned everyone. Muslims had come to accept that at the very least, the crusaders would regain Jerusalem and its kingdom, and many expected Egypt to fall as well. The Christians of Europe agreed with this assessment. The sudden and complete collapse of the crusade filled Muslim hearts with joy and Christian mouths with words of disgust. Pelagius received much of the blame, and rightly so, for it was his opposition to the exchange of Jerusalem and his disastrously led campaign against Mansurah that doomed the crusade.

Fingers also were pointed at Frederick II. His vow was now six years old, and, despite repeated promises, he was no closer to Egypt. His empty promises had profoundly shaped the events of the Fifth Crusade. Returning soldiers accused Frederick of reckless disregard for the crusade. He had strung them along, insisting that he and his vast armies were just beyond the horizon, thus keeping the enterprise in a limbo that ultimately proved fatal. Pope Honorius III shared these sentiments. On November 19, 1221, he wrote to the emperor, reproaching him for his repeated delays and blaming himself for allowing Frederick to get away with them.

In a personal meeting, Frederick convinced the pope that he was not to blame for the delays and reaffirmed his strong intention to lead a great crusade. With the pope's blessings, Frederick again renewed his crusading vow and set the departure date for the fleet at June 24, 1225—ten years after his original vow. At once, the crusade preachers were sent out, but recruits gathered only slowly. To stir interest, John of Brienne made a much-celebrated tour of Europe. Everywhere, the king of Jerusalem was received with pomp and joyous greetings, but with few recruits and less money. By the spring of 1224, Frederick had assembled a sizable fleet, but the poor response to the crusade among the German nobility meant that he would not have an army to fill it. At last, he requested from Honorius yet another delay.

By right, and by his own advice, Frederick should have been excommunicated long before. Honorius had been patient with him because he recognized the real difficulties the emperor encountered and because he desperately wanted the glorious crusade that he promised. But his patience and the patience of Christendom were nearly exhausted. To avoid excommunication, Frederick suggested another face-to-face meeting. It was held on July 25, 1225, at San Germano. Once again, Frederick assured the pope of his unswerving commitment to the crusade and outlined even bolder plans for a massive expedition. The pope responded that he was willing to grant one final delay, but only if he had tangible assurances of the size, scope, and departure date of the crusade. Frederick agreed wholeheartedly. In the treaty of San Germano, Frederick committed himself to sailing with a large crusading army on August 15, 1227, and prosecuting a war in the East for no less than two years. As security for his word, he agreed to render 100,000 ounces of gold to the king and patriarch of Jerusalem and the master of the Teutonic Knights. The funds would be returned to him when he arrived in Acre. If he failed to crusade or died, the money would be forfeit. If he failed to keep any of the promises made at San Germano, Frederick agreed that he should be immediately excommunicated. With the document signed, Frederick headed north to prepare for the crusade.

In June 1222, Frederick's wife, Constance, died. To make clear his crusading intentions, Frederick suggested that he marry Isabella, the daughter of King John of Brienne of Jerusalem, but John was reluctant. He had acquired the crown of Jerusalem through his marriage to Maria of Montferrat. After her death in 1211, he ruled as guardian of his daughter. John feared that if Frederick married Isabella, he would claim the throne of Jerusalem for himself as the husband of the heir. Frederick assured John that he would do no such thing. The pope was eager to see the match because it would bind together the Holy Roman Empire and the kingdom of Jerusalem. Such a union, he hoped, would ensure the long-term defense of the Holy Land. Reluctantly, John consented; in November 1225, Frederick and Isabella were married. Despite his promises, Frederick declared himself king of Jerusalem immediately after the nuptials and altered the imperial seal to include the new title. John was outraged, and he denounced the emperor to the pope in the strongest terms. Not only had Frederick doomed the Fifth Crusade, he complained, but now he had usurped the crusader kingdom from one who had fought for it all of his life. Honorius wrote to Frederick, condemning his scandalous action, but there was little more that he could do. Although acquired through deceit, Frederick now had the legal right to claim John's crown.

As king of Jerusalem, Frederick acquired more tangible reasons to crusade than that of eternal salvation. He was determined to win his new kingdom and properly take the crown in the Church of the Holy Sepulcher. Now, more than ever, he cursed Louis of Bavaria and Pelagius for the collapse of the crusade in Egypt, for if he still had Damietta, he could have traded it for Jerusalem. As it happened, though, the time for deals was not yet past.

After the defeat of the Christians, the harmony of the three sons of al-Adil crumbled. Al-Kamil and al-Mu'uazzam became enemies, and al-Ashraf wavered from one side to the other. If Frederick were to arrive in Egypt with a large crusade army, al-Kamil was certain that his brother would move against him. To forestall that possibility, the sultan sent an envoy to Frederick in 1226. The envoy, the emir Fakhr-ad-Din, arrived in the emperor's court with rich gifts. Frederick was deeply impressed by the emir. The two men became fast friends, and Frederick even knighted his Muslim guest. The terms of the deal were not yet precise, but it is clear that the sultan offered Jerusalem and its kingdom if the crusade avoided Egypt and turned instead against Damascus. Frederick was more than intrigued. He sent his own envoy to Egypt to discuss the specifics. The envoy even traveled to the court of al-Mu'uazzam to see if the ruler of Damascus could make a more appealing counteroffer. "Tell your master," al-Mu'uazzam replied, "that I have for him only a sword."

Honorius III never did see the crusade he had expected for so long. On March 18, 1227, he died. His successor, Gregory IX (1227–41), was deeply pious, learned, and energetic. Like Honorius, he was committed to the salvation of the Holy Land and eager to see Frederick fulfill his vow. It had been from Gregory's own hands that Frederick took the cross during his imperial coronation in 1220. Also like Honorius, Gregory found that his patience was at an end. He would brook no further delays. In his letter announcing his election, Gregory called Europe to join the emperor in his holy cause, while at the same time warning Frederick that if he failed to crusade again it would mean excommunication. Frederick had every intention of sailing as promised. Recruitment efforts were starting to bear fruit across Europe, with the exception of France, where Louis VIII was leading his crusaders against Raymond of Toulouse.

In the summer of 1227, the crusading hosts converged on the embarkation point at Brindisi. The south Italian heat was intense that year. Water became a problem, and disease struck down many of the crusaders. A good portion of the army gave up and went home. Those who remained boarded the vessels in August. The long-anticipated crusade departed, right on schedule, but the emperor did not. He and his court were delayed. When they finally did set sail, their vessel was struck by plague. Many died, and the emperor himself became quite ill, so they put into port at Otranto to recuperate. When Frederick subsequently moved to the lavish spas of Pozzuoli near Naples, it was clear that he would not be sailing to the East after all. He sent envoys to Gregory IX to explain the tragic misfiring of the crusade and to affirm his intention to join the crusaders the following year. Gregory had heard this song before. By his own words and by his own agreements, Frederick stood condemned. On September 29, 1227, Gregory excommunicated the Holy Roman Emperor.

Although the pope suspected that Frederick was faking his illness to avoid the crusade, there is no reason to doubt the reports that the emperor was truly at death's door. Frederick had every reason to sail to the Levant. His negotiations with al-Kamil were going very well. When he arrived with his troops, poised to attack al-Mu'uazzam, he expected that al-Kamil would hand over Jerusalem and its kingdom. For Frederick, the time to strike the deal was now. Time, indeed, was his enemy. If either side in the fraternal dispute gained the upper hand, the terms would not be so attractive. That, in fact, is what happened: Al-Mu'uazzam died suddenly in November 1227, and al-Kamil quickly seized Palestine. Had Frederick sailed as planned, he would have recovered all the crusaders' lost territories for the promise to fight a dead man. The year's delay meant that he had much less with which to bargain when he finally did arrive.

Frederick's crusade arrived at Acre without him in October. When word came that the emperor had again delayed his departure, many abandoned the enterprise, and many more made plans to leave when they heard of Frederick's excommunication. Those who remained had little to do, because the terms of the truce with the Muslims stated that only Frederick could initiate hostilities. They spent the winter repairing fortifications along the coast.

The emperor publicly announced that he would set sail for the Levant the following May, excommunication or no. Gregory warned against such an action. It must be remembered that a crusade was not simply a military campaign but an act of devotion and a means of salvation; as such, it could not be undertaken, let alone led, by an excommunicate. For an excommunicate to lead a crusade would be to defile the army of Christ. If he wished to crusade, the pope insisted, the emperor must first seek absolution for his sins; otherwise, he was no crusader and his mission no crusade. Frederick ignored these technicalities. After more than a decade of troubles with popes, Frederick's youthful piety had given way to a dry cynicism in matters of religion. The state of his soul was no longer his concern, but rather the state of his kingdom in Palestine. He would sail to the Levant and claim his prize. When he had won Jerusalem, then he would speak of absolution with the pope.

When May arrived, Frederick again delayed his departure. He had been awaiting the birth of his son, Conrad, which occurred on April 25,

1228. Unfortunately, Isabella died in childbirth. John of Brienne, now bereft of both his kingdom and his daughter, became Frederick's most intractable enemy, putting himself in the service of the pope. Frederick, too, was upset by the death of Isabella, for it made his claim to the throne of Jerusalem tenuous. As husband to the heir, Frederick could legally be crowned in the Holy Land, but the death of his wife and birth of her son meant that the most he could claim was a regency for Conrad. Only Conrad could wear the crown and don the royal title. Frederick ignored these technicalities as well.

Finally, at the end of June, Frederick departed for the Holy Land. The pope wrote to Patriarch Gerald of Jerusalem and the masters of the military orders, informing them that the emperor was not a crusader but an enemy of the faith. Despite papal prohibitions, he was en route to Acre, where he planned to take command of the crusade army. They should by no means swear allegiance to him, nor take part in any of his plans. As with any excommunicate, the crusaders were to avoid any dealings with him.

There was plenty of time for the pope's letter to arrive, because Frederick took his time traveling to Palestine. After spending five weeks on Cyprus, he arrived at Acre on September 7, 1228, a decade after crusaders first expected him. He did not receive the warmest of welcomes. The crusaders were deeply split in their attitudes toward the emperor. He was supported by most of his own vassals—the Normans, Germans, and Italians, as well as the knights of the Teutonic order, who prospered greatly during his reign. The rest of the crusaders, as well as the Hospitallers, Templars, patriarch, and clergy, would not follow him.

Frederick was not overly concerned about the division in the army because he saw the host only as a tool to be used in negotiations with al-Kamil. Shortly after his arrival, Frederick sent envoys to the sultan proclaiming that he was now ready to accept the previously agreed upon deal. Al-Kamil was gracious and friendly, sending kind words and many gifts to Frederick, but he was no longer willing to hand over the kingdom of Jerusalem. Too many things had changed. The death of al-Mu'uazzam not only secured al-Kamil's hold on Egypt but also allowed him to expand his domain to Palestine, including Jerusalem itself. In return for this expansion, the sultan had agreed to help al-Ashraf capture Damascus, which was defended by the heir of al-Mu'uazzam. The siege was still in process when Frederick arrived. Al-Kamil clearly did not want Frederick to attack Palestine, because that would force him to divert troops from Damascus. He was also concerned about Frederick's fleet, which could pose a serious threat to Egypt. Al-Kamil therefore drew out negotiations in order to keep the Christians at bay until the fall of Damascus.

The crusaders' distrust of Frederick intensified as they watched Muslim envoys ushered in and out of imperial audiences. Even the emperor's own vassals began to fear that he had come not to fight the Muslims but to betray the crusade. For his part, Frederick soon realized that the sultan was stalling. Time remained his enemy. When Damascus fell, al-Kamil would have the means to defend himself against the emperor's meager and divided forces. Frederick needed to convince the sultan of the immediacy of the danger to him. A show of force would do it. In council, he suggested that the crusaders march to Jaffa to repair the city's fortifications. From there, they could launch an attack on Jerusalem, which still had no walls. The Templars, Hospitallers, crusading barons, and much of the crusading host at first refused to follow him, but they changed their minds when it was agreed that orders would be issued not in the name of the emperor but in the name of God and Christianity.

As Frederick expected, the refortification of Jaffa grabbed al-Kamil's attention. The sultan was still unwilling to trade away the former kingdom of Jerusalem, but perhaps a compromise could be worked out that would allow Frederick to declare victory and put an end to his crusade. Al-Kamil made an offer, and Frederick instantly accepted it.

The treaty itself does not survive, but its contents can be surmised from numerous contemporary descriptions. In return for a ten-year truce between the kingdom of Jerusalem and the Muslims, al-Kamil would give to Frederick Jerusalem, Bethlehem, and Nazareth, as well as a thin strip of land connecting the Holy Sites to the coast. The conditions for the transferal of Jerusalem were far-reaching and unprecedented. Frederick agreed that henceforth the city would remain defenseless and unfortified. Muslim residents would be free to remain there, retaining their homes and possessions. In addition, they would have their own city officials to administer their own separate justice system and safeguard their religious interests. The el-Aqsa Mosque and the

Dome of the Rock on the Temple Mount would remain in Muslim hands. As ruler of Jerusalem, Frederick also agreed to remain neutral in any war between Muslims and the Christians of Tripoli or Antioch, and he vowed to ally with Muslim forces if any Christian broke the truce.

Unbridled joy broke out among the crusaders when Frederick announced that Jerusalem had been surrendered by al-Kamil, but the joy soon turned to suspicion and then contempt as people learned more about the terms of the deal. Unfazed, Frederick began preparing for his triumphal entry into the holy city and his coronation in the Church of the Holy Sepulcher. When he asked the patriarch to perform the ceremony, as was customary, Gerald responded that he was confused by the extraordinary situation and asked to see the treaty. Instead, Frederick delivered a sanitized abstract of the agreement. When Gerald finally learned the terms of the deal, the patriarch was outraged. Refusing to crown Frederick, he condemned him and the treaty in the strongest terms.

For the patriarch and most of the crusaders, the agreement between the emperor and the sultan represented the prostitution of the crusade and the Holy Land. They saw it as a legalistic victory achieved by a clever excommunicate, not the rescue of Jerusalem from the stain of Islam. The Templars and Hospitallers solidly opposed the deal. They considered it a political sham, not a military victory. Unfortified Jerusalem would remain in Christian hands only as long as Muslim leaders wished it to be. Indeed, it could hardly be said to be in Christian hands at all, since the Muslims of the city were themselves a self-governing entity who retained control over the Temple. As al-Kamil told his own people,

> We have only conceded to them [the Christians] some churches and ruined houses. The sacred precincts, the venerated Rock and all the other sanctuaries to which we make our pilgrimage remain ours as they were; Muslim rites continue to flourish as they did before, and the Muslims have their own governor of the rural provinces and districts.[3]

When the truce expired, the sultan promised to "purify Jerusalem of the Franks and chase them out."

When it became clear to Frederick that the patriarch would not give him his coronation, or even journey to Jerusalem with him, the emperor quickly set off for the city with a body of his own armed men. When Gerald learned of the emperor's departure, he sent a letter to Jerusalem threatening excommunication for anyone who followed Frederick and placing the city under interdict. The letter was too late. On March 17, 1229, Frederick and his men entered the Holy City. The Muslim mayor was on hand to give him the keys. There was an attempt at a ceremony, but it was a joyless event. Both Muslims and Christians felt betrayed by their leaders. The Christian recapture of Jerusalem, which should have been a time of great celebration, evoked only angry grumbling.

On the following morning, Frederick entered the Church of the Holy Sepulcher for his coronation. None of the usual attendees were there. Most of the local barons did not recognize Frederick's right to his son's crown. The Hospitallers and Templars boycotted the ceremony, although the Teutonic Knights attended. Neither the patriarch nor any of the clergy, save Frederick's own vassals, were in attendance. They could not even perform a Mass because Frederick remained an excommunicate. Defiantly, Frederick strode through the church to the high altar, where the crown of Jerusalem rested. With no one to anoint him, he lifted the crown himself and set it on his head. The next day, March 19, the patriarch's interdict of Jerusalem arrived. Frederick gathered his men and left the city to its own devices.

Acre seethed with anger over Frederick's entry into Jerusalem and the mockery that he called a coronation. The crusading barons and military orders rallied around the patriarch, who began raising troops to occupy and garrison Jerusalem against Muslim invasion. The Hospitallers and Templars were particularly angry that Jerusalem was to remain defenseless, because of a truce with al-Kamil, while no such truce was negotiated with al-Ashraf, the ruler of Damascus.

When Frederick arrived in Acre with his forces, he was appalled. In a heated exchange, he demanded that the patriarch cease his efforts to raise an army and immediately acknowledge him as king of Jerusalem. Gerald replied that he did not take orders from excommunicates and traitors. In response, the emperor seized control of Acre. Those who were recruited for the patriarch's army were expelled. Guards were stationed at all city gates with orders to allow no one entry who did not recognize

Frederick as king. The patriarch and Templars were besieged in their own houses, unable to leave lest Frederick's men capture them. Clergy who preached against Frederick were publicly flogged. Gerald sent numerous letters to the pope reporting Frederick's conduct at Jerusalem and Acre, but the emperor's men intercepted all but a few.

Back in Rome, Gregory IX was energetically working to weaken Frederick in Italy. John of Brienne had his revenge by leading a number of successful campaigns against Frederick's lands in the South. The emperor was kept apprised of the situation. He knew that he could remain in the East no longer. At the end of April, he prepared his vessels for departure. Before leaving, he made certain to destroy all the crusaders' weapons and siege machinery, leaving them virtually defenseless. He did not want them attacking his own agents or the Muslims after he left.

Very early in the morning of May 1, 1229, Frederick and his retinue moved swiftly and quietly down the streets of Acre toward their waiting fleet. Frederick hoped to slip out of town before anyone awoke, but he was noticed, and people began pouring out into the streets, shouting curses and showering the emperor with rotten meat and garbage. In this humiliating procession, Frederick's much-anticipated journey to the Holy Land came to an end.

In purely secular terms, the crusade of Frederick II was a success. With no bloodshed, the emperor succeeded in winning back the most treasured objectives of the crusades, including Jerusalem itself. A crusade, however, was not a secular event. In its purest form, it was an act of selfless piety for the salvation of one's soul. It was not that Frederick struck a bargain to acquire Jerusalem that so angered his contemporaries. If Pelagius had accepted the restoration of the crusader states in 1220, the event would have been greeted with joy throughout Christendom. What Christians and Muslims alike considered reprehensible was the state of Jerusalem itself. With the stroke of a pen, the Holy City was transformed from a citadel of faith into a defenseless bauble. Despite the assurances of al-Kamil and Frederick, Jerusalem could not meaningfully be said to be under Christian or Muslim control. Instead, it became a place where religion mattered so little that it no longer formed the basis of government. The holiest of cities had become a secular state. In the modern world, this is applauded as religious tolerance; in the medieval world, it was treason.

NOTES

1. Oliver of Paderborn, *The Capture of Damietta,* trans. Joseph J. Gavigan, repr. in *Christian Society and the Crusades, 1198–1229,* ed. Edward Peters (Philadelphia: University of Pennsylvania Press, 1971), 94.

2. Ibid., 132.

3. Ibn Wasil, in Francesco Gabrieli, *Arab Historians of the Crusades,* trans. E. J. Costello (New York: Routledge, 1969), 271.

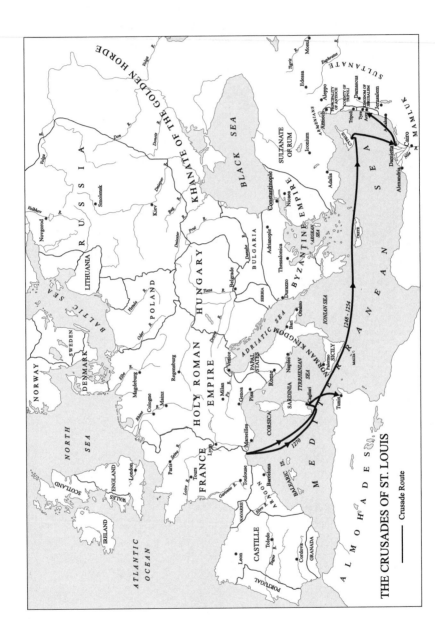

Map 12.   The Crusades of St. Louis

8

THE CRUSADES OF ST. LOUIS

When the garbage-adorned Frederick II sailed from Acre harbor, he left behind a kingdom devastated by the attainment of its most cherished goals. The Templars, Hospitallers, and local barons watched with horror as the Holy Roman Emperor destroyed their weapons and garrisoned their towns with his own troops. They were incensed by what they saw as the humiliation of Jerusalem: The Holy City was filled with Muslims, lacked fortifications, and had been handed over to an excommunicate. Frederick's "coronation" in the Church of Holy Sepulcher was an affront to their laws and the traditions of the kingdom of Jerusalem, a blatantly illegal action bordering on sacrilege. It is no wonder, then, that the Christians of the East saw the crusade of Frederick II as a war aimed not at the Muslims but themselves.

STRIFE AND CONQUEST IN
THE CRUSADER KINGDOM

Frederick's reconciliation with Pope Gregory IX in 1230 did nothing to make his rule in the Levant more palatable. Resistance and open rebellion were everywhere. The lord of Beirut, John of Ibelin, became the leader of an opposition party that included virtually all the barons as well as the Hospitallers and Templars. Before Frederick replaced him with his own men, John had been regent (*bailli*) of Cyprus. He was easily the most powerful member of the native aristocracy, so it was natural that he should become the rebellion's focus. In 1232, the city of Acre went so far as to declare itself an independent commune, separate from the kingdom of Jerusalem. John was elected the city's first mayor. War between Frederick's Hohenstaufen forces and the crusaders continued until 1233, when John captured Cyprus. Henceforth, the trappings of imperial government remained, but the real power lay in the well-connected Ibelin family.

Fortunately for the Christians, the Muslims were also in a state of disarray. The brotherly love of al-Kamil and al-Ashraf expired shortly after the conquest of Damascus. The two fought a bitter civil war until 1237, when al-Ashraf died and al-Kamil took Syria. The sultan did not have long to savor his victory; he died one year later. The Ayyubid Empire was split between his two sons: As-Salih ruled in Damascus, and al-Adil took Egypt. The two brothers quickly followed the example of their father and uncle by declaring war on each other. As-Salih succeeded in capturing Egypt but lost Syria in the process. He would spend much of his energy over the years attempting to regain it.

In 1239, Frederick II's truce expired. The Muslims wasted no time in taking back Jerusalem, a task made simple by the fact that the city was undefended and surrounded. In a real sense, it had only been on loan to the Christians anyway.

During the tensions between Syria and Egypt in 1240 and 1241, two crusades from the West arrived at Acre in rapid succession. Neither the first, led by Thibaut of Champagne, nor the second, led by Richard of Cornwall, had any important military victories, but together they successfully played the sides in the Muslim dispute against each other to gain territorial concessions. In return for an alliance with Egypt, the Christians recovered Jerusalem as well as other lost territories, including Ascalon, Sidon, Tiberias, and Galilee. It was a remarkable deal, one that brought the kingdom of Jerusalem to its largest size since 1187.

The last vestiges of Frederick II's power in the Holy Land were eradicated in 1242 or 1243, when his son Conrad came of age. The barons declared the emperor's regency at an end and invited the young Conrad to assume his throne in Jerusalem. They knew, of course, that he would do no such thing; Alice of Cyprus, the next in line for the throne, became regent. Conrad's own nominations for his regency were ignored; indeed, Alice instructed the barons to henceforth ignore all orders from the king—which they happily did. She also revoked all grants made by Frederick in Conrad's name. The last stronghold of imperial power was Tyre, which the barons besieged and captured. Hohenstaufen rule in Jerusalem was effectively at an end.

The sands of regional power shifted again when as-Salih allied with the Khorezmians of northern Syria to regain Syria and Palestine. In response, the crusaders allied with Damascus for the promise of additional land concessions. As part of the deal, the Muslim residents evacuated Jerusalem, leaving it for one last moment a Christian city. It still lacked serious fortifications. When the Khorezmians poured into the region in 1244, they easily captured it, massacred the Christians, and burned their churches, including the Church of the Holy Sepulcher. The allied army of the Egyptians and Khorezmians was formidable. After dealing a crushing blow to the crusader-Syrian forces, as-Salih took Syria and reunited the Ayyubid Empire. In one devastating campaign, the Christians had lost all the gains won by Frederick II, Thibaut of Champagne, and Richard of Cornwall. Once again, they were confined to a strip of ports along the Mediterranean coast.

THE FIRST CRUSADE OF ST. LOUIS

The catastrophic events in the Holy Land did not escape the notice of the young king of France, Louis IX (1226–70). A man of great piety and enormous courage, Louis was eager to use the resources of his kingdom in the service of Christ. Those resources were considerable. Thanks to the wise policies of Philip II Augustus and Louis's mother and regent, Blanche of Castille, France had emerged as the wealthiest and most powerful state in Europe. Much has been written about the character of Louis IX—all of it good. Even his staunchest enemies agreed that Louis was a man of integrity whose moral character was unassailable and whose devotion to justice was legendary. Like all men of his class, Louis was raised in a culture of chivalry that celebrated the crusade as the greatest use of Christian arms. It is no exaggeration to say that the liberation of Jerusalem was the single most cherished goal in his life.

Like Richard the Lionheart, Louis IX was a consummate crusader-king. The spirit of the crusade energized both men, and each had a wealthy state at his disposal with which to pursue his goals. Both were gifted leaders of men, inspiring their troops to endure great hardships for the good of the crusade. Louis was much more cautious and deliberative than Richard, qualities that also made him a better king. Louis's piety ran deeper as well. He saw the conquest of Jerusalem as the greatest act of devotion to Christ, whereas Richard viewed it as the greatest achievement of a chivalric warrior. In the field, Louis was a skillful tactician, although never the equal of Richard on that score.

Louis IX came to crusading honestly. He was the product of generations of crusaders on both sides of his family. His father, Louis VIII, devoted his final years to the Albigensian Crusade. By engaging France in a new crusade, Louis may have felt that he was fulfilling the dreams of a father whom he never knew. After coming of age, he considered crusading frequently, although his mother did her best to discourage him. At last, in December 1244, after a serious illness, Louis took the cross. When Blanche arranged to have the vow commuted, Louis stubbornly took it again. On this matter, he would not be moved, despite protests from many in his court.

Louis's crusade was from the beginning a French affair—no one else was available. The aging Frederick II was once again in open warfare with the church and in his customary state of excommunication. Although the emperor had promised vast and numerous crusades to conquer Palestine and protect the Latin Empire of Constantinople, the popes no longer expected anything from him but lies. The English were busy with their own turmoil between Henry III (1216–72) and his nobles.

The king of France was determined that his crusade would be well supplied, well funded, and meticulously organized. He oversaw every aspect of the long preparation. Pope Innocent IV (1243–54) granted him the right to receive a tenth of ecclesiastical revenues in his kingdom, and Louis instituted additional special taxes on his subjects to fund the enterprise. A large fleet was contracted from the merchants of Genoa and Marseilles, and enormous stores of provisions were stockpiled on Cyprus to provide support for the crusaders wherever they chose to operate.

Louis and his main fleet sailed on August 25, 1248. On September 17, they arrived at Cyprus, where they spent the winter waiting for more troops. By spring, a sizable force had assembled. The destination of the crusade had not been formally announced, although Louis had clearly decided on Egypt long before he arrived on Cyprus. Like many Christians, Louis thought often about the tragic failure of the Fifth Crusade. He studied the event and was determined to improve on history. In a council of war, the crusaders settled on Damietta, the Nile port captured and then lost by the Fifth Crusade, as their initial destination. None of this was a surprise to the sultan of Egypt, who sent a garrison to the city and

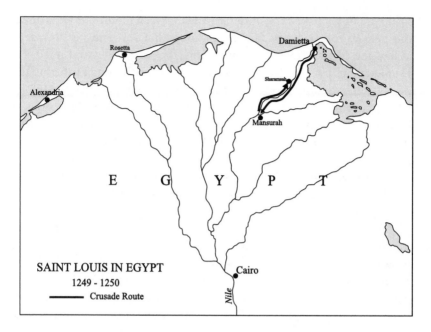

Map 13.   St. Louis in Egypt, 1249–1250

made camp with his own forces nearby. The sultan, too, was well ac-
quainted with the Fifth Crusade.

The crusade fleet sailed from Cyprus in late May 1249, arriving at
Damietta on June 4. Thirty-one years earlier, the Fifth Crusade had pros-
ecuted their siege of this city from a fortified camp on the west bank of
the Nile. Louis planned to do the same. Determined to deny the French
that beachhead, as-Salih arrayed troops along the shore. The crusaders
were prepared. Many of the knights boarded shallow-bottomed boats
that could be maneuvered right up to the banks of the river. The French
then struck with a bold amphibious assault. When the vessels opened,
knights poured out, splashing through waist-deep water to fight the
Muslim defense forces on the shore. Louis was among the knights, wield-
ing his sword with righteous determination. When the Muslim cavalry
came thundering down the beach, the French thrust their lances into the
sands, breaking up the charge. Soon, the Egyptians were in full retreat
and the crusaders had won their camp.

At this point, the Christians expected to begin a long siege of

Damietta. It had taken the Fifth Crusade eighteen months to wear down the heavily fortified city, but luck was with Louis and his crusaders. When the Muslim forces retreated from the shore, they did not enter Damietta but instead marched directly to the sultan's camp further up the Nile. Seeing this, the garrison in the city began to suspect that they alone would have to suffer the depredations of a siege. The horrible stories of conditions in Damietta during the siege of 1218–19 were still vividly told in Egypt; the garrison, therefore, followed the cue of the shore defense forces and marched back to the sultan's camp. Seeing themselves abandoned, the citizens of Damietta also made a quick retreat from the city. To their astonishment, the crusaders discovered the city undefended and empty. They occupied it at once.

As al-Kamil had done in 1219, as-Salih moved his forces upriver to the fortified town of Mansurah. Louis did not give chase, for he did not want to repeat the Fifth Crusade's mistake of getting caught by the Nile's summer flood. He also wanted to wait for the arrival of his brother, Alphonse of Poitiers, who was bringing additional troops. Alphonse arrived on October 24, 1248, and Louis immediately called a council of war.

The arguments presented at the council in Damietta exposed the two contradictory motivations for leading crusades into Egypt. When Richard the Lionheart proposed an attack on Egypt during the Third Crusade, he envisioned it as a means of breaking the back of Muslim power in the Near East, thereby ensuring the permanent safety of Jerusalem. This also was the initial motivation behind the Fourth Crusade and the Fifth Crusade. In Louis IX's council, this position was championed by the king's brother, Robert of Artois, who proclaimed that the surest way to kill a serpent was to smash its head. The goal, therefore, should be Cairo, the capital of the Ayyubid Empire. Only with Egypt under their control, he argued, could they hope to bring peace to the Holy Land.

The majority of the council opposed this plan. They saw conquests in Egypt not as an end in themselves but as a means to bargain for the return of the holy places. This idea was more recently developed during the Fifth Crusade, when the sultan was willing to return the entire kingdom of Jerusalem in exchange for Damietta. It was further supported by the diplomatic successes of the crusades of Frederick II, Thibaut of Champagne, and Richard of Cornwall. The majority argued that the French should not risk the treacherous Nile Delta but instead should sail to Alexandria. There, they could capture a rich and important city while remaining well supplied from Cyprus. Because they ruled the waves, the French could hold Damietta and Alexandria indefinitely, or until the sultan offered them enough in Palestine to make them relinquish their Egyptian prizes. This proposal was pragmatic, but it did not offer a long-term solution to the survival of the crusader states. The view of Robert of Artois was more ambitious, but as the debacle of the Fifth Crusade demonstrated, the risks were great. Louis deeply believed that God was eager to bestow great victories on his army of crusaders, and the ease with which they had taken Damietta confirmed this for him. He felt certain that similar victories awaited them at Mansurah and Cairo if only they put their trust in God rather than in clever bargaining. They would march to Mansurah.

The crusade headed south on November 20. Louis took his time, ensuring that lines of communication and supply from Damietta to the Nile were established and maintained. It took the army a month to reach Mansurah. They made camp on the same spot chosen by the Fifth Crusade, a wedge of land between the Nile and a tributary. During their journey south, the sultan died. Because his heir was in Syria, Emir Fakhr-ad-Din took command of the forces and managed to maintain order.

Across the river from the French camp lay the town of Mansurah and the camp of Fakhr-ad-Din. The latter had sufficient forces to repulse any landing of troops by boat. The French began constructing a causeway, but the Muslims bombarded it with stones and Greek fire. They also began to dig away the shore where it would make land. Weeks dragged by with little progress. Then an opportunity fell into Louis's lap. An Egyptian informant, in exchange for a rich reward, revealed the location of a ford further down the tributary. At once, Louis and his men made plans for a surprise attack on Mansurah. They decided to send an advance force, commanded by Robert of Artois, to the ford under cover of night. Robert would cross the river and establish a secure base on the other side. Louis would then follow with the main body of the army, and the combined forces would sweep down on Mansurah. Hugh of Burgundy was given command over a small defensive force to hold the current crusader camp.

On February 7, 1250, Robert of Artois crossed the ford as planned, but rather than wait for Louis, he decided to seize the moment and attack the Muslim encampment. It was a foolish risk but enormously successful. The Egyptians were caught completely unaware. Fakhr-ad-Din did not even have time to find his sword before he was cut down. In short order, the camp was taken. Flushed with victory, Robert then gave the order to attack Mansurah itself. This too was a foolish risk, and this time the results were disastrous. Robert and his knights could not fight effectively in the tight and winding streets of the city. They were also greatly outnumbered—the bulk of the Egyptian forces were quartered in the city. Almost the entire advance force was killed, including Robert himself.

As planned, the king crossed the ford, but he found no trace of his brother. He did not have long to wonder about him, though, as he could soon hear the thunder of hoofbeats as the Muslim army charged to the ford. Retreat was impossible, so Louis's forces prepared to fight. The difficult and bloody battle lasted all day. Louis and his men slowly fought their way along the river until they brought themselves just opposite the crusader camp. From there, Hugh of Burgundy was able to provide missile support and ferry reinforcements across. The Egyptians retreated back into Mansurah. When the sun set, the French had won the opposite shore of the river and were in possession of the Muslim camp.

Because of the botched surprise attack, the crusaders had acquired much less than they anticipated and paid much more than they planned. Casualty rates were high, and the frequent Muslim sorties drove them higher. Louis now lacked sufficient numbers to take the city of Mansurah, let alone contemplate the conquest of Cairo, yet he refused to lose hope. So strong was his belief that God would continue to bless his army with victories that Louis would not hear of retreat back to Damietta. He knew that the new sultan was not popular with the elite Turkish slave army (known as the Mamluks), so he held on to the hope that a coup would throw the Muslims into disarray, leaving Mansurah vulnerable. That was not to be. On February 28, the new sultan, Turan-Shah, arrived to take command of the Egyptian forces. He ordered dismantled vessels to be carried by camel down the Nile past the crusader camp, where they were to be reassembled. Catching the crusaders by surprise, the Egyptian galleys severed the shipping lines back to Damietta. It was the worst possible news. Despite all their careful preparations, the crusaders found themselves in precisely the same predicament that had destroyed the Fifth Crusade. The king refused to give up his position, despite starvation and sickness in the ranks. By the end of March, though, he had no choice. Clearly, Turan-Shah's hold on power would outlast the French food reserves. The king abandoned the hard-won camp outside the city and returned to the crusader camp across the river.

The weakest were put aboard the few remaining crusader vessels, which then attempted to run the Muslim blockade. Only one made it back to Damietta. Louis refused to board a vessel, despite a dangerous illness that had sapped all of his strength. When his brother angrily told him that his gallantry would slow the progress of the army, he replied, "Count of Anjou, count of Anjou, if you think I am a burden to you, get rid of me; but I will never leave my people." On April 5, the weak and starving army headed north. Muslim forces harassed them the entire way. After the army had trudged halfway to Damietta, Louis's advisers informed him that further progress was impossible. With great sorrow, Louis sent envoys to the sultan of Egypt, offering his surrender.

Turan-Shah immediately ordered the massacre of the poor and the sick in the Christian army. The rest, including the king and the nobility, he took as hostage. At the end of April, Louis and the sultan struck a bargain. In return for the release of all hostages, the Christians would hand over Damietta, evacuate Egypt, and agree to pay 800,000 bezants. Louis himself was to remain in Egypt until half of the ransom had been paid. Things did not go quite as planned. The coup that Louis had anticipated finally occurred. The Mamluks revolted against the sultan, killed him, and seized control of Egypt. The Mamluks were at first unwilling to abide by the terms of the agreement, but at last they realized that they needed both the money and Damietta.

On May 6, Damietta was once again surrendered to the Muslims. Louis was released, along with many, but not all, of the upper nobility. On May 8, the French paid 400,000 bezants, thus allowing the king to leave Egypt. Contrary to the agreement, the Mamluks did not release the thousands of hostages they still held.

It was a somber group that assembled for Louis's next council of war. With one voice, the royal vassals, including Louis's own brothers, proclaimed the obvious: The crusade was over. It was time to go home. Back in France, Blanche of Castille agreed. She urged Louis to return, but the king was not finished in the East. If his vassals wished to go home, he could not gainsay it. Each had done all that could be expected of a crusader. He announced his intention to travel to the Holy Land and do whatever he could for the Christians there. He was also determined not to leave the Levant until he had won the release of his countrymen in Egyptian dungeons.

St. Louis in the Holy Land

Louis arrived at Acre on May 13. The patriarch of Jerusalem, the masters of the military orders, and the cheering citizens of the city welcomed him in a splendid ceremony. Louis had no legal authority in the crusader kingdom, which remained under the titular control of the Hohenstaufen. Neither did he have claim to power through military strength, because he arrived with only about a thousand troops. In truth, however, Louis's authority was vast. During the next four years, he was the virtual ruler of the kingdom. His power flowed not from raw might, but from what the ancient Romans called *auctoritas,* the authority that one obtains through fame, glory, and moral uprightness. As in Europe, the barons of the East saw the king of France as the epitome of chivalric and Christian virtue. No one dared to contradict him, for they were absolutely certain that his interests were solely for the good of the Holy Land. His mere presence helped to cool the factionalism that had torn the crusader states asunder. The contrast between the visits of Louis IX and Frederick II could not be more stark.

There was more opportunity to make progress in the kingdom of Jerusalem than Louis might have thought. After the assassination of Turan-Shah, the Muslims of Syria and Egypt were once again at war. Because the two sides were evenly matched, both were willing to offer much to the crusaders in exchange for an alliance. Louis bargained cleverly, playing each side off of the other. Both promised to restore Jerusalem and its kingdom to the Christians after the war, but Egypt also offered to release the remaining French captives and cancel the outstanding debt of 400,000 bezants. As had occurred during the crusade of Thibaut of Champagne, there was considerable debate among the Christians over which side they should favor. In their customary way, the Templars and Hospitallers strongly disagreed on the question, with the former supporting the Syrians and the latter arguing for the Egyptians. For Louis, there was no real question. Egypt offered the liberation of his men and the cancellation of a sizable debt. In early 1252, he made an alliance with his former enemies, the Mamluks.

The war was plagued with fits and starts, and as it turned out, the Christians were never able to link up with the Egyptians. Finally, on April 1, 1253, Egypt and Syria made peace. There was no longer any need to court the crusaders. Diplomatically left out in the cold, Louis turned his attention to building projects he was sponsoring in the kingdom. With his own funds, he improved the defenses of Acre, Caesarea, Jaffa, Sidon, and other smaller fortresses along the coast.

Throughout his stay in Palestine, Louis continued to receive letters from home asking him to return. His mother had died at the end of 1252, and Louis's two brothers, Alphonse of Poitiers and Charles of Anjou, had taken over the royal government. There were plenty of reasons why he should return to his own kingdom and fewer and fewer reasons why he should remain in the East. By the end of 1253, it was clear that without many more troops there was nothing more he could do. He had calmed the internal dissension of the crusader kingdom while greatly improving its defensive position. His last act was to establish a permanent garrison of one hundred knights in Acre that would henceforth be maintained by the French crown. On April 24, 1254, almost six years after his departure from Europe, Louis IX sailed home.

Louis never forgot the Holy Land; indeed, the thought of its restoration animated his entire reign. Over the next decade and a half, he sought to perform his duties as a Christian king so well, and to care for his subjects with such devotion, that God would deem him worthy to rescue the land of his Son. As William Chester Jordan has argued, Louis's reforms at home can best be understood when viewed through the king's intense desire to win Jerusalem. He wanted to build a government that could efficiently and effectively fight the wars of God. He kept a sharp eye on events in the East and sent funds regularly to assist the crusader kingdom. The news from the East was not good.

The Mongols

After the king's departure from Palestine, the crusader states appeared secure for the foreseeable future. In 1255, they made a ten-year truce with the Mamluks, a reason for some optimism concerning the relations between the Christians and the new masters of Egypt. The arrival of the Mongols, however, changed everything.

The Mongols, an Asiatic people, already had built through conquest the largest empire the world had ever seen, stretching from the Black Sea to the Pacific Ocean. They were ferocious fighters, mercilessly cruel and fantastically successful. After conquering China and other parts of the Far East, they stormed through the heart of the Muslim world, rapidly capturing Persia, Mesopotamia, and Anatolia. Christians did not shed a tear to see the most opulent areas of Islam destroyed. A few of the Mongols were known to be Nestorian Christians, members of a heretical sect that held that Christ's divine and human natures were distinct and separate. This was hardly a vast theological gap to be bridged. Various popes expressed the belief that the European Catholics and Mongolian Nestorians could come to an agreement if it meant the defeat of Islam.

The arrival of the Mongols appeared to be presaged by the legend of Prester John, a popular tale familiar to almost all Europeans. It held that a great and powerful Christian monarch, perhaps the successor of one of the magi who attended the Nativity of Christ, ruled a mighty empire in the Far East. When he learned of the Muslim conquests in the Mediterranean, he would make plans to lead the forces of his empire to defend the Holy Sepulcher and his fellow Christians in the West. No one was certain where the story came from, but there was not a Christian alive who did not hope that it was true. Naturally, expectations were raised when the Mongols appeared in the East, trampling Muslim armies in their powerful advance. Over the course of the last six centuries, Islam had conquered three-quarters of the Christian world. It is not surprising, then, that Christians prayed that the Mongols were their long awaited rescuers—but they were not, at least not directly.

While he was still in the Holy Land, St. Louis himself had opened negotiations with the ruler of the Mongol Empire, the Great Khan. The king proposed mending their minor theological differences so that they could ally against the Muslim conquerors of the land of Christ. Although these words were translated for the Mongols, they were still unintelligible. Nestorianism was the religion of only a tiny handful of Mongols. In any case, religion was not why they waged their wars of conquest; it was a side issue for the Mongols, a matter of personal taste. They expanded their territory because they had the power to do so and because they wanted still more power. As the Khan responded to a similar letter from Pope Innocent IV in 1246:

You have also said that supplication and prayer have been offered by you, that I might find a good entry into baptism. This prayer of thine is not understood. Other words which thou hast sent me: "I am surprised that thou has seized all the lands of the Magyar and the Christians. Tell us what their fault is." These words of thine I have also not understood. The eternal God has slain and annihilated these lands and peoples, because they have neither adhered to Jenghiz Khan, nor the Khagan, nor to the command of God.[1]

The Mongols' ultimate goal was nothing less than world conquest, which, they believed, would usher in a new era of order under the control of an all-powerful Khan. From their perspective, Louis was a petty chieftain, a ruler of a small kingdom that they would conquer or assimilate in due course. In reply, they demanded that Louis surrender France and prepare to send an annual tribute to the Great Khan. Needless to say, talks got nowhere.

Christian applause for the Mongol conquests began to subside a bit when the Mongols entered Syria, capturing Aleppo and Damascus. They were led by Kitbogha, a Nestorian Christian. The Christians in the north, at Antioch and in Armenia, had already submitted to the Mongols and thereby survived. When Kitbogha entered Damascus, he was accompanied by the king of Armenia and the prince of Antioch, putting three Christians at the head of the Mongol advance. This did not put the crusaders in the kingdom of Jerusalem at ease. They counted all three men as traitors to the faith who would just as happily deprive the crusaders of their own lands if given the chance.

In fact, Kitbogha did not attack their kingdom, nor did he make plans to. Instead, he sent an ambassador to Cairo demanding the immediate submission of Egypt to the Mongols. The Mamluk sultan, Kutuz, responded by killing the ambassador and mobilizing his own forces for war. His timing was good, for at that moment news arrived that the Khan had died, and civil war erupted four thousand miles away in Karakorum. Kitbogha's forces were depleted. The Mamluk troops were led by the brilliant but thoroughly ruthless General Baybars, a Kipchak Turk. At the Battle of Ain Jalud in September 1260, the Mamluks decisively defeated the Mongols and captured Syria. It was a momentous victory: No one on three continents had ever pushed back a Mongol conquest. With Baghdad already in Mongol hands, it was Egypt that now took center stage in the Islamic world.

CHANGE AND DECAY IN THE CRUSADER KINGDOM

Not long after his victory at Ain Jalud, Baybars became sultan of Egypt. This was bad news for the crusaders. Although Egypt was rich and prosperous, its chaotic and capricious governments kept it relatively weak. The Mamluks changed that. Under the command of Baybars, it was a powerful threat. The new sultan initially was kept busy establishing control over Syria, but there could be no doubt that he would soon turn his attention to Palestine.

While external threats grew in magnitude, internal dissension again weakened the struggling kingdom. For decades, the Templars and Hospitallers had been at odds. Aside from their mutual refusal to recognize Frederick II as king in 1229, the two military orders agreed on nothing. Even trivial issues found them staking out opposing positions. The tension grew to such levels that it erupted in open warfare. One of the vehicles for internecine fighting was the War of St. Sabas, which began as a case in the civil courts. In 1251, the Venetians and the Genoese disputed ownership of some houses that belonged to the monastery of St. Sabas in Acre. After five years of legal wrangling, the case was no closer to resolution, and tempers flared violently. In 1256, the Genoese armed themselves, seized the disputed houses, and attacked the Venetian Quarter of Acre. The Venetian merchants rallied and drove out the Genoese. Philip of Montfort, the lord of Tyre, took advantage of the disturbance to expel the Venetians, who had owned one-third of that city since their crusade of 1122. Quickly, the opposing factions in the crusader kingdom chose sides in the war. The Templars and Teutonic Knights supported Venice, whereas the Hospitallers and most of the barons backed Genoa. The war climaxed with a massive naval battle between the two maritime states fought just off the port of Acre in June 1258. Venice was the victor. Genoa abandoned Acre altogether and concentrated its resources on Tyre. The Genoese got their revenge a few years later when they backed Emperor Michael VIII Palaeologus (1261–82), who reconquered Constantinople in 1261 and expelled the Venetians.

The nature of the crusader kingdom was changing fundamentally in response to changes in the world. The Mongol conquests made possible new trade routes to the Far East that allowed a merchant to travel from the Black Sea to the Sea of Japan while remaining in the Mongol Empire. The route was safe, quick, and free from numerous and shifting customs duties that plagued routes through Muslim lands. Black Sea ports started to bustle with activity as goods from the Far East were loaded aboard vessels bound for Europe. Constantinople also did well because it commanded the Bosporus strait, the only connection between the Black Sea and the Mediterranean. As a result, business slowed noticeably in the markets of the crusader states. The Italians made due with less exotic payloads, but the local barons could not afford the loss in revenue. One by one, they began to sell their lands to the military orders, which were always well off thanks to pious contributions to their houses in Europe. Soon, power in the kingdom resided primarily with the Italians and the military orders—and they were usually at each other's throats.

MAMLUK CONQUESTS

It did not take long for Baybars to settle matters in Syria and turn his attention to the Christians. Unlike Saladin, the Mamluk sultan did not cloak his war against the crusaders in the rhetoric of *jihad*. It was merely a matter of conquest, aimed at removing once and for all the problem of the Christian presence in Palestine. In 1263, he led a successful raid into Galilee and destroyed the cathedral of Nazareth. Two years later, he conquered Caesarea and Arsuf. In 1266, he took the Templar fortress of Safad, massacring the inhabitants after promising to spare their lives. Indeed, Baybars made it a point to massacre or enslave Christians wherever he found them, be they in great citadels or in modest villages. In 1268, he captured Jaffa and brutally sacked the city.

Later that same year, Baybars led his forces north against the great city of Antioch. It fell after only four days. The sultan ordered the doors of the city closed and the inhabitants, including women and children, massacred. This atrocity shocked even the Muslim chroniclers. It was probably the single greatest massacre of the entire crusading era. Upset to see that Count Bohemund VI was not in his city, Baybars wrote to him to describe the carnage that he missed:

> You would have seen your knights prostrate beneath the horses' hooves, your houses stormed by pillagers and ransacked by looters, your wealth weighed by the quintal, your women sold four at a time and bought for a dinar of your own money! You would have seen

the crosses in your churches smashed, the pages of the false Testaments scattered, the Patriarchs' tombs overturned. You would have seen your Muslim enemy trampling on the place where you celebrate the Mass, cutting the throats of monks, priests and deacons upon the altars, bringing sudden death to the Patriarchs and slavery to the royal princes. You would have seen fire running through your palaces, your dead burned in this world before going down to the fires of the next, your palace lying unrecognizable, the Church of St. Paul and that of the Cathedral of St. Peter pulled down and destroyed; then you would have said: "Would that I were dust, and that no letter had ever brought me such tidings!"[2]

The loss of Antioch was a terrible blow to the Christians. It was the oldest of the crusader states, having stood firm for 170 years. What remained of the Latin East was in desperate need of aid from the West.

THE SECOND CRUSADE OF ST. LOUIS

No sizable crusading force had arrived in the Holy Land for almost three decades. This was not for lack of interest in Europe, nor because of popular disillusionment with the crusades; rather, it was the result of the proliferation of crusades to destinations other than the Levant. Crusade fervor in Europe was just as strong as ever; it was simply directed elsewhere. Crusades in Spain and the Baltic continued to attract recruits. The popes also had responsibility for the safety of the Latin Empire of Constantinople, which was always in desperate need of help. After Constantinople fell in 1261, the pope proclaimed a new crusade to reconquer it. Closer to home, there was the continual problem of the Hohenstaufen in Italy. After the death of Frederick II's son, Conrad, in 1254, Pope Alexander IV (1254–61) proclaimed a crusade against his illegitimate brother, Manfred. That crusade continued well after Alexander's death. In 1264, Pope Urban IV (1261–64) invited Charles of Anjou to invade the Kingdom of Two Sicilies, defining the war as a crusade. Louis IX, who had earlier attempted to arbitrate a peace, fully supported his brother's crusade against the Hohenstaufen, although he worried about expending crusade energy in wars against Christians. In 1266, Charles defeated Manfred and became king of Sicily.

The Christian losses in the Levant were a source of great anguish to the king of France. Although he continued to send money and men to the East, Louis longed to be able to lead a crusade in defense of Jerusalem once again. After his brother's victory in Sicily, Louis saw no reason to wait any longer. He discussed his plans with Pope Clement IV (1265–68), who was pleased by the prospect but somewhat concerned with what would become of southern Italy in the absence of both Louis and Charles of Anjou. Charles and Louis spoke often about the crusade. Charles made no secret about his desire to go to Constantinople and wrest the city from the newly restored Byzantine emperor. Having just won the crown of Sicily, Charles dreamed of wearing the imperial diadem in the city of Constantine. Louis, however, would hear no more of wars against Christians.

At an assembly of the barons of France on March 24, 1267, Louis and his three sons proudly took the cross of the crusade. The barons were unimpressed. Louis was not the swashbuckling warrior of his youth; he was in his fifties and becoming frail. To many, Louis's desire to win Jerusalem seemed the unrealistic dream of a young man, one that should have faded away long ago. His friend and comrade in the previous crusade, Jean de Joinville, expressed the changing values of the time when he excused himself from again accompanying the king on the expedition to the East:

> And I told him [Louis IX] this, that if I wished to do what was pleasing to God, I should remain here, to help and defend my people; and if I put my body in danger in the pilgrimage of the cross, while seeing quite clearly that this would be to the hurt and damage of my people, I should move God to anger, Who gave His body to save His people.[3]

The royal court was unanimously opposed to the expedition, but Louis was granitic in his resolve. The king's brothers, Charles of Anjou and Alphonse of Poitiers, announced that they would join him. Outside France, the crusade attracted other royal adherents: King James I of Aragon (1213–76) and King Henry III of England (1216–72).

Now the governmental reforms that Louis had instituted in France were put to the test, and they performed marvelously. The king had little problem in collecting the ecclesiastical and secular tithes for his expedition and was easily able to procure the necessary supplies. He arranged for a fleet to be waiting in Genoa and Marseilles. If anything, Louis's second crusade was even better organized than his first.

The crusade was to depart in June 1270, but the Genoese were late providing vessels, so it did not sail until July. The rendezvous point was Cagliari in southern Sardinia, where Louis convened a council of war. The Spanish were not there. Their fleet had been broken up by storms, and most of the survivors returned home. Henry III of England had decided not to crusade after all, but he sent his son, Edward, to lead the English crusaders. They too had not yet arrived.

The destination of the crusade had not been announced. Most, including even the owners of the vessels, expected that Louis would again take the crusaders to Egypt. The assembly was stunned, therefore, to learn that they were headed for Tunis.

Scholars have long wondered at Louis's reasons for attacking a relatively weak Muslim state in the western Mediterranean. Although it appears that Charles of Anjou did not have a hand in the decision, he could scarcely have opposed it. Tunis lay directly across the sea from Sicily, and the emir continued to support Hohenstaufen sympathizers there. The conquest of Tunis not only would deny an outpost for rebels in the south but would also give Charles solid control over the western Mediterranean. Because Louis would not allow the crusade to go to Constantinople, for Charles, Tunis was second best. Louis may have believed that the capture of Tunis would harm Egypt and thus make its subsequent conquest easier. If so, he was misinformed. Egypt received almost nothing from Tunis; indeed, the sultan in Cairo was delighted when he learned of the crusade's destination. The king may also have received information that the emir of Tunis, Muhammad I, was willing to convert to Christianity if a strong Christian army would support him. If Louis believed this story, it might have convinced him to head to Tunis. That information, too, was faulty.

Whatever the reason for Louis's decision, it is clear that he envisioned the trip to Tunis as only a brief stop on his way to the East. The city was neither well fortified nor well defended. Once captured, it could serve as a useful place to await further recruits. Scrupulous crusaders might question whether this western town was a legitimate target for a crusade, but the word of Louis IX was sufficient to dispel any doubts.

The crusade landed in Tunisia on July 18, 1270. The crusaders quickly captured a fortress on the site of ancient Carthage and established their camp. Charles of Anjou had been detained in Italy, and Louis decided to wait until his arrival with more troops before launching an attack. Muhammad sent a few sorties to harass the crusaders, but Louis strictly ordered his men to avoid skirmishes. He did not want headstrong and glory-hungry knights to harm the crusade as his brother, Robert of Artois, had done in Egypt. The summer sun beat down on the crusaders and nurtured an outbreak of deadly diseases in the camp. Soldiers began to die in greater numbers. Soon, even members of the royal family fell ill. Louis's eldest son, Philip, became extremely sick, and another son, John of Nevers, died. Louis was stricken with grief over the loss of John, who had been born in Damietta during the king's first crusade and now died in the ruins of Carthage on his second. It seemed that God was sending down an angel of death to ravage the crusade army, and Louis could not guess why. Eventually, Louis himself fell ill. Day by day, he grew weaker, until it was clear to all that he would not recover. On the night of August 24 he asked to be laid out on a bed of penitential ashes. That night, in his sleeping delirium, he could be heard to cry out, "Jerusalem! Jerusalem!" The next day, the Most Christian King of France died.

A few days later, Charles of Anjou arrived. Legally, Philip III (1270–85) was in command of the crusade, but because he remained ill, he deferred to his uncle. Charles immediately opened negotiations with the emir. Muhammad was eager to talk, and in short order the two men came to an agreement. In exchange for the departure of the crusade, the emir granted a series of concessions to Charles's kingdom of Sicily and paid a large war indemnity, of which Charles would receive one-third. The rank-and-file crusaders were incensed when the deal was announced. Charles had successfully negotiated a great victory for himself, although he had taken no part in the crusade. Some even blamed him for Louis's death, for if he had arrived sooner, they would not have had to endure the heat and disease of the crusader camp for six agonizing weeks.

The second crusade of Louis IX was a success for no one but Charles of Anjou, and he profited mightily. Despite very high casualties, the French had failed to achieve anything, or even to reach their final destination. But the reputation of Louis IX did not suffer in the slightest. After a life of exemplary piety and Christian kingship, he died as he lived, in the service of the faith. A mere twenty-seven years later, the church honored her defender by canonizing him as a saint.

Shortly after Charles struck his bargain with the emir, Prince Edward arrived with his English crusaders. He was understandably upset to find the French preparing to depart. After wintering in Sicily, Edward led his small force to Acre, where he landed on May 9, 1271. He found the crusader kingdom in a pitiful state. When Baybars learned of the French decision to attack Tunis, he immediately continued his attacks on Christian strongholds. In March, he took the huge Hospitaller fortress of Krak des Chevaliers, the greatest Christian outpost in the Levant. Edward lacked the troops to threaten Baybars, but he possessed diplomatic skills. He roused the Mongols to raid and plunder in Syria, then negotiated a truce of ten years and ten months with the sultan of Egypt. Unable to do more, he returned to England, where he discovered that his father had died and he was king.

The crusades of St. Louis were the best-funded, best-organized enterprises that Christendom had ever launched. They were led by a king of enormous piety, skilled in the art of war and devoted to the restoration of Jerusalem. If they could not succeed, what could? One might expect that disillusionment and despair would be the natural result, yet despite these failures and a century of similar ones the Christians of Europe remained steadfast in their commitment to the Holy Land. The crusade remained a central part of life and the restoration of the Holy Land a constant prayer of all the faithful. The fire of crusading zeal still burned brightly, and, despite his failures, St. Louis became the model of the selfless warrior of Christ. Few could shake the foreboding feeling, however, that perhaps the forces of Islam were becoming simply too powerful to resist.

NOTES

1. Brundage, *The Crusades: A Documentary Survey*, 260.

2. Gabrieli, *Arab Historians of the Crusades*, 311.

3. *Memoirs of the Crusades*, trans. Frank T. Marzials (New York: E. P. Dutton, 1951), 320.

9

THE DECLINE OF CRUSADING

THE FALL OF THE CRUSADER STATES

After the failure of his brother's crusade, Charles of Anjou did not lead the French forces to the Holy Land, but he did purchase the crown of Jerusalem for himself in 1277. The sale was unprecedented, but the pope approved it in the hope that Charles would pay more attention to the Levant than to his plans to conquer Constantinople. Charles never did sail to the East, and his regent, Roger of San Severino, received only partial recognition in the crusader kingdom. Hugh of Cyprus became a rival king, causing the kingdom of Jerusalem to divide its allegiance, with Acre supporting Charles and Tyre endorsing Hugh.

Fortunately for the Christians, the Mamluks could not at first take advantage of the division. The dreaded Baybars died in 1277, and it was not until 1280 that the emir, Kalavun, was able to close his grip around the sultanate. Kalavun matched Baybars in ruthlessness and in his desire to eradicate the Christians from Palestine. He quickly exploited the crusaders' factionalism by making separate treaties with various cities. Invariably, this pitted the interests of different portions of the kingdom against each other.

Charles of Anjou's empire building came to a crashing halt on March 30, 1282, when the revolt of the Sicilian Vespers ejected him from Sicily. Because he could no longer afford to be king of Jerusalem, he ordered his forces in Acre to return home. When Charles died in 1284, the barons and military orders overcame their mutual distrust and at last settled on a single king. They offered the crown to young Henry of Cyprus, who had only just succeeded his father Hugh on the island. Henry was crowned in Tyre on August 15, 1286. After the coronation, the king and his nobles rode to Acre, where they enjoyed two weeks of feasting, pageants, tournaments, and other courtly entertainment. It was a splendid event but the last of its kind to take place in Palestine.

Henry had little success quelling the infighting among the Italians and military orders that had already so damaged the kingdom. He had even less success with the sultan of Egypt. In 1287, Kalavun captured the important port of Latakia, the last remnant of the old Principality of Antioch. Then, despite a treaty of peace, he launched an attack on Tripoli in March 1289. The city fell, and the county was quickly assimilated into the Mamluk Empire. Although the sultan renewed his truce with Acre, his word obviously meant little now.

The barons and military orders at Acre sent urgent appeals to the West for aid. Much was promised, but little arrived. Venice sent war galleys, and the pope raised money to fund an army of Tuscan and Lombard crusaders. The latter arrived in Acre in August 1290, but they were troops of very poor quality. After a few weeks, the new recruits killed some unarmed Muslim merchants who entered the city to sell their produce. The ringleaders were arrested and an apology for the deaths sent to Cairo. Kalavun seized on the altercation as a useful excuse to resume hostilities with the Christians. He demanded that the military orders turn the offenders over to him. The high council in Acre considered the sultan's request, but the members could not bring themselves to surrender Christians to a Muslim leader for certain torture and death. Instead, they sent word to Kalavun that the Muslim merchants had really started the whole thing. Unamused, the sultan declared war.

Kalavun arrived at Acre with a vast army equipped with more than one hundred siege engines. It was probably the largest single force ever assembled during the crusade era, and it was arrayed before the mighty walls of Acre, the greatest of the Christian strongholds in Palestine. It was lost on no one that this was the crusaders' last stand. All the factionalism and rancor that had so weakened the crusader kingdom in the past was now forgotten in the face of the common foe. The Templars, Hospitallers, and Teutonic Knights summoned all available men from Europe to assist in the defense. The brothers were led by the grand masters themselves, all three of whom were in Acre. King Henry was ill in Cyprus, but he sent troops and his brother, Amalric, who commanded the defense. Thanks to the constant support of the French crown, the fortifications of Acre were in excellent shape, but the Christians were faced with an army that outnumbered them seven to one.

The siege of Acre began on April 6, 1291. The engines relentlessly pounded the walls of the city night and day. Thousands of Muslim sappers were put to work digging tunnels under the walls to destroy their foundations. The fortifications held firm for a month but then began to collapse. On May 18, the Muslims breached the city's inner wall and swarmed inside. Women and children fled to the harbor, where they boarded escape vessels. The military orders refused to surrender, continuing the battle in house-to-house fighting, but it was hopeless. The slaughter was immense. Those who could not escape were put to the sword.

By evening, the entire city was in Muslim hands, with the lone exception of the Templars' house, which was partially protected by the harbor. As the last Christian possession, it became a refuge for those who could not escape. After a week, the sultan finally abandoned his attempts to take the building. He offered to allow the knights and refugees to leave Acre with their lives if they would surrender their position. They agreed, but when the Muslim soldiers entered the house, they at once began to sexually abuse the women and boys. Outraged, the Templar knights expelled the Muslims and secured the stronghold. The Muslims responded by undermining the building. When the outer wall collapsed, the Muslim troops rushed in to gather loot and refugees, but they had done their work too well. The building collapsed utterly, killing attackers and defenders alike.

In the bloody battles to save Acre, the Christians lost their last effective army. Tyre, which had withstood even Saladin, surrendered to Kalavun without a fight. The last remaining crusader possessions quickly followed suit. Sidon capitulated at the end of June, and Beirut on July 31. The last Templar castles of Chateau Pèlerin and Tortosa surrendered in August. The crusader states founded by the First Crusade almost two centuries earlier were wiped away without a trace. All that was left was the island of Cyprus, captured by Richard I during the Third Crusade. To ensure that the Franks never returned, Kalavun ordered the destruction of all fortifications along the Mediterranean coast. Arab historian Abu L-Fida summed it up:

> With these conquests the whole of Palestine was now in Muslim hands, a result that no one would have dared to hope for or to desire. Thus the whole of Syria and the coastal zones were purified of the Franks, who had once been on the point of conquering Egypt and subduing Damascus and other cities. Praise be to God![1]

The wealthy and splendid cities of Acre, Tyre, and Tripoli became ruined and empty ghost towns, sad remnants of a world that had forever passed away.

The loss of the crusader kingdom was taken hard in Europe. A flurry of plans to reconquer Palestine swirled between Rome and the thrones of western Christendom, but none of them would be easy to implement. The absence of a fortified beachhead meant that any crusader army would have to constitute a major invasion force. Not surprisingly, most plans envisioned the conquest of Egypt as the necessary precursor to successful campaigning in Syria. In preparation, Pope Boniface VIII (1294–1303) imposed a trade embargo on Egypt, but the great retaliatory crusade never materialized. The pope soon found himself embroiled in a fierce dispute with King Philip IV of France (1285–1314) over the taxation of clergy. Matters turned ugly in 1303, when Philip declared Boniface a usurper and murderer and sent men to Italy to arrest him. The pope died of shock. Determined to make peace with the French crown, Pope Clement V (1305–14) spent the first years of his pontificate in Gascony, finally settling in Avignon, where the papacy remained throughout most of the fourteenth century.

THE TRANSFORMATION OF THE MILITARY ORDERS

As one might expect, there was quite a lot of finger pointing after the fall of the crusader states. The lion's share of criticism fell upon the military orders. They were highly visible, for they had houses across Europe where they collected funds for the sake of the Holy Land. Over the course of the last century, they had also become quite wealthy and had even become involved in banking. Many Christians now derisively asked just how all that wealth had helped the land of Christ. Had the military orders enriched the Holy Land or just themselves? Was it not the incessant fighting between the Templars and Hospitallers that had so seriously weakened the crusader kingdom? Many wondered what need there was for military orders with the extinction of the Latin East. Even their supporters in the church began to argue that the various military orders should consider merging into a single entity.

Like all kings in the late Middle Ages, Philip IV had an insatiable appetite for money. After consuming his clerical tithes, he began to look for other sources of wealth to devour. In 1291 and in 1311, he ordered the arrest of Italian bankers and the confiscation of their wealth. In 1306, he claimed the wealth and property of all Jews in France, then expelled them from his kingdom. His gaze then turned toward the wealthiest bankers in Europe, the Knights Templar. Taking advantage of the unpopularity of the military orders, Philip, on October 13, 1307, ordered the mass arrest of all Templars in France. Under torture, Templar leaders admitted to a host of trumped-up charges, including sodomy, black magic, and heresy. Those who refused to confess were burned at the stake. Not surprisingly, most Templars confessed. In an attempt to appease Philip, Clement V ordered the arrest of all Templars in Europe and launched a papal inquiry into the charges. Rational inquiry was not Philip's desire. At last, under extreme pressure, Clement V suppressed the Knights Templar on April 3, 1312. The grand master of the order, who recanted his forced confession to imagined crimes, was burned at the stake in 1314.

The violent demolition of the Templars naturally led the Knights Hospitaller to fear that they would be next. In an attempt to prove their effectiveness, the Hospitallers launched an attack on the island of Rhodes in 1307. With the help of the Genoese, the Knights subdued the island in less than three years. Rhodes was an excellent strategic port commanding the naval routes between the Levant and the West. Over time, the Hospitallers turned the island into a well-fortified Christian citadel, one that became a regular stopping point for pilgrims. Using Rhodes as a base, the knights extended their control over neighboring islands, including Cos, as well as coastal cities including Bodrum (Halicarnassus). These well-publicized successes turned public opinion around. The Knights of Rhodes, as they came to be called, were applauded as the defenders of Christianity in the East.

As the rulers of their own strong feudal state in northern Europe, the Teutonic Knights were in no danger of suppression after the fall of the crusader kingdom. They continued to wage war against pagans in the eastern Baltic, particularly in Lithuania, where they did not meet with much success. They were successful, however, in expanding their holdings by purchase and conquest, becoming so powerful that Poland began to regret inviting them into the region.

CRUSADING IN THE FOURTEENTH CENTURY

The fourteenth century witnessed fundamental changes in Europe with profound effects on the crusading movement. A strong papacy had given birth to the crusades and nurtured them across the centuries. Without powerful popes able to rally the knights of Christendom, a great crusade—or *passagium generale*—was impossible. The fourteenth century saw the political authority of the papacy declining noticeably, with the power of kings dramatically on the rise. As a result, popes found it increasingly difficult to enlist nobles directly, for the latter now had pressing responsibilities to their kings. The church alone could no longer launch a *passagium generale:* It needed the active support of kings.

To be sure, most Christian monarchs held dear the idea of liberating Palestine, and many genuinely longed to lead their armies against the Muslims. By definition, however, kings were easily distracted by matters of state. They were also plagued by the sure knowledge that any state that took up the cross could expect to be preyed upon by those that did not. Thus, although the French monarchy undertook plenty of initiatives to prepare for a great crusade in the first half of the fourteenth century, and despite the sincerest of motives, they never went anywhere.

The best that popes could do on their own was to organize smaller crusades aimed at limited goals, the so-called *passagium particulare.* During the fourteenth century, these were usually fought at home for political or religious reasons. When an expedition to the East was considered at all, it was usually to assist the remaining Latin states in Greece. These kinds of objectives, as well as the proposed targets of the greater crusades, finalized in the popular mind the divorce of the concepts of crusade and pilgrimage. The change had been a century in coming. When Richard I favored an attack on Egypt rather than Jerusalem during the Third Crusade, he was widely denounced by the soldiers. When the Fourth Crusade made a treaty for transportation to Egypt, the leaders carefully kept the destination secret, lest the rank and file discover that they were not bound for Jerusalem. The Fifth Crusade legitimized Egypt as a worthy crusading goal, and the first crusade of St. Louis sanctified it. The Albigensian Crusade and various political crusades of the thirteenth century only served to underline the point. Crusades were no longer armed pilgrimages but papally sanctioned wars against the enemies of the faith.

THE KINGDOM OF CYPRUS

The heir to the kingdom of Jerusalem was the kingdom of Cyprus; indeed, the monarchs there retained the titular kingship of the holy city. A number of the older crusading families had retreated to Cyprus, so the island had the feel of a government in exile. Famagusta became a wealthy city, steeped in the chivalric culture of the old crusader kingdom. Its most famous king, Peter I (1359–69), was himself thoroughly imbued with the ways of the past. Young, brave, dashing, and charismatic, Peter devoted himself absolutely to the task of raising a mighty crusade to reconquer the East. Immediately after taking the throne in 1359, he began raiding Turkish possessions in Asia Minor. In 1361, he added the port of Adalia to his possessions. He then traveled to Europe, where he spent the next two years, as well as a great deal of money, in an attempt to raise troops for a crusade. He was received by the great and powerful with glittering pomp and ceremony. Monarchs were moved to tears by the stories that this valiant warrior brought of the plight of the Holy Land, but they did not join his crusade.

By sheer determination, Peter cobbled together a crusader army, although it was of very uneven quality. The crusader fleet gathered at Rhodes in 1365 to plan its attack. Expecting the Christians to land in Palestine, the Muslims beefed up their defensive forces there. Instead, on October 9, the crusade appeared in the harbor of Alexandria. A crusade army was so unexpected that the merchants of the city opened the gates to trade. They soon learned their mistake, but it was too late to make an effective defense. Mighty Alexandria fell in just one day. Inside, the crusaders found a sea of wealth. In revenge for Antioch and Acre, they massacred many of the citizens.

After the booty was divided, a council of war was called to decide on the next move. The majority of barons argued that they should abandon the city rather than defend it. Peter was thunderstruck. He reminded them that this was the first major victory against the Muslims in almost a century. Alexandria could serve as a defensible beachhead from which future crusades could continue the conquest of Egypt. The king's arguments fell on deaf ears. The ragtag soldiery wanted nothing more than to return home with their loot; they had no interest in risking life or limb defending an Egyptian city. As the sultan approached Alexandria, he was delighted to learn that the Christians were departing. Peter remained until the last possible moment, boarding his vessel only when the Egyptian forces entered the city.

News of the surrender of Alexandria was greeted with roars of indignation in Europe. Peter's reputation as a great crusader grew exponentially. Monarchs and barons bitterly lamented that there had been but one good and brave Christian at Alexandria, but aside from sympathy, they offered very little. Undeterred by the dispiriting failure, Peter launched a series of raids along the Syrian coast. In 1368, he returned to Europe in another attempt to raise a crusade. He was again received with every courtesy and honor but no help whatsoever. When Peter returned to Cyprus, he found the local barons seething over the vast sums he had spent on his crusading activities. Cyprus was also heir to the factionalism and intrigue of the crusader kingdom. Soon, a plot was hatched to remove the king, and Peter was assassinated in his bedchamber. The people of Europe cursed the treachery of the Cypriots and mourned the loss of their last crusader-king.

After the death of Peter I, Cyprus began its slow slide into ruin. A war with Genoa in the late fourteenth century was particularly destructive. In 1426, Mamluk Egypt attacked the island, captured the king, and forced the inhabitants to accept the sultan as their overlord. By that time, however, the island was in difficult economic straits. Aside from titles and a few ceremonies, almost nothing was left of the old crusader ways. In 1489, the island passed by inheritance to the Republic of Venice.

THE RISE OF THE OTTOMAN TURKS

Events in the East became more troubling with the rise of the Ottoman Turks. In the wake of the Mongol defeat of the Seljuk Turks in 1243, Seljuk rule declined and then shattered into an array of petty emirates. From the ashes of this chaos rose one emir, Osman, for whom the new dynasty was named. Osman established a solid government with well-disciplined troops. With them, he conquered the other emirates, including a good portion of Anatolia. After his death in 1326, his son, Orkhan, continued the expansion, conquering Nicaea and pressing on to the shores of the Bosporus. Across the water was Europe, and defending it, as always, was Constantinople.

Although restored to Byzantine rule, Constantinople had never recovered from the crusader sack of 1204. Since then, the city had lost more than 90 percent of its population. Its palaces and forums lay in ruin, and much of the city space was turned over to cultivation. The empire simply lacked the resources, organization, and will to support a grand and opulent capital city. Constantinople still had its mighty walls, however, and they had been kept in good repair. As long as the Byzantines opposed them, the Turks could go no further west.

Byzantium did not oppose them. During a civil war, John Cantacuzenus, a claimant to the imperial throne, allied with the Ottoman Turks. In 1348, he allowed them to cross over the Dardanelles into Europe. Cantacuzenus was successful in his bid for the throne, but he sealed the eventual fate of his empire. The gates to Europe, so long closed, were now wide open. In 1354, the Turks occupied Gallipoli and secured control of the straits. Waves of Turks began to cross over. All of Europe lay before them.

After Orkhan's death in 1360, the Ottomans began their European conquests in earnest. In 1361, they captured most of Thrace, including Adrianople, which became their capital in the West. By the end of the fourteenth century, they controlled all of Bulgaria and most of Greece. Constantinople itself was completely surrounded—a citizen could leave the empire simply by walking outside the city gates.

The rise of the Ottoman Turks and their successful campaigns to the West drastically changed the stakes in the crusading movement. It was no longer faraway Palestine that was in danger but western Europe itself. Crusaders had always seen themselves as fighting a defensive war, defending the Christians in the East, Jerusalem, or the faith. Now they were called on to defend themselves. Henceforth, crusades were no longer wars to expand Christendom but desperate attempts to slow the advance of Islam. Crusading had become a matter of simple survival.

The Ottoman conquests were not the only bad news for Europeans. After an extended stay in Avignon, the papacy at last returned to Rome, but only fitfully. By 1378, Christendom was split between two popes, one in Avignon and one in Rome. The Great Schism continued for more than thirty years, further degrading the image of the papacy. On top of that was the Black Death, which took the lives of at least one-third of the population. Few doubted that God was pouring down punishments on his sinful people and his fractured church. Calls for renewal and reform echoed across the countryside, as did calls for a crusade.

As in centuries past, France became the nexus of crusades in the late fourteenth century. Chivalric culture remained powerfully strong there, indeed, stronger than it had been in the High Middle Ages. The world was changing, however, and leaving the knight behind. Chivalry was already becoming just a literary device, spoon-fed to aristocrats with little serious experience in warfare. Nevertheless, it filled noble hearts with the desire to win glory on crusade, to slash down the infidel hordes with ease as the heroes in courtly romances did at every opportunity. Charles VI of France (1380–1422) was thoroughly committed to crusading, and he urged his vassals and members of his court to take up the cross. He wrote to Richard II of England (1377–99), suggesting that they both commit themselves to the defense of the faith. Because Richard did not so commit, neither did Charles, but many French did prepare to march in the footsteps of their ancestors.

In 1390, France joined with Genoa in a new crusade against Tunisia, the object of St. Louis's second crusade. They garnered the approval of one of the popes and set sail for Mahdia, a notorious refuge for Muslim pirates. The siege lasted almost ten days before the crusaders returned home, having accomplished nothing.

THE CRUSADE OF NICOPOLIS

Much larger was the Crusade of Nicopolis. In 1395, King Sigismund of Hungary (1387–1437) sent a desperate plea for assistance to the French court. Charles responded enthusiastically with money and men, and he urged his subjects to contribute their time and money to the cause. Both popes endorsed the proposed crusade and issued indulgences for whichever troops recognized them. Many Burgundian and German barons also joined the expedition. The troops rendezvoused in 1396 at Buda, where they were joined by Sigismund and his armies. It was an impressive force, one of the largest crusades ever assembled.

In a council of war, the king of Hungary argued for a cautious advance into Turkish territory, but the knights, eager to cover themselves with glory, would not hear of it. They wanted to follow the example of the First Crusade, fighting the infidel directly and winning conquests all the way to Jerusalem. The crusaders crossed the Danube into Bulgaria, where they took a few small towns. Next they laid siege to Nicopolis, a well-fortified town overlooking the Danube. Sultan Bayazid I (1389–1402) was prosecuting his own siege at Constantinople when he heard of Nicopolis's distress. At once, he marched his forces to meet the crusaders. The two sides had armies of equal size but unequal quality. Unlike the Christians, Bayazid's men were well disciplined and under a unified command. The sultan took up a position on a hill and waited. Sigismund again counseled caution, but the French and Burgundian knights insisted on an immediate attack. They also demanded the honor of leading the assault.

The thunder of the Frankish charge echoed in the valley outside Nicopolis as the brightly adorned knights galloped toward the Turkish lines. Quickly and decisively, they defeated the Turkish light cavalry. Beyond was a forest of wooden stakes driven into the soil to break up a charge. When the knights dismounted and began removing the stakes, archers approached and showered arrows down on them. The Franks fell ferociously on the archers, who ran up the hill to safety. On foot, the knights pursued them. As they crested the hill, they found an unexpected sight. Waiting for them was the sultan himself with his elite Turkish cavalry and Serbian army. The flower of chivalry turned tail and ran back down the hill, but it was too late. The Turks advanced in good order, crushing the crusading army. The defeat was total. Most of the crusaders were captured or killed; a few escaped into the woods. Those barons who could arrange ransoms were allowed to go free. The rest, about three thousand in all, were stripped naked, tied together with ropes, and led before Bayazid, where they were decapitated.

The destruction of the Crusade of Nicopolis was a devastating defeat for western Europe. Hungary lay virtually defenseless before the sultan's armies, and beyond that was the German Empire. For the first time, Europeans began to consider seriously what life would be like under Turkish occupation, in a world in which there were no Christian states. Prophecies circulated that all of Europe would be conquered by the Turks before a great warrior would rise up to defeat them. Yet, it was not a savior at home that spared Europe, but someone altogether different.

TIMUR

The rescuing monarch from the East did not look like the Prester John of legend, but his actions had a similar effect. Timur (Tamerlane) rose to power by violence and treachery in Transoxania. He was a Muslim, half Turkish and half Mongol. By 1360, he was ready to begin his own conquests, building a new empire from the scattered remains of the original Mongol conquests. With enormous brutality, he conquered Persia and invaded India. Behind him he left rivers of blood and towers of skulls. By 1399, he had returned to his capital at Samarkand and was examining the situation in the West. During Timur's campaigns, Bayazid and the Mamluk sultan of Egypt had seized some of his lands. He was determined to punish them for that. In 1400, he marched into Syria and stormed Aleppo. The following year, he captured Damascus. In 1402, he seized Baghdad, massacring twenty thousand of its inhabitants. That was enough for the Mamluks. The sultan offered his submission to Timur, promising to pay an annual tribute.

Sultan Bayazid had no intention of groveling before this Mongolian upstart. When Timur invaded Anatolia, Ottoman forces were waiting for him at Ankara. An epic battle took place on July 20, 1402. At the end of the day, the Turkish army was annihilated, and Bayazid himself had been captured and killed. The defeat was a stunning blow to the prestige and power of the Ottomans. The death of the sultan plunged the Turks into a destructive civil war. The Ottoman threat, for the moment, was neutralized. Satisfied, Timur began his planned invasion of China. On the march, in 1405, he died. Although it was by no means his intention, Timur's defeat of the Turks may well have saved Christendom.

In the West, there was no move to take advantage of the Turkish disarray. France, the traditional homeland of the crusades, was itself torn by civil war and on the brink of conquest by England. The Great Schism, which did not end until 1417, took up much of Christendom's attention, as did the problem of the Hussites, a heretical sect in Bohemia. A number of crusades were directed against the heretics, but none met with much success.

THE LAST YEARS OF THE BYZANTINE EMPIRE

Timur's defeat of the Ottomans gave a last-minute reprieve to the Byzantine Empire. Emperor Manuel II Palaeologus (1391–1425) seized every opportunity to bolster Byzantium's position while the Turks were down. He reclaimed Thessalonica as well as other areas in Greece. With extraordinary diplomatic skill, he became a central figure in the Ottoman dynastic disputes, playing various sides off the others while retaining pretenders to the sultan's throne in Constantinople as bargaining chips. He regularly requested aid from the West while dangling the promise of the reunion of the churches before both the Roman and Avignonese papal courts. Neither pope, however, was in a position to launch a major crusade.

By 1422, the embers of rebellion were dying down in the Ottoman Empire, and the aged Manuel II retired to a monastery. His son, John VIII (1421–48), quickly made poor decisions. Upon assuming full power, John promptly released and supported a rival to Sultan Murad II (1421–51). When the sultan defeated the pretender and solidified his control over the empire, he was obviously not well disposed to the Byzantines; indeed, he was determined to crush the troublesome Roman Empire once and for all. Byzantine ambassadors who attempted to convince Murad that it was all a misunderstanding were sent back to Constantinople with the ominous message, "Go and tell the emperor that I will be coming soon." On June 8, 1422, Murad began a massive attack along the Theodosian land walls of Constantinople. All the citizens of the capital, including women and children, manned the fortifications. Their heroic efforts saved their city. Despite his numbers, Murad had no effective means to deal with Constantinople's ancient fortifications. Sappers were useless against their sheer size. It was widely rumored among the Turks that the walls of Constantinople were made of solid steel.

The siege of 1422 made it clear to John that the empire could not survive without western aid. With the Great Schism at an end in Europe, a single pope could stir the forces of the West to come to the rescue of Byzantium. At least that is what the popes claimed. Military assistance, however, carried a price. Although the papacy was committed to preserving a Christian Constantinople, they rather doubted that the warriors of Europe could be stirred to fight for schismatics who did not recognize the primacy of Rome. John was eager for aid but reluctant to accept reunification with Rome, largely because he knew that his citizens were strongly opposed to it. When Murad captured Thessalonica in 1430 and imposed a naval blockade on Constantinople, the emperor realized that he no longer had any choice.

The Byzantine emperor, patriarch, and upper clergy traveled to the West to attend the Council of Florence in 1437. There the various questions of theology, authority, and ritual that separated East from West were honestly and frankly debated. But no amount of debate could change the basic calculus that the Byzantine Empire would fall without western help. At last, the emperor and patriarch accepted every position of the western church, including papal primacy. The reunification of the Christian church was solemnly decreed at the ecumenical council and joyfully celebrated across Europe.

The news was not so welcome in Constantinople. The Byzantine people were enraged when they discovered what their leaders were up to. The streets were filled with their cries of defiance, and they insisted that they would rather be conquered by the Turks than abjure their faith for the sake of western aid. If they embraced this agreement, many argued, God would not fail to punish their apostasy. Without popular approval, the reunification of the churches was nothing more than paper and ink. John VIII remained Catholic, as did his successor, Constantine XI, but the people, clergy, and patriarch were Greek Orthodox.

THE CRUSADE OF VARNA

Although the Byzantines did not make good on their part of the bargain, Pope Eugenius IV (1431–47) nevertheless worked energetically to send a crusade to their rescue. On January 1, 1443, he issued a crusade encyclical calling on the faithful to take up the cross and hurry to the defense of Byzantium. There was no response in central Europe. England and France were still locked in the Hundred Years War, and Germany had its own internal problems. The crusade was taken up by those states in eastern Europe for whom the Turkish threat was most dire: Poland, Wallachia, and Hungary. The Crusade of Varna, as it came to be called, was led by John Hunyadi, the ruler of Transylvania, and King Ladislas of Hungary. It enlisted a sizable force of approximately twenty thousand men. In 1444, the crusaders entered Serbia and captured Nish. In an attempt to neutralize the crusade, Murad opened negotiations with King Ladislas, offering Hungary a ten-year truce. Ladislas seized the opportunity and prepared to return home, but he was rebuked by the other crusaders and the papal legate. The latter absolved him from his oath of truce, and the crusade continued on its way, laying siege to Varna in Bulgaria. Angered by Ladislas's bad faith, the sultan led his troops to Varna, where he crushed the crusade. The papal legate and king of Hungary were killed in battle. Once again, a major crusade against the Ottomans had ended in humiliating defeat.

CRUSADING IN THE FIFTEENTH CENTURY

Two of the already weakened foundations of the crusading movement—a powerful and respected papacy and the culture of Christian chivalry—crumbled into dust in the fifteenth century. The papacy was discredited by its stay in Avignon and disgraced by the Great Schism. The wealth of the Renaissance popes and their support for distasteful abuses like indulgence sales further tarnished their image as the leaders of Christendom. Instead, the pope was increasingly viewed as just another ecclesiastical prince, exploiting the piety of the people for his own personal ends. Christian chivalry began a transformation in the fourteenth century. The fifteenth century saw further changes with the introduction of the longbow, the pike, and gunpowder, which made heavy mounted warriors militarily useless. As a result, the culture of chivalry became nothing more that a system of manners, a body of literature, and a collection of antiquarian pastimes. The warrior aristocracy of Europe was transforming itself into a landed gentry concerned with martial skill only in the most academic sense. Although they were still regaled with stories of glorious crusades, most of the nobility lacked the will or the means to take part in any such enterprise.

The Fall of Constantinople

The 2,206-year-old Roman state came to an end on May 29, 1453. The new Ottoman sultan, Mehmed II (1451–81), was determined to have Constantinople for his capital. After a two-month siege and round-the-clock artillery bombardment of the ancient walls, the city of the Caesars fell at last. The greatest Christian church in the world, Hagia Sophia, was turned into a mosque. News of the fall of Constantinople shook the West in a way that is hard to understand today. Dire predictions of the conquest of the city had circulated for more than a century, yet few took them seriously. Like the Byzantines, most Europeans believed that Christ and the Virgin would preserve the city from the Muslims. The Ottomans' repeated failures to capture it seemed to confirm this view. Following the loss of the greatest Christian city in the world, many asked themselves what would be next. Mehmed II left no doubt. He vowed that he would reunite the younger sister (Constantinople) with the elder sister (Rome), boasting that his horse would eat oats from the high altar of St. Peter's.

The loss of Constantinople meant that Latin Christendom now stood alone against the Ottoman Empire. The popes were determined to get the city back. Pope Nicholas V (1447–55) called a crusade to recapture Constantinople, and his successor, Calixtus III (1455–58) did the same. But the crowned heads of Europe were otherwise occupied, so no major crusade ever developed. John Hunyadi did save Belgrade in July 1456, when he led a crusade of Hungarians to break a Turkish siege of the city. The following year, a papal fleet occupied several Greek islands and captured some Turkish vessels. But that was all.

No pope felt more strongly about the reconquest of Constantinople than Pius II (1458–64). With extraordinary vigor, he succeeded in bringing representatives from most of Europe's states to a congress at Mantua in 1460. There they unanimously agreed that they should put aside their quarrels and launch a great crusade against the Turks. Altogether, the delegates promised eighty thousand troops for a three-year campaign. Nothing of the sort occurred. The monarchs of France and Germany had their own agendas at home, and they suspected the pope's motives were just as insincere. Pius, however, was sincere. He took the cross himself and, in 1464, prepared to depart for the East. When he arrived at Ancona to embark, he contracted the plague and died, waiting in vain for a crusade army that never materialized.

The Turks Land in Italy

Mehmed II kept busy consolidating his power in the Balkans and transforming Constantinople into the capital of a mighty empire once more. By 1480, he was finally in a position to make good on his threats against the West. He waged a two-front war on the Christians, launching large-scale attacks on Rhodes and the coast of Italy. The Hospitallers on Rhodes held out, but in Europe, Otranto fell, providing the sultan with an excellent beachhead to begin his invasion of Italy. Panic broke out in Rome as people packed their bags and fled the city. Pope Sixtus IV

(1471–84) at once issued a crusading bull, calling on all Christians to fight the Turks:

> [I]f the faithful, and especially the Italians, want to keep their lands, homes, wives, children, liberty, and the very faith in which we are baptized and reborn, let them believe us that they must now take up arms and go to war![2]

Despite the urgency of events, only the Italians took an interest in the pope's call. The dire emergency evaporated, though, when Mehmed II died on May 3, 1481. Turkish attention shifted to the inevitable struggle for power among the sultan's sons. A few months later, a papal fleet took advantage of the situation by recapturing Otranto.

Reconquest of Spain

One of the few places in which crusading news was good was Spain. In 1479, the two Christian Spanish states of Aragon and Castille united in the marriage of Ferdinand and Isabella. Their court was a place of martial splendor and crusading zeal. The knights of Spain committed themselves to crusading against the Spanish Muslims, just as their ancestors had done in previous centuries. They campaigned energetically throughout the 1480s. Finally, on January 2, 1492, Grenada, the last Muslim possession on the Iberian peninsula, surrendered. After seven centuries of warfare, the *reconquista* was complete. Christians across Europe rang church bells and marched in processions of thanksgiving. It was the first victory they had to celebrate in a very long time.

European Inaction

By the end of the fifteenth century, crusade preaching had fallen into a recognizable pattern. Popes wrote encyclicals and gave orations about the necessity of a crusade against the Turks. Monarchs expressed the desire, often sincere, to join in the enterprise, but they insisted on a peace in Europe favorable to themselves. Popes then acted as international referees, trying to mediate Europe's internal disputes, but the task was thankless and nearly impossible. Everyone knew that the stakes were enormous, for Christendom itself seemed on the brink of extinction. There was widespread frustration that Europeans could not shake themselves from their petty quarrels long enough to defend against the wolf at the door. These sentiments were expressed in one of the most popular books of the time, Sebastian Brant's *The Ship of Fools,* first published in 1494 and subsequently translated into most of Europe's languages. In a chapter titled "Of the Decline of the Faith," Brant echoed the thoughts of isolation, despair, and fear that plagued Christians:

> Our faith was strong in th' Orient,
> It ruled in all of Asia,
> In Moorish lands and Africa.
> But now for us these lands are gone,
> 'Twould even grieve the hardest stone.
>
> . . .
>
> We perish sleeping one and all,
> The wolf has come into the stall
> And steals the Holy Church's sheep
> The while the shepherd lies asleep.
> Four sisters of our Church you find,
> They're of the patriarchic kind:
> Constantinople, Alexandria,
> Jerusalem, Antiochia,
> But they've been forfeited and sacked
> And soon the head will be attacked.[3]

CRUSADE PLANS OF LEO X

The final serious attempt to launch a major crusade to the East occurred on the very eve of the Protestant Reformation. Pope Leo X (1513–21) believed that he had no greater task than to organize the defense of Latin Christendom. Sultan Selim I ("the Grim") (1512–20) was among the most ruthless and effective rulers of the Ottoman Empire. His name struck fear in the hearts of Christians, for they knew of his plans to conquer Europe. Leo invoked Selim's name when he wrote to Europe's leaders begging them to put aside their disputes and make ready to take up the cross of Christ. The new king of France, Francis I (1515–47), expressed youthful, bold, and probably sincere promises to put the resources of his kingdom at the disposal of the crusade. In the interim, he requested and received Leo's permission to tax the French clergy for the crusade. Overjoyed, the pope wrote to King Henry VIII of England (1491–1547), Maximilian I of the German Empire (1486–1519), Charles I of Spain and the Netherlands (1516–56), and Manuel I of Portugal (1495–1521), urging them to join with Francis in this holy enterprise. All the monarchs were enthusiastic about the crusade, but not about Francis. They doubted his sincerity, suggesting that he was interested only in collecting tithes. Maximilian even proposed that Germany, England, and Spain should organize their own crusade, which could then conquer France before heading off to the East.

The urgency for a crusade was ratcheted up in 1517, when, in the space of two years, Selim and his armies conquered Syria and Egypt. The Ottoman Empire was now truly massive, encompassing the entire eastern Mediterranean. Europeans were terrified. All the monarchs reiterated their firm intention to crusade, but all insisted that a truce must first be in place. As Henry VIII told a Venetian ambassador in his court:

> No general expedition against the Turks will ever be effected so long as such treachery prevails among the Christian powers, that their sole thought is to destroy one another; and I think how I could quit this kingdom when such ill will is borne me by certain persons.[4]

To get the ball rolling, Leo appointed a committee of cardinals to gather data concerning Ottoman movements and make recommendations for a general crusade. The committee finished its work efficiently and in a timely fashion. It recommended that a universal truce be imposed on Europe that would last until six months after the crusade ended. Because it was clear that the kingdoms would not line up behind one ruler, the committee proposed two great armies, one led by the Holy Roman Emperor and one by the king of France. As in the Second Crusade, the two forces would work separately but cooperatively. The army should consist of a minimum of sixty thousand infantry, drawn from Germany, Spain, and Bohemia. In addition, four thousand cavalry would come from Italy and France, and another twelve thousand light cavalry from Spain, Italy, Dalmatia, and Greece. The crusader fleet would be donated by Venice, Genoa, France, Brittany, Portugal, and England and

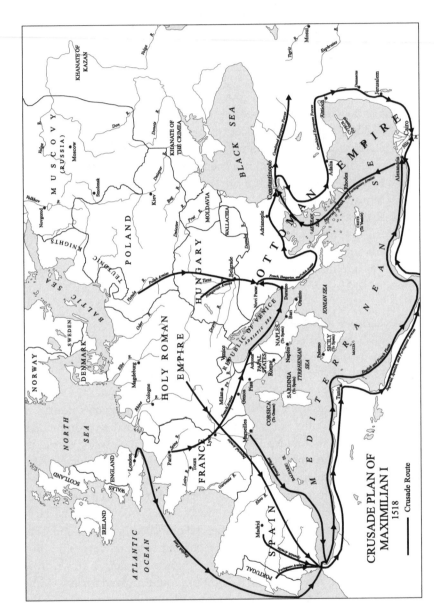

Map 14.   Crusade Plan of Maximilian I, 1518

would be under the joint command of the kings of England and Portugal. The land forces should march into Italy and assemble at Ancona and Brindisi, where the fleet would ferry them across to Durazzo. From there, they could follow the ancient *via Egnatia* straight to Constantinople. They reckoned the total cost of the expedition at eight million ducats. A general ecclesiastical tithe could pay part of the sum; the rest would come from the kings and barons, who, after all, had the most to lose if the Turks conquered Europe.

Francis committed himself and his armies fully to the plan and began collecting the new clerical tithes without delay. Maximilian offered a more ambitious counterproposal. He suggested that the crusade be organized along a three-year plan. In the first year, he, Charles of Spain, and Manuel of Portugal would land in North Africa and begin marching east. With naval support from England and France, Maximilian felt certain they could conquer Egypt within the year. Meanwhile, an army of Hungarians, Poles, and other east Europeans would attack the Turks in the Balkans. The second year, Francis and his armies would march to Ancona, as the papal commission suggested, and sail to Durazzo. They would then meet the Hungarian and Polish troops at Novi Pazar and conquer all of Greece. The third year, they would close the trap. The French, Hungarian, and Polish troops would besiege Constantinople by land, and the German, Spanish, and Portuguese would surround it on the sea. When the capital surrendered, they would join into one huge army and push the Turks out of Anatolia and Syria. In three years, Maximilian proposed undoing the Muslim conquests of the last millennium.

In March 1518, Leo proclaimed a five-year truce in Europe. England and Venice ratified it immediately. The pope sent legates to France, Germany, Spain, and England to oversee crusade preparations. A tangible excitement filled the courts of Europe, particularly that of England. Young Henry VIII and his Lord Chancellor Cardinal Wolsey were dead serious about getting the crusade on its feet. Wolsey realized that for a truce to be taken seriously, it must rest on more than just papal words; it would have to be hammered out among Europe's most powerful states. He rightly saw that France was the greatest obstacle to such a truce. Without papal assistance, Wolsey negotiated a peace between France and England as a precursor to a universal peace. On October 3, 1518, the French and English were the first to sign Wolsey's Treaty of London, which proclaimed an eternal peace throughout Christendom. Signatories agreed to attack in unison any other signatory that broke the general peace. The pope was overjoyed. In his ratification of the treaty, he proclaimed, "Be glad and rejoice, O Jerusalem, for now your deliverance can be hoped for!" Within a year, twenty-five princes had signed the peace treaty. In gratitude, Leo granted Cardinal Wolsey full authority over the forming crusade.

It seemed that at last the states of Europe would organize a powerful crusade against the Turks. A summit meeting between Francis I and Henry VIII was scheduled, and all countries were informed that they should send ambassadors to the meeting to coordinate preparations for the expedition. But, on January 12, 1519, Emperor Maximilian I died, and the crusade died with him as Europe was plunged into a struggle of imperial succession. Charles I and Francis I wanted the imperial crown, and both promised to lead even greater crusades against the Turks if they got it. The reality was rather different. Whichever monarch won the German throne would hardly be on good terms with the loser, and Europe would again be divided. All of Wolsey's work was for nothing. Pope Leo watched in horror as this bold new crusade became merely a tool of political rhetoric.

When King Charles I became Emperor Charles V (1519–58), Francis washed his hands of everyone and everything. Within a few years, he had allied France with the Ottoman Empire, an alliance that was to last for centuries. The homeland of the crusades was now in league with the infidel. Leo continued to promote the crusade to Charles V, but even the pope abandoned it in 1520 when news of Selim's death arrived in Rome. The new sultan, Suleiman, was known to be a quiet and scholarly man committed to peace. All of Europe breathed a sigh of relief.

Europe was wrong—the new sultan was quiet and scholarly, but not peaceful. Suleiman the Magnificent (1520–66) was the most dangerous foe the West had ever faced. He brought the Ottoman Empire to new heights of prosperity while pursuing an aggressive policy of conquest. In 1521, he captured Belgrade. The next year, he began a massive naval bombardment of the Hospitallers at Rhodes. With their fortresses in ruins, the knights were allowed to leave the island with honor, but it was a bitter defeat for the West. Suleiman decisively defeated Christian armies at the battle of Mohács in 1526, opening the way for him to besiege Vienna in 1529. The battle was close, but Vienna held out. Had it fallen, all of Germany would have been at the mercy of the Turkish armies.

The Protestants, the Turks, and the Crusades

Pope Leo X was so involved in preserving Christendom from the dire threat to the east that he failed to recognize the greater danger from within. In 1517, Martin Luther, an Augustinian friar and professor of theology at the University of Wittenburg, published his famous Ninety-Five Theses. Within a few years, a "monkish quarrel" had developed into a widespread break with the church in Saxony and northern Germany. With the help of the printing press, Luther's ideas spread quickly across Europe, inspiring other reformers to devise their own brands of Christianity. Western Europe was already fractured along national lines; the Protestant Reformation now shredded it along religious ones as well.

The Protestants and the Turks had a mutually beneficial, although unintentional, relationship. The Turkish threat distracted the pope and the Holy Roman Emperor long enough for Luther to nurture his movement and secure his position. Because of his wars with the Turks and their allies, Charles V was unable to remove Protestantism from his northern domains. As Kenneth Setton has noted, "without them [the Turks], Protestantism might conceivably have gone the way of Albigensianism."[5] Simply put, the Turkish threat allowed the Protestants to flourish.

The Turks benefited from the arrangement as well. Within a few decades, much of Europe was lost to the Catholic church. For Protestants, crusading was impossible, for it presupposed obedience to the pope, the unity of Christendom, and the spiritual benefits of indulgences. The religious division of Europe was the best possible news for the Turks because it removed the ever-present threat of a major crusade. It was said that when Suleiman learned of Martin Luther, he expressed an interest in protecting him. When Luther heard this, he hastily crossed himself and asked God to save him from such a "gracious lord," but whether Luther knew it or not, Suleiman was indeed his protector.

Luther set the tone for Protestant thought on the Turkish threat. When Leo X was still trying to resurrect his crusade in 1520, Luther wrote that "to fight against the Turks is to oppose the judgement God visits upon our iniquities through them."[6] In Luther's view, crusades against the Ottomans were wars against God. Not only were they ineffectual, he contended, but they also helped the evil institution of the Catholic church. In 1521, he wrote:

How shamefully the pope has this long time baited us with the war against the Turks, gotten our money, destroyed so many Christians and made so much mischief! When will we learn that the pope is the devil's most dangerous cat's paw?[7]

After the siege of Vienna in 1529, the Turkish threat became much more dire to Germans, and so Luther changed his mind. In letters, he urged Christian princes to set aside their quarrels and take up their swords against the Muslims. He envisioned a great army of Catholic and Protestant troops marching to the East, called not by papal encyclical but by Luther's own pamphlets and letters. Still, what Luther was preaching was a secular war, not a religious one, and it was by no means a crusade. As he wrote:

If in my turn I were a soldier and saw in the battlefield a priest's banner or cross, even if it were the very crucifix, I should want to run away as though the devil were chasing me![8]

As the greatest source of disunity in Europe, Luther's calls for unity went nowhere.

HOLY LEAGUES

After the Protestant Reformation, crusades were naturally confined to Catholic Europe. In some cases, crusade status was given to religious wars between Catholics and Protestants, but the East was not forgotten. Popes routinely called for peace in Europe to prepare for crusades against the Turks. They had some success in negotiating new crusades with other Catholic states, which now took the form of Holy Leagues. Aside from the papacy, the greatest champions of crusades to the East were the Spanish and the Venetians. France, which remained Catholic, wanted nothing to do with wars against its ally, the sultan.

Several leagues bankrolled by the popes had limited successes against the Turks. The greatest victory, however, came in 1571, when a Holy League of the papacy, Spain, and Venice launched an armada of more than two hundred vessels carrying approximately thirty thousand men. On October 7, the fleet engaged a Turkish fleet of 275 vessels at Lepanto and destroyed it utterly. The Battle of Lepanto was the first major victory Christians had ever scored against the Ottoman Turks. Although the sultan was able to build an even larger fleet within a year, the news of his defeat gave a psychological boost to all Europeans, Catholic and Protestant. The Turks were no longer invincible.

The rhetoric of crusade in Catholic Europe continued during the seventeenth century, but it was rarely more than that. Wars that acquired the moniker of a crusade, such as the attack by the Holy League of Poland, Germany, and Venice against the Turks in 1684, were actions that would have occurred without an indulgence. In any event, by the late seventeenth century the Turks were no longer a serious threat to Europe. Indeed, no power on earth was a serious threat to Europeans, who were expanding on a planetary scale.

THE FATE OF THE MILITARY ORDERS

The last tangible vestige of the crusades can be found in the military orders, most prominently the Knights Hospitaller of St. John and the Teutonic Knights. After Suleiman ejected the Hospitallers from Rhodes in 1522, Charles V donated the island of Malta to them. In this way, the Knights of Rhodes became the Knights of Malta. Suleiman later pursued them, laying siege to Malta in 1565. Against all odds, the knights not only held the island but also dealt a harsh blow to the Turkish navy. They followed up this victory by sending a fleet to take part in the Battle of Lepanto in 1571. The Knights of Malta never abandoned their mission to the poor and sick. On Malta, they built a great hospital in the capital city of Valletta that attracted patients from across Europe. They remained militarily active into the seventeenth century, but after that their numbers dropped as the need for their services evaporated. By the eighteenth century, the Hospitallers were little more than rulers of an island. On June 13, 1798, Napoleon captured Malta and expelled the knights. Their military function was forever finished. After the defeat of Napoleon, the order attempted to regain its island home, but it was given to Great Britain instead. Thus, in 1834 the order permanently established itself in Rome, becoming a government without a country. The order still exists. In Rome, it issues passports, and the Vatican and a few other Catholic states recognize it as a sovereign state. More important, across the globe the Knights of Malta still devote themselves to the care of the poor and the sick.

The Teutonic Knights began to decline after the combined armies of Poland and Lithuania defeated them in 1410. Over the course of the fifteenth century, their Baltic holdings began to peel away one by one. When the Protestant Reformation swept through northern Europe, there was no longer room for a crusading order ruling a prosperous state. In 1525, the grand master, under Protestant influence, dissolved the order in Prussia and took the lands for himself as a vassal of the Polish crown. The knights' other properties in Europe were taken from them by various secular leaders over the course of the following centuries. By the beginning of the nineteenth century, the Teutonic Knights were reduced to only a few tiny holdings in Austria. In 1809, the order was dissolved, yet it survived. In 1834, the emperor re-established the order, headquartering it in Vienna, where it remains today. Henceforth, it was to be a religious institution. New rules were approved for the order by the Holy See in 1871 and 1929. Today, the Teutonic Knights are dedicated to charitable work and care for the sick.

In the fullness of time, the history of the last crusading orders, the Knights Hospitaller and the Teutonic Knights, came full circle. Both were founded by selfless people to care for the sick and the "holy poor." Both later embraced holy war, carving out independent states and exercising significant worldly power. Today, both are shorn of those states, yet they continue to carry out their original mission—caring for the least of Christ's brothers and sisters.

NOTES

1. Gabrieli, *Arab Historians of the Crusades,* 346.

2. Kenneth M. Setton, *Papacy and the Levant (1204–1571),* vol. 2 (Philadelphia: American Philosophical Society, 1978), 364.

3. Sebastian Brant, *The Ship of Fools,* trans. Edwin H. Zedel (New York: Columbia University Press, 1944), 316–18.

4. *Four Years at the Court of Henry VIII,* trans. Rawdon Brown (London: 1854), 58.

5. Quoted in Kenneth M. Setton, "Lutheranism and the Turkish Peril," *Balkan Studies* 3 (1962): 133.

6. Ibid., 142.

7. Ibid.

8. Ibid., 150.

AFTERWORD

For medieval men and women, the crusade was an act of piety, charity, and love, but it was also a means of defending their world, their culture, and their way of life. It is not surprising, then, that the crusades lost their appeal when Christians no longer identified themselves first and foremost as members of one body of Christ. By the sixteenth century, Europe was dividing itself along political rather than religious lines. In that new world, the crusade had no place.

It is easy for modern people to dismiss the crusades as morally repugnant, cynically evil, or, as Runciman summed them up, "nothing more than a long act of intolerance in the name of God."[1] Such judgments, however, tell us more about the observer than the observed. They are based on uniquely modern (and, therefore, Western) values. If, from the safety of our desks, we are quick to condemn the medieval crusader, we should be mindful that he would be just as quick to condemn us. Our infinitely more destructive wars waged for the sake of political and social ideologies would, in his opinion, be lamentable wastes of human life. In both societies, the medieval and the modern, people fight for what is most dear to them. That is a fact of human nature that is not so changeable.

It is common today to brand the crusades a failure even at attaining their original goals. Jerusalem was conquered, it is often asserted, but the crusader kingdom was short-lived. It may seem so from our own day, but it is not so. Jerusalem remained in crusader hands for eighty-eight years, and the kingdom lasted in Palestine for 192 years. By any measure of human institutions, that is a long time. Many countries today have shorter histories. The planting of the crusader states was not a fleeting show but the creation of a new entity in the Middle East—one that would remain pivotal for almost two centuries.

The other goal of the crusades was the defense of the Christian East, and many believe that they failed most dramatically at this. It is certainly true that the crusades did not do much for mutual understanding. The sack of Constantinople by the Fourth Crusade in 1204 closed an iron door between the Catholic West and Orthodox East. So great was the hatred engendered by this event that even when the Byzantines faced the extinction of their state, they preferred Turkish conquest to union with the pope in Rome. We cannot say with certainty, as some do, that the crusades actually shortened the life of the Byzantine Empire. The crusader kingdoms not only distracted Muslim powers; they also formed a buffer between the Arabs and Turks and the vulnerable Byzantine Empire. It is true that the Fourth Crusade did immeasurable damage to the city of Constantinople, but it was Byzantium's subsequent weakness that made the damage permanent. It cannot be said (although it often is said) that the conquest of Constantinople in 1204 was responsible for the fall of the empire in 1453: Byzantium survived for 249 years after it regained its capital. It is in those years that the seeds of the empire's downfall can be found. Despite the many tragedies, the crusades may well have added years to the life span of the Byzantine Empire.

For good or ill, the crusading movement did have long-term effects. In the judgment of Enlightenment historian Edward Gibbon, the crusades sapped wealth from western Europe, as well as human lives that would have been better spent at home working hard and fostering friendly relations with the Muslim world. Like all scholars of that era, Gibbon saw medieval Christianity as a vile superstition, and those who fought for it as ignorant or deceived. It is highly questionable, however, whether Europeans would have beaten their swords into plowshares merely because they lacked an external enemy. More likely, they simply would have continued to wage internal warfare with greater vigor. Given the steady Muslim conquest of Christian lands over the centuries, it also seems unlikely that good relations could have been forged between the two religions without first establishing firm and secure borders.

There can be little doubt that the crusades slowed the advance of Islam, although how much is an open question. The presence of the crusader states in the Near East for almost two centuries certainly destabilized Muslim power and therefore hindered unification into a single Islamic state. Even the crusades that failed or did not materialize forced Muslim powers to divert resources from conquest to their own defense. At the very least, then, the crusades bought western Europe some time. Judging by the number of occasions on which it narrowly escaped Turkish invasion in the fifteenth and sixteenth centuries, Europe had need of that time.

In a less direct sense, the crusades did play a part in the eventual neutralization of the Muslim threat. In Spain, where traditional crusade chivalry lasted longer than anywhere else, veterans of the *reconquista* and crusades in North Africa became the conquistadors of the New World. Although the conquests of Mexico and Peru were not themselves crusades, crusading culture played a crucial role in them. Popes, Spanish monarchs, and conquistadors naturally viewed the people of the New World through the lens of four centuries of crusading. The conquistadors were warriors of Christ in an infidel land. There, they carved out new Christian states. Without hesitation, they raised their swords against the barbaric cruelties of Aztec human sacrifice, which, they were convinced, were Satanic in origin. They also were desirous of booty, which the New World had in abundance. These facts all match well-established characteristics of the crusades.

Spanish galleons laden with New World gold and silver financed more than one Holy League against the Turks. More than that, the new wealth, coupled with a rise in industrial technology, allowed Europe to purchase raw materials from the Ottomans and sell back to them finished goods at bargain prices. The resulting trade deficit, along with the repeated failure of the Ottoman Empire to embrace technological advances in anything other than military applications, ultimately doomed the Turkish economy. Europe never did win a decisive war against the Turks until World War I, when the Ottoman Empire was already a dilapidated shell. Instead, unable to compete with Europe's skyrocketing economy, the Ottoman Empire slowly bled to death. In the end, the discovery and exploitation of the New World not only saved western Europe but also propelled it to world hegemony. The Muslim threat was neutralized not by the crusades to the East, but by those to the West.

NOTE

1. Steven Runciman, *A History of the Crusades,* vol. 3 (Cambridge: Cambridge University Press, 1951–54), 480.

GLOSSARY

Abbasid: Sunni Arab dynasty in Iraq and Baghdad, 750–1258, and in Cairo, 1261–1517.

Almohads: Muslim rulers in Northwest Africa, 1130–1269.

Almoravids: Muslim Berber rulers in Northwest Africa, 1056–1147.

Anatolia: *See* Asia Minor.

Asia Minor: A peninsula of western Asia between the Black Sea and the Mediterranean Sea. Also called Anatolia.

Assassins: Secret order of Muslim extremists and terrorists.

Atabeg: Originally a Turkish regent, it came to mean an actual ruler.

Ayyubid: Muslim dynasty in Egypt and Syria founded by Saladin.

Benefice: Land tenure associated with an ecclesiastical or secular office.

Bezant: Gold coin of the Byzantine Empire.

Caliph: Literally "successor." The title of the supreme ruler of the Islamic state.

Canon Law: Law of the church.

Dalmatia: Lands on the eastern shore of the Adriatic Sea.

Danishmend: Turkish dynasty that ruled in central and northeastern Anatolia from about 1071 to 1178.

Emir: Turkish local governor or commander in the field.

Excommunication: Ecclesiastical sanction barring one from the sacraments. An excommunicate was to be avoided by all Christians.

Fatimids: Shi'ite dynasty in Egypt, North Africa, and Syria, 909–1171.

Fief: Land or incomes given by a feudal lord to a vassal in return for military service and fealty.

Frank: Originally the name of a Germanic tribe of the Rhine region, the name was used by Byzantines and Muslims in the Middle Ages to refer to most western Europeans.

German Empire: *See* Holy Roman Empire.

217

Great Schism: Period when two popes claimed sovereignty over the church, 1378–1417. One pope resided in Rome and the other in Avignon.

Greek Fire: A petroleum based mixture used by Byzantines and later others to set fire to the surface of the water, thus engulfing vessels. It could be thrown in pots or expelled through copper tubes. Because the secret of the mixture was so closely guarded, its composition is still not known with certainty.

Hagia Sophia: "Church of the Holy Wisdom." Enormous church built by Emperor Justinian I in Constantinople. Completed in 537.

Hohenstaufen: Ruling family in the German Empire, 1125–1250.

Holy Roman Empire: Loosely organized state encompassing central Europe and northern Italy. Ruled by a German king, who could be crowned emperor by a pope. Also called German Empire.

Hospitallers: The Order of the Hospital of St. John of Jerusalem.

Imam: Muslim religious leader.

Interdict: Ecclesiastical sanction barring the administration of sacraments in a defined region.

Jihad: Muslim holy war or struggle against infidels.

Khorezmians: Formerly holding an empire stretching from Persia to Samarkand, they were displaced by Genghis Khan. When their shah died in 1231, leaderless Khorezmian troops migrated in Mesopotamia and Syria.

Legate: *See* papal legate.

Mangonel: A form of catapult used in medieval sieges.

Mark: Approximately 8 ounces (usually of silver).

Normans: Originally Scandinavian people who settled in southern Italy and Sicily, as well as northern France and elsewhere.

Outremer: "Across the sea." French term for the Levant.

Papal legate: One who is empowered to act in the name of the pope.

Patriarchates: The five major episcopal sees of Christianity in the ancient and late ancient world. They were Rome, Antioch, Alexandria, Jerusalem, and Constantinople.

Pechenegs: Nomadic Turkic people who occupied the steppes north of the Black Sea.

Schism: Division in the church. *See* Great Schism.

Seljuks: Sunni Turks who conquered Iran and Iraq before invading Syria and Asia Minor.

Shia: Minority Muslim sect that recognizes Ali and his successors as the legitimate rulers of Islam.

Sultan: Muslim ruler, usually independent.

Sunni: Majority Muslim sect.

Vassal: One who swears fealty and military service to a feudal lord in return for land tenure or money.

Veneto: Lands bordering Venice.

Vizier: Muslim official, often with effective powers approaching or even exceeding those of the ruler.

Wends: Pagan Slavs who settled along the Baltic Sea.

SELECT BIBLIOGRAPHY

Scholarly interest in the crusades has exploded over the course of the last few decades, and there appears to be no end in sight. As of this writing, the Society for the Study of the Crusades and the Latin East, a professional organization devoted to crusade studies, has 435 members in 31 countries. The amount of scholarly literature produced each year is staggering. For that reason, I have limited myself in this essay to mentioning only the most important works published in the recent past. The footnotes and bibliographies in these books will lead interested readers to older or more specialized studies.

General histories of the crusades have proliferated at a rapid rate. The best known of these is Sir Steven Runciman's three-volume *A History of the Crusades* (Cambridge: Cambridge University Press, 1951–54). Runciman provides a compelling and beautifully written narration of the crusading movement from the Council of Clermont to the fall of Acre. In an epilogue, he also mentions crusades up to the fall of Constantinople in 1453. Runciman is best when discussing the First Crusade and the history of the crusader states; errors appear more frequently when he reaches the thirteenth century. Throughout his history, he sees Byzantium in the best possible light. Despite its age, this work remains widely available and influential. Hans Eberhard Mayer's *The Crusades,* 2d ed., trans. John Gillingham (Oxford: Oxford University Press, 1988) is a well-written synthesis of the crusades within the traditional chronological framework. Mayer puts special emphasis on the history of the Latin East. Jean Richard's *The Crusades, c. 1071– c. 1291,* trans. Jean Birrell (Cambridge: Cambridge University Press, 1999) also approaches the crusades from the traditional emphasis on expeditions to the East before 1291. The more expansive view of the crusading movement is presented by Jonathan Riley-Smith in *The Crusades: A Short History* (New Haven,

Conn.: Yale University Press, 1987). Riley-Smith manages to touch on almost every aspect of crusading within the space of a single volume. Eschewing the traditional organization of crusade history into major expeditions, he tackles the subject by describing the birth, maturity, and death of the movement. The largest collection of crusade scholarship can be found in *A History of the Crusades,* 6 vols., ed. Kenneth M. Setton (Madison: University of Wisconsin Press, 1958–89). This compendium has chapters on almost every subject discussed in this book. Because the chapters are written by various authors, they are necessarily of uneven quality; some are excellent, others forgettable.

The starting point for all studies on the idea of the crusade is Carl Erdmann's *Origins of the Idea of the Crusade* (Stuttgart: W. Kohlhammer, 1935; English trans., Princeton: Princeton University Press, 1977). Although the "Erdmann Thesis" is the subject of recent debate, it remains the foundation for discussion. Whereas Erdmann attempted to understand what factors led to the development of the crusading idea, Paul Alphandéry in *La chrétienté et l'idée de croisade,* 2 vols. (Paris: Albin Michel, 1954–59) examines the development of the idea within the context of medieval Christianity, particularly the concepts of the humanity of Christ and the expectation of the Last Judgment. Alphandéry stresses the uniquely medieval nature of the crusades and scorns the imposition of modern stereotypes on people of the past. James A. Brundage examines the crusade's legal underpinnings, including the crusader's vow, obligations, and privileges, in *Medieval Law and the Crusader* (Madison: University of Wisconsin Press, 1969). Jonathan Riley-Smith emphasizes the pious idealism that lay behind crusader motivations in his informative little book *What Were the Crusades?* (Totowa, N.J.: Rowman & Littlefield, 1977). In a seminal article, "Crusading as an Act of Love," *History* 65 (1980): 177–92, Riley-Smith delves into the crusade propaganda behind the pious idealism, noting that it stressed Christian charity and fraternal love while omitting reference to the love of one's enemies. Crusade preaching is described by Penny J. Cole in *The Preaching of the Crusades to the Holy Land, 1095–1270* (Cambridge, Mass.: Medieval Academy of America, 1991) and by Christoph T. Maier in *Preaching the Crusade: Mendicant Friars and the Cross in the Thirteenth Century* (Cambridge: Cambridge University Press, 1994). Two works examine other aspects of crusader motivations: Paul Rousset, *Histoire d'une idéologie: La croisade* (Lausanne: L'age d'homme, 1983), and Benjamin Z. Kedar, *Crusade and Mission: Eu-*

ropean Approaches toward the Muslims (Princeton: Princeton University Press, 1984). Kedar's study is particularly interesting, for it seeks to understand the relationship between the crusades and missions of conversion. Elizabeth Siberry's *Criticism of Crusading, 1095–1274* (Oxford: Clarendon, 1985) looks at Europe's favorable and unfavorable reactions to the crusades. Finally, Christopher Tyerman's *The Invention of the Crusades* (Toronto: University of Toronto Press, 1998) challenges, not altogether successfully, the whole notion of the crusades before the thirteenth century.

Scholarship on medieval Spain is vibrant, but much work remains to be done on the *reconquista* and its relationship to the larger crusading movement. The only monograph on the subject is Derek W. Lomax's *The Reconquest of Spain* (New York: Longman, 1978). Robert I. Burns has written a number of studies on local portions of the religious wars. Among the best is *The Crusader Kingdom of Valencia,* 2 vols. (Cambridge: Harvard University Press, 1967). Of similar importance are Bernard F. Reilly, *The Contest of Christian and Muslim Spain, 1031–1157* (Cambridge, Mass.: Blackwell, 1992), and Olivia R. Constable, *Trade and Traders in Medieval Spain* (Philadelphia: University of Pennsylvania Press, 1994).

No crusade has been studied more than the First Crusade. There are hundreds of books on the campaign, the participants, and the implications of the expedition. Among the best recent works is Jonathan Riley-Smith's *The First Crusade and the Idea of Crusading* (Philadelphia: University of Pennsylvania Press, 1986). This excellent short study emphasizes the motivations of the various crusaders and the conditions they experienced during the campaign. It is by no means, however, a military history. For that, one should consult the first-rate work by John France, *Victory in the East: A Military History of the First Crusade* (Cambridge: Cambridge University Press, 1994). Robert Chazan's *In the Year 1096: The First Crusade and the Jews* (Philadelphia: Jewish Publication Society, 1996) zeroes in on the motivations, extent, and aftermath of the anti-Jewish massacres in the wake of the "People's Crusade." In a somewhat controversial thesis, Marcus Bull argues in *Knightly Piety and the Lay Response to the First Crusade: Limousin and Gascony, c. 970–c. 1130* (Oxford: Clarendon, 1993) that scholars have misunderstood the motivations of the lay crusaders because of their reliance on ecclesiastical sources. Bull believes that lay piety and the close relationship between the laity and religious orders at the local level explains better the response to the call of Urban II.

Most recently, Jonathan Riley-Smith, in *The First Crusaders, 1095–1131* (Cambridge: Cambridge University Press, 1997), has brought the fruits of his many years of cartulary studies to bear on fundamental questions about the identity and character of those who took the cross.

There exist many excellent histories of the Latin Kingdom of Jerusalem. The old, but still useful, standard is D. C. Munro's *The Kingdom of the Crusaders* (New York: D. Appleton-Century, 1935). Another excellent introduction is Jean Richard's *The Latin Kingdom of Jerusalem*, trans. Janet Shirley (New York: North Holland, 1979).

A number of studies have examined the relationship of the crusader states to outside powers. Joshua Prawer, in *The Latin Kingdom of Jerusalem: European Colonialism in the Middle Ages* (London: Weidenfeld and Nicolson, 1972), approaches the Franks from the perspective of their relations with the Muslim majority. Of related interest is Ronnie Ellenblum's *Frankish Rural Settlement in the Latin Kingdom of Jerusalem* (Cambridge: Cambridge University Press, 1998). Ralph-Johannes Lilie, in *Byzantium and the Crusader States, 1096–1204*, trans. J. C. Morris and Jean E. Ridings (Oxford: Clarendon, 1993), uncovers the importance of the crusaders' relationship with Constantinople. Jonathan Phillips, in *Defenders of the Holy Land: Relations between the Latin East and the West, 1119–1187* (Oxford: Clarendon, 1996), looks at contacts between the Latin East and western Europe, also touching on their relationship with Byzantium.

Military histories of the Latin East can be found in the classic study by R. C. Smail, *Crusading Warfare, 1097–1193*, 2d ed. (Cambridge: Cambridge University Press, 1995), as well as in Christopher Marshall's *Warfare in the Latin East, 1192–1291* (Cambridge: Cambridge University Press, 1992), which deals with the second century of the kingdom's history. Hugh Kennedy's *Crusader Castles* (Cambridge: Cambridge University Press, 1994) expertly describes the role of massive strongholds in the East and describes the citadels themselves. Jaroslav Folda's beautiful volume, *The Art of the Crusaders in the Holy Land, 1098–1187* (Cambridge: Cambridge University Press, 1995), explores the artistic component of this unique society.

Many books have been written on the Knights Templar, but only a few are good. The best history of the order is Malcolm Barber's *The New Knighthood: A History of the Order of the Temple* (Cambridge: Cambridge University Press, 1994). Building on his copious work on medieval chivalry, Barber presents a balanced and learned history of the Templars. Peter Partner, in *The Murdered Magicians: The Templars and Their Myth* (Oxford: Oxford University Press, 1982), provides a much more concise history of the order; he is more concerned with the growth of Templar legends. Unlike Barber, Partner discounts the idea that Philip IV moved against the Templars for their money. The best history of the medieval Hospitallers is Jonathan Riley-Smith's *The Knights of St. John in Jerusalem and Cyprus, c. 1050–1310* (New York: St. Martin's, 1967). For the activities of the Teutonic Knights in northern Europe, see Eric Christiansen, *The Northern Crusades: The Baltic and Catholic Frontier, 1100–1525,* 2d ed. (New York: Penguin, 1997), and William Urban, *The Baltic Crusade,* 2d ed. (Chicago: Lithuanian Research and Studies Center, 1994).

No monograph exists on the Second Crusade; indeed, scholarship on the event outside Cistercian studies is very sparse. The best study remains Giles Constable's important article, "The Second Crusade as Seen by Contemporaries," *Traditio* 9 (1953): 213–79. *The Second Crusade and the Cistercians,* ed. Michael Gervers (New York: St. Martin's, 1992) is a good collection of recent essays on the subject. Despite the somewhat misleading title, this book includes a number of studies that have nothing to do with the Cistercians.

Given the prolific nature of crusade studies, it is particularly surprising that there is no monograph on the Third Crusade. The history of the expedition must be pieced together from biographies of the leaders. Peter Munz, in *Frederick Barbarossa: A Study in Medieval Politics* (London: Eyre & Spottiswoode, 1969), provides a good overview of the German contribution to the crusade. Malcolm Cameron Lyons and D.E.P. Jackson, in *Saladin: The Politics of the Holy War* (Cambridge: Cambridge University Press, 1982), approach it from the Muslim side. Biographies of Richard I naturally devote considerable attention to his primary role in the crusade. Among the best are James A. Brundage's *Richard Lion Heart* (New York: Scribner, 1974) and John Gillingham's *Richard the Lionheart* (New York: Times, 1978).

Because of the oddity of the event and its controversial nature, the Fourth Crusade has always enjoyed a great deal of scholarly interest. The standard treatment is Donald E. Queller and my *The Fourth Crusade: The Conquest of Constantinople,* 2d ed. (Philadelphia: University of Pennsylvania Press, 1997). Charles M. Brand sets the crusade within the framework of Byzantine foreign policy in *Byzantium Confronts the West,*

1180–1204 (Cambridge: Harvard University Press, 1968). John Godfrey has produced a short and colorfully written account of the crusade, *1204: The Unholy Crusade* (Oxford: Oxford University Press, 1980). Unfortunately, it is marred by many serious errors. The standard histories of the Latin Empire of Constantinople are Jean Longnon's *L'empire latin de Constantinople et la principauté de Morée* (Paris: Payot, 1949) and Freddy Thiriet's *La Romanie vénitienne au moyen âge* (Paris: E. de Boccard, 1959).

The Albigensian Crusade has received renewed interest of late. The best monograph, however, remains Joseph R. Strayer's *The Albigensian Crusades,* with a new epilogue by Carol Lansing (Ann Arbor: University of Michigan Press, 1992). No good book exists for the Children's Crusade. The current state of understanding of the event can be found in Giovanni Miccoli, "La 'Crociata dei fanciulli' del 1212," *Studi medievali* 3 (1961): 407–43; Peter Raedts, "The Children's Crusade of 1212," *Journal of Medieval History* 3 (1977): 279–323; and Gary Dickson, "La genese de la croisade des enfants (1212)," *Bibliotheque de l'ecole des chartes* 153 (1995): 53–102.

A useful introduction to the Baltic Crusades is Eric Christiansen's *The Northern Crusades: The Baltic and the Catholic Frontier, 1100–1525* (Minneapolis: University of Minnesota Press, 1980). The political crusades of the thirteenth and fourteenth centuries are described by Norman J. Housley in *The Italian Crusades: The Papal-Angevin Alliance and the Crusades against Christian Lay Powers, 1254–1343* (Oxford: Oxford University Press, 1982).

The standard work on the Fifth Crusade is by James M. Powell, *Anatomy of a Crusade, 1213–1221* (Philadelphia: University of Pennsylvania Press, 1986). In a brilliant statistical analysis, Powell sheds light on the fluid and often precarious nature of the army at Damietta. Older, but still useful, is Joseph P. Donovan's *Pelagius and the Fifth Crusade* (Philadelphia: University of Pennsylvania Press, 1950).

The Crusade of Frederick II is treated in biographies of the emperor. Ernst Kantorowicz's *Frederick II* (Berlin: G. Bondi, 1931; English trans., New York: F. Ungar, 1957) is the foundation for all studies of the emperor. Thomas C. Van Cleve, in *The Emperor Frederick II of Hohenstaufen, Immutator Mundi* (Oxford: Oxford University Press, 1972), provides a well-researched narrative of the emperor's journey to the East. David Abulafia's *Frederick II: A Medieval Emperor* (Oxford: Oxford University Press, 1988) does the same, although it views Frederick in a consistently positive light.

Understanding of the central role of the crusade in the life and reign of Louis IX of France was greatly enhanced by William Chester Jordan's *Louis IX and the Challenge of the Crusade* (Princeton: Princeton University Press, 1979). Another excellent study is Jean Richard's *Saint Louis: Crusader King of France,* trans. Jean Birrell (Cambridge: Cambridge University Press, 1992). Jacques Le Goff's *Saint Louis* (Paris: Gallimard, 1996) provides an exhaustive treatment of Louis's reign. Le Goff notes the importance of the crusade to the king but questions whether it was the cause or the result of Louis's reforms.

The single best resource for the later crusades is Kenneth M. Setton's *The Papacy and the Levant (1204–1571),* 4 vols. (Philadelphia: American Philosophical Society, 1978–85). In an amazing piece of scholarship, Setton brings a lifetime of archival and library research to bear on the pope's efforts to bring peace to Europe and organize an effective defense against the Muslims. Many of the footnotes could be articles in their own right. Much more concise, but extremely useful, is Norman Housley's *The Later Crusades, 1274–1580: From Lyons to Alcazar* (Oxford: Oxford University Press, 1992). Housley's *The Avignon Papacy and the Crusades, 1305–1378* (Oxford: Clarendon, 1986) is indispensable for understanding the crusades of the fourteenth century. The role of Cyprus and the campaigns of Peter I are briefly described by Peter W. Edbury in *The Kingdom of Cyprus and the Crusades,* 1191–1374 (Cambridge: Cambridge University Press, 1991).

SOURCES IN TRANSLATION

Few topics in medieval history are more accessible to English-speaking students than the crusades. Below is a select list of some of the more important sources in translation.

SOURCE ANTHOLOGIES

Brundage, James A. *The Crusades: A Documentary Survey*. Milwaukee: Marquette University Press, 1962.

Gabrieli, Francesco. *Arab Historians of the Crusades*. New York: Routledge, 1969.

Pernoud, Régine. *The Crusades*. New York: G. P. Putnam's Sons, 1963.

Riley-Smith, Louise, and Jonathan Riley-Smith. *The Crusades: Idea and Reality, 1095–1274*. London: Edward Arnold, 1981.

THE FIRST CRUSADE

Comnena, Anna. *The Alexiad*. Translated by Elizabeth A. S. Dawes. London: K. Paul, 1928.

Eidelberg, Shlomo. *The Jews and the Crusaders: The Hebrew Chronicles of the First and Second Crusades*. Madison: University of Wisconsin Press, 1977.

Fulcher of Chartres. *A History of the Expedition to Jerusalem, 1095–1127*. Translated by Frances Rita Ryan, edited by Harold S. Fink. Knoxville: University of Tennessee Press, 1969.

Guibert of Nogent. *The Deeds of God through the Franks*. Translated and edited by Robert Levine. Rochester: Boydell, 1997.

Hill, Rosalind, ed. and trans. *Gesta Francorum et aliorum Hierosolymitanorum*. London: T. Nelson, 1962.

Krey, August C. *The First Crusade: The Accounts of Eye Witnesses and Participants.* Princeton: Princeton University Press, 1921.

Peters, Edward, ed. *The First Crusade: The Chronicle of Fulcher of Chartres and Other Source Materials.* 2d ed. Philadelphia: University of Pennsylvania Press, 1998.

Raymond of Aquilers. *Historia Francorum qui ceperunt Iherusalem.* Translated by John Hugh Hill and Laurita L. Hill. Philadelphia: American Philosophical Society, 1968.

Tudebode, Peter. *Historia de Hierosolymitano itinere.* Translated by John Hugh Hill and Laurita L. Hill. Philadelphia: American Philosophical Society, 1974.

THE CRUSADER STATES

An Arab-Syrian Gentleman and Warrior: Memoirs of Usamah Ibn Munqidh. Translated by Philip K. Hitti. Princeton: Princeton University Press, 1987.

William of Tyre. *History of Deeds Done beyond the Sea.* Translated by Emily Babcock and A. C. Krey. 2 vols. New York: Columbia University Press, 1943.

THE SECOND CRUSADE

The Chronicle of the Slavs. Translated by Joseph Tschan. New York: Columbia University Press, 1935.

De expugantione Lyxbonensi (The Capture of Lisbon). Translated by Charles Wendell David. New York: Columbia University Press, 1936.

Odo of Deuil. *De profectione Ludovici VII in orientem.* Translated and edited by Virginia Gingerick Berry. New York: Columbia University Press, 1948.

THE THIRD CRUSADE

Ambroise. *The Crusade of Richard Lion-heart.* Translated by Merton Jerome Hubert and John L. La Monte. New York: Columbia University Press, 1941.

Archer, Thomas A. *The Crusade of Richard I, 1189–92.* New York: G. P. Putnam's Sons, 1889.

Baha ad-Din. *The Life of Saladin.* Translated by Charles William Wilson. London: Palestine Exploration Fund, 1897.

The Chronicle of the Third Crusade: A Translation of the "Itinerarium Peregrinorum et Gesta Regis Ricardi." Translated by Helen Nicholson. Brookfield, Vt.: Ashgate, 1997.

Edbury, Peter W. *The Conquest of Jerusalem and the Third Crusade: Sources in Translation*. Aldershot: Ashgate, 1998.

THE FOURTH CRUSADE

Geoffrey of Villehardouin. *The Conquest of Constantinople*. Translated by M. R. B. Shaw. Baltimore: Penguin Books, 1967. (A slightly better translation is by Sir Frank Marzials [New York: E. P. Dutton, 1908]. Both have been reprinted frequently.)

Gunther of Pairis. *The Capture of Constantinople: The "Hystoria Constantinopolitana" of Gunther of Pairis*. Translated and edited by Alfred J. Andrea. Philadelphia: University of Pennsylvania Press, 1997.

Nicetas Choniates. *O City of Byzantium*. Translated by Harry J. Magoulias. Detroit: Wayne State University Press, 1984.

Robert of Clari. *The Conquest of Constantinople*. Translated by Edgar Holmes McNeal. New York: Columbia University Press, 1936.

THE LATIN EMPIRE OF CONSTANTINOPLE

Crusaders as Conquerors: The Chronicle of Morea. Translated by Harold E. Lurier. New York: Columbia University Press, 1964.

THE ALBIGENSIAN CRUSADE

Guillaume de Tudèle. *The Song of the Cathar Wars: A History of the Albigensian Crusade*. Translated and edited by Janet Shirley. Brookfield, Vt.: Ashgate, 1996.

Peter of Vaux-de-Cernay. *The History of the Albigensian Crusade*. Rochester, N.Y.: Boydell, 1998.

Peters, Edward, ed. *Christian Society and the Crusades, 1198–1229*. Philadelphia: University of Pennsylvania Press, 1971.

THE FIFTH CRUSADE

Peters, Edward, ed. *Christian Society and the Crusades, 1198–1229*. Philadelphia: University of Pennsylvania Press, 1971.

THE CRUSADE OF FREDERICK II

Peters, Edward, ed. *Christian Society and the Crusades, 1198–1229.* Philadelphia: University of Pennsylvania Press, 1971.

Philip of Novara. *The Wars of Frederick II against the Ibelins in Syria and Cyprus.* Translated by John L. La Monte and Merton Jerome Hubert. New York: Columbia University Press, 1936.

THE CRUSADES OF ST. LOUIS

Crusader Syria in the Thirteenth Century: The Rothelin Continuation of William of Tyre. Translated by Janet Shirley. Brookfield, Vt.: Ashgate, 1999.

John of Joinville. *The Life of St. Louis.* Translated by M. R. B. Shaw. Baltimore: Penguin Books, 1967. (Also translated by Sir Frank Marzials [New York: E. P. Dutton, 1908].)

LATER CRUSADES

Housley, Norman, ed. and trans. *Documents on the Later Crusades, 1274–1580.* New York: St. Martin's Press, 1996.

INDEX

For alphabetical sorting, the Arabic articles *al* and *as* are ignored.

ABOUT THE AUTHOR

Thomas F. Madden is associate professor of medieval history at Saint Louis University. He is coauthor of *The Fourth Crusade: The Conquest of Constantinople* (Philadelphia: University of Pennsylvania Press, 1997) and coeditor of *Medieval and Renaissance Venice* (Urbana: University of Illinois Press, 1999). He has written numerous other studies on the history of the crusades, Venice, and Constantinople.